MICHAEL JOSEPH MILLER

MURDER IN THE DELTA: THE EMMETT TILL STORY

MJM Publishing LLC
Bellwood, Illinois.

The opinions expressed in this manuscript are solely the opinions of the author and do not represent the opinions or thoughts of the publisher. The author has represented and warranted full ownership and/or legal right to publish all the materials in this book.

Murder in The Delta: The Emmett Till Story
All Rights Reserved.
Copyright © 2016 Michael Joseph Miller
v6.0

Cover Photo © 2016 thinkstockphotos.com. All rights reserved - used with permission.

This book may not be reproduced, transmitted, or stored in whole or in part by any means, including graphic, electronic, or mechanical without the express written consent of the publisher except in the case of brief quotations embodied in critical articles and reviews.

MJM Publishing LLC.
Bellwood, Illinois

ISBN: 978-0-578-17288-0

PRINTED IN THE UNITED STATES OF AMERICA

TABLE OF CONTENTS

PREFACE i
PROLOGUE: The Early Years v
CHAPTER ONE:
    ARRIVAL 1
CHAPTER TWO:
    THE GATHERING 6
CHAPTER THREE:
    DEPARTURE 20
CHAPTER FOUR:
    THE DELTA 28
CHAPTER FIVE:
    BRYANT'S GENERAL STORE 37
CHAPTER SIX:
    RUMORS 44
CHAPTER SEVEN:
    THE KIDNAPPING 50
CHAPTER EIGHT:
    THE SEARCH 60

CHAPTER NINE:
    CLINT SHERIDAN 65
CHAPTER TEN:
    DILAPIDATED SHED...73
CHAPTER ELEVEN:
    THE CALL...82
CHAPTER TWELVE:
    ARREST 87
CHAPTER THIRTEEN:
    STORMY NIGHT 95
CHAPTER FOURTEEN:
    THE RIVER'S EDGE 105
CHAPTER FIFTEEN:
    REVELATION.. 113
CHAPTER SIXTEEN:
    GOING HOME 121
CHAPTER SEVENTEEN:
    NATIONAL INTEREST 130
CHAPTER EIGHTEEN:
    A MOTHER'S TASK 137
CHAPTER NINETEEN:
    OPEN IT UP!.. 145
CHAPTER TWENTY:
    UNIVERSAL CHILD 154
CHAPTER TWENTY-ONE:
    NIGHT OF CHAOS 164
CHAPTER TWENTY-TWO:
    ARRAIGMENT 173

CHAPTER TWENTY-THREE:
PROTEST RISING 180
CHAPTER TWENTY-FOUR:
PRE-TRIAL BLUES 189
CHAPTER TWENTY-FIVE:
MURDER-TRIAL: Day One 204
CHAPTER TWENTY-SIX:
STEAL AWAY IN THE NIGHT 217
CHAPTER TWENTY-SEVEN:
MURDER-TRIAL: Day Two 228
CHAPTER TWENTY-EIGHT:
THE MEETING PLACE 237
CHAPTER TWENTY-NINE:
MURDER-TRIAL: Day Three 250
CHAPTER THIRTY:
MURDER-TRIAL: Day Four 263
CHAPTER THIRTY-ONE:
MURDER-TRIAL: Afternoon Session 277
CHAPTER THIRTY-TWO:
MOUND BAYOU HOTEL 288
CHAPTER THIRTY-THREE:
THE VERDICT 296
CHAPTER THIRTY-FOUR:
STEPS TOWARD SOCIAL CHANGE 309
CHAPTER THRITY-FIVE:
MURDER CONFESSION 319

PREFACE

*"There is a way which seemeth right unto a man,
but the ends thereof are the ways of death."*
PROVERBS 14:12

Since the inception of civilization, man's systematic concept has been to rule. There are many reasons for man's dictatorial temperament, the most prevalent being multi-racial existence, predomination of power and difference in social class backgrounds. Because of man's superior mindset, the evil machinations of man have sought with unswerving determinations to enslave and eradicate those whom man designated as being less superlative than man is. As such, the prolonged inhumanity of racial conflict has produced some of the most hideous examples of brutality ever conceived. The chronicle of events to which you are about to peruse is a case in point.

It was on a humid Wednesday evening around 7:30 p.m., August 24, 1955 when the "wolf-whistling incident" involving fourteen-year-old Emmett Till occurred at the Bryant's General

Store in Money, Mississippi. Almost three months later on November 11, 1955, a grand jury in Greenwood, Mississippi declined the indictments of twenty-four year-old Roy Bryant and thirty-six-year-old John Williams Milam (half-brothers) on a charge of kidnapping. At the conclusion of the five day murder trial on Friday, September 23, 1955, an all-white male jury in Sumner, Mississippi had contemplated for sixty-seven minutes to return a "not guilty" verdict against the two men on a charge of murder.

To this extent, Mississippi justice brought to an "official close" one of the most notorious cases in modern history, yet even now over five decades later, the napping question surrounding the "mystery" still remains, **who really murdered Emmett Louis Till** on August 28, 1955.

The story of Emmett Till was one of unbelievable torture and cruelty. It highlighted the courage of simple black sharecroppers who braved death to testify at the murder trial, in spite of death threats and intimidations from their white southern neighbors. It was a tragic story, which involved the unwilling participation of two black field hands: Henry Lee Loggins and Leroy (Too-Tight) Collins. The two men had witnessed the brutal murder on the Clint Sheridan plantation near Drew, Mississippi. They were later incarcerated by Sheriff H. C. Strider, who had concealed their names in an effort to prevent their testimonies in the sensational murder trial, which had captivated media coverage from around the world. A story which elucidated the utter contempt and defiance of an all-white Mississippi male jury and Sheriff H. C. Strider who, callously, with boldness, told a startled world:

"We don't believe the body found in the Tallahatchie River was that of Emmett Till."

The story of Emmett Till epitomized many heroic deeds, most notably, by members of the black press. The twelve-member press forged ahead without the support of state agencies or the Department of Justice and at imminent danger to themselves combed the racially tense backwoods and plantation counties of the Mississippi Delta in search of witnesses. It was the black press that uncovered facts encompassing the incarceration of the two "missing field hands" as they were held in the county jail in Charleston, Mississippi.

When Emmett's body arrived in Chicago from Mississippi, his mother Mamie (Till) Bradley ordered the casket opened, **"Open it up! Let the people see what they did to my son,"** sobbed the grief-stricken mother. More than one-hundred thousand people viewed the young child's body during the four-day obsequy from September 2nd to September 6th. The large outpouring dramatically accentuated the calamity of the case.

During the research into Emmett Till's brutal murder, which many refer to as an historical American tragedy, this story held me entrenched for over three decades. I ascertained the contents of this story to be both astonishing and prophetic how the Lord played such an exceptional role in **"to loose the bands of wickedness, undoing the heavy burdens and letting the oppressed go free"(Isaiah 58:6).** My research and personal interviews had taken me far beyond a story based on facts and a miscarriage of justice. It became apparent that this story must be recounted against the background of a time, in the nineteen-fifties, when racial tension was so fierce, that hatred and violence consumed a person of color, when "Jim Crow" boundaries were socially invaded. A story which exposed the barbarity of racism in a state which had spawned such supporters of white supremacy as the Ku Klux Klan, the White Citizens Council and numerous right wing ultra-conservative constituents, committed to dogmatic traditional values, whether the rationale was through subversive or perilous deeds.

It is noteworthy to mention that because of this young child who in his short life never knew what a symbol he would become: **a spark ignited a flame.** And that flame kindled one of the most extensive civil rights movements in U.S. History. A movement, which inspired Americans of African lineage to seek vigorously for themselves the rights denied for so long.

"…And a little child shall lead them…"

I present to you the true story of Emmett Louis Till: **"MURDER IN THE DELTA."**

PROLOGUE: THE EARLY YEARS

The story of Emmett Till began with the courtship of his prospective parents, Louis Till and Mamie Elizabeth Carthan. Mamie met Louis during her last year in high school. Louis Till had migrated to Argo, Illinois during the late 1930's to pursue opportunities which had eluded him in his endemic home of Madrid, Missouri, where he was a resident with his foster parents for many years of his young life. When Louis reached the age of sixteen, his decision to move North was like many Americans of African ancestry who felt that by relocating to the North, they would receive better opportunities to advance their lives as opposed to the harsh segregated oppression in the South. In the South, the lack of equality and fair treatment was a degree of law. During the time that Louis resided in Argo with foster relatives, when he became eighteen years of age, like other inhabitants there, he found employment at the Argo Corn Products Company.

Mamie, the only child of her parents, John and Alma Smith Carthan, moved from Webb, Mississippi, where she was born, to

Argo, Illinois in 1924, when she was just fourteen months old. Her father settled in Argo where he also found employment at the Argo Corn Products Company, having arrived several months ahead of his wife and daughter from his native state of Mississippi. The Carthan family adjusted to life in Argo, an upwardly mobile, small-town community near Chicago, where Mamie's parents raised her in a strict middle-class environment. Her mother, Alma, was a member of the Church of God in Christ and she reared her in that essential faith. Mamie described her mother as a firm disciplinarian and she credits her mother with raising her by an unyielding code of supervision.

Mamie first met Louis Till through her best friend; Bertha while they were both in their senior year in high school, Louis had only lived in Argo for three years after arriving from his innate home in Missouri. Mamie's interest in Louis began to intensify after she graduated from Argo Community High School in 1940. She described him as a big, strapping fellow with a devil-may-care air and rather dashing. Louis was an amateur boxer and regarded by many who knew him as a local hero. Since her parents, (who had divorced when she was thirteen), reared her in a strict upbringing they considered Louis too worldly for her. Contrary to their beliefs, she continued dating him. On one particular date, Louis took Mamie to the local ice cream parlor where they had banana splits, which she said humorously was her very first one. Mamie disclosed with fond memories that dating Louis often reminded her of a favorite movie, Beau Brummel and she further explained that she was very pleased with her prowess in getting the man she desired. They were both eighteen at the time of their courtship. Mamie continued to elucidate about their growing relationship by saying she felt that Louis was much more sophisticated than she was about life. She said she occasionally felt that Louis treated her like a little girl and had taken her for granted. Mamie explicated, "Like a doll you would sit on a shelf and find it there when you returned."

Louis and Mamie's courtship like any relationship had its unexpected obstacles and challenges. Alma recalled she was after her daughter repeatedly to end her relationship with him and Mamie finally gave in and decided not to see Louis anymore. During their brief separation, some Chicago male friends that Mamie and her friends knew came to Argo to visit. Mamie disclosed that one of the males had asked her out without her mother's consent and she slipped off and went to see a movie with him. Alma said one of her rules she insisted upon was not allowing her daughter to attend movies without her permission and at times without her supervision. Now Argo was a small town like many in the 1930's and 40's, where the male youths of the community had a rule that if boys from anywhere else invaded their turf, they were considered outsiders and intruders. To the gang it did not matter who they were calling on or whether the girls preferred them or not. The "whaling parties" dealt with outsiders and intruders in a harsh way and ran them out of town as trespassers. Therefore, her Chicago friend had to take a beating from the gang, but nothing comparable to today's standards. In other words, they just punched him around a bit and sent him on his way.

Louis confronted Mamie regarding her date with the Chicago male visitor, which he had heard about through some of their acquaintances, so when he saw Mamie near her mother's home, the revelation caused a heated argument between them and as she recalled the episode, Mamie remembered him speaking to her in loud tones as he held her arm. Apparently, her mother and her Uncle Crosby Smith, her mother's younger brother who was living in Chicago at the time, heard them quarreling in front of her mother's home. The confrontation prompted her uncle to say to his sister, "Alma, you better go out there and get your daughter. She's out there with Louis again and you need to put a stop to it." When her mother rushed out of her home and challenged Louis, there was quite a stormy scene. Alma said she really berated Louis and when she got her daughter in the house, she gave Mamie the bawling out of her life. During their heated discussion, Mamie angrily stated to her mother that she was no longer a child and that she would no longer tolerate such treatment. It was then Mamie said she had made up her mind to marry Louis Till.

At this point in my conversation with Mamie and her mother; Alma told me that she did not want to convey that she vehemently disliked Louis. She said that based on her opinion, he did not seem to be one reared in a cultured background, and as a mother she just wanted the best for her daughter. Alma concluded the conversation by saying that as she became better acquainted with Louis; she became more tolerant of his quick-tempered behavior for the sake of her daughter.

Louis and Mamie were married on October 14, 1940. They got a little place to themselves, in the hopes of being as independent of their folks as possible; but in fact, Mamie admitted to her lack of preparation for independence in a new marriage, as she illustrated, "I felt like a new born lamb strayed from its mother." Naturally, she found herself turning to her mother for everything from advice on cooking to the little disagreements between Mamie and her new husband. Soon after her marriage, she became pregnant. Inasmuch as, she was a woman always conscious of her weight, she started filling out rapidly. As a matter of course, she said her sudden weight gain caused a lot of talk and whispered speculation from her neighbors. Emmett Louis Till made his postnatal debut into the world on July 25, 1941. Mamie recalled that prior to his birth there was a great deal of excitement from family and friends who had wagers on whether her delivery date would possibly be in June or more likely July. Her parents were elated about the anticipated arrival of their first grandchild, whom they were praying would be a boy to carry on the family name. Mamie said pensively, "I had a long difficult labor. My baby weighed six and three quarter pounds and the medical instruments left a scar. His right hand was swollen and his left knee was bruised, because it was a breech birth."

The doctors at the hospital informed her mother that because of the breech birth, some of the doctors felt that her baby might be permanently crippled. At birth, Emmett was blond and blue-eyed; this caused Mamie and Louis some concern until Alma convinced them not to worry, because the baby's natural color would return. Shortly after Mamie had given birth to Emmett, she became very ill with childbed fever, which caused her confinement in an emergency ward. Mamie talked about the anguish she felt during that time, "I guess I made my condition worse by crying and worrying over my baby's condition. The doctor's suggested that I put him in a home for cripples, but I firmly refuted that and determined that between my mama, my husband and me, he would someday be normal. Louis was kind and patient with me. However, there were times when it became overwhelming for him. In his way, he meant well and I guess he tried to do the best he could. We were both young and foolish." Although, she was released from the hospital, Mamie was still weak and ailing and it took almost a year before she recovered from her illness. During her recovery, she spent most of her time in bed.

In the meantime, little Emmett improved steadily under the care of his father and grandmother. By the time he was two months old, he was a beautiful baby with a sunny disposition and showing every sign of being normal. He would stretch and flex his muscles and the exercise was good for his limbs, his mother said. She said it seemed to her that the baby grew so fast that he was soon too big for his bassinet. Mamie recalled that one-day, when her mother had come over to their small apartment, she saw the baby lying in the dresser drawer that Mamie had pulled out as a bed for him. Indignantly, her mother asked why she had him there and Mamie replied that she had no place else to put him because the baby was growing so fast. Alma said she became incensed over the situation and she snatched the baby up, took him home with her, and purchased a crib for him that day. It would not take long before baby Emmett kicked the sides out of his new crib as well. Mamie said from that time on, her mother adopted Emmett (not in the legal sense) as her second child; therefore, it was as if she had two children.

Naturally, curiosity led to concerns about her husband's temperament, and she explained, "Louis was a happy-go-lucky guy by nature, but he had a hot, gusty temper that sometimes got him in trouble. As I look back on it now, I can see many things that I did not realize then. Louis was an orphan who had been switched around from place to place. Part of his swaggering was really to cover up the loneliness he felt and the affection he craved. I know he resented my close attachment to mama and looked at this as family interference. Emmett was just a few weeks old when we had a bad quarrel. Louis had come home from work and found that I was visiting my mother and I had forgotten to prepare his dinner. I didn't get back until late and he was hungry and angry." When she arrived home, they had what she described as, "a stormy verbal altercation." Because of their verbal confrontation, she stayed the night at her mother's home. The following day after a night of contemplation by himself, Louis felt very remorseful about their argument and they resolved the tense situation temporarily. Yet Mamie related that the disputation was a turning point in their marriage, which resulted in the two of them drifting apart. Although, they did not file for divorce, they separated permanently in November 1942.

Louis and Mamie were planning reconciliation when he was drafted into the United States Army in March 1943. She disclosed that Louis listed himself as a single man, with his next of kin being his Uncle Lee Green of Argo. Soon after his residence in camp, he began writing her regularly and all he talked about was the two of them being reconciled, for the sake of their son and keeping his family together. She agreed to his proposal to try and salvage their marriage. Sometime in May 1943, while stationed temporarily in Casablanca, Morocco and during his transient duty, Louis purchased a ring on which he had his initials and the date, May 25, 1943, engraved. In July 1943, he made out an allotment for his wife and young son. Around Thanksgiving the same year, he came home to visit his family and they spent an exciting and fun filled time together. Surprisingly, she said that he even helped with some of the cooking. Louis enjoyed playing with his young son, he was so proud of him. Mamie said at the time that she did not know he was AWOL from the Army. During the time he spent with her, she said Louis often spoke of the harsh racist mistreatment of black soldiers in the Army. Moreover, how such treatment held him mentally in a place where he was tired of the abuse. The military police picked him up later and sent him to the stockade. Mamie said that was the last time she saw him.

Immediately after his release from the stockade, the Army shipped him overseas. Private Louis Till found himself assigned to the Jim-Crow 397th Port Battalion, a unit of the United States Army that consisted of non-commissioned officers and men who were draftees, mostly from the Chicago land area. During Louis overseas military duty, he corresponded invariably with his wife until about three months prior to the letter she had received from the Army. The letter informed her that he had died. Mamie explained that after her husband's death, she found herself embroiled in controversy with the Army over the circumstances surrounding his demise, "I would like to make it very clear here about my part in this terrible tragedy. On the thirteenth of July 1945, I received a telegram from the Department of Defense saying that my husband had died on the second of July 1945. The cause of death was listed as 'willful misconduct'." Mamie continued by stating that she fainted for the first and only time in her life when she had received word of her husband's death. She went on to say that she did not understand the Army's terminology of 'willful misconduct' nor did a letter she had received a few days later from a chaplain in Italy shed any light on the circumstances surrounding her husband's death. Mamie said her tenacious drive to uncover the facts, led her to numerous investigations, but she never received a complete explanation from the Army. It was not until ten years later, during the brutal murder of her only child in Mississippi, that she learned the Army's official version. James O. Eastland, an ultra-conservative Senator from the State of Mississippi had the Army release to the public the accounts of her late husband's death.

According to official records from the Army's account, Louis Till was convicted of alleged rape and murder of a white woman based on the testimony from white soldiers stationed with him overseas and he was hanged. Mamie said she contacted Joseph Tobias, a lawyer and an old friend of the family, in July 1948. She asked for his assistance in ascertaining information regarding the death of her late husband. He wrote to the Department of the Army to get information on her legal rights as a widow. The Army informed him by letter and stated that in 'willful misconduct cases' family members of the deceased received no benefits from the government. Although, her lawyer friend tried to ascertain an explanation for them shedding some light on Louis' death, they never received a satisfactory answer. Mamie concluded our conversation by saying she had no further knowledge about the case.

Many friends of Louis', who served with him overseas, said he met with an unfortunate event in a mysterious clandestine racially charged atmosphere while he was in Italy. They described Louis Till as a 210 pound, six-foot giant who, "licked every man in the outfit with boxing gloves," as friendly and easygoing, a fun lover, who always got into mischief, "but nothing serious," they said. One friend remembered the time when Louis had put on a robe, took off his shoes and went into an area populated with Arabs. He further explained, "The M.P.'s spotted him because he was trying to walk around broken glass and debris to protect his aching feet." Another former war buddy recalled Louis buying the 'ring' in Casablanca for his wife. They described him as a sentimental guy, always talking about his wife and young son whom he held in high esteem. One of Louis' closest friend who had worked with him at the Argo Corn Products Company and then served with him overseas, said, "I remember there was a group of about a 135 of us black non-coms who got busted following North African riots when white military police sought to enforce non-fraternization bans. We were known as the most militant unit in Italy, but we also esblished new tonnage records in unloading ships under fire." Still another friend related, "Louis never confessed the crime and we felt that he was innocent. It is inconceivable that the big, playful fellow could be a criminal. If the facts stood up the army should not have been so mysterious about killing him."

After Louis' death, Alma made a solemn promise to her daughter to help support Emmett until his eighteenth birthday. Emmett began walking when he was eleven months old. According to Mamie, Emmett was as cute and mischievous as any curious and energetic young child could be. When he would indulge in harmless mischief, he had this trick of hiding under the bed. Then he would peek out at his mother and of course, Mamie said she was completely ineffective in her ability to discipline him and Emmett would get away with a much-deserved spanking. "Bobo" received his nickname from a close friend of the family. Mamie said she preferred "Mickey," but she settled for Bobo as a nickname, which his neighborhood friends later shorten to "Bo".

Our next topic of conversation concerned Emmett's attack with polio at a young age and his mother said, "Bo, started in kindergarten when he was five years old. At age six, he entered first grade. This was the year he was stricken with polio. When the doctor came to my home, he diagnosed the case and told us to get him to the hospital at once. Neverthless, we could not get a friend or relative to loan us their car. Everyone was deathly afraid of the disease. In desperation, mother called to get a private ambulance, but the ambulance operator turned us down because of our race. We finally ended up getting a police squad car to take him to the Contagious Disease Hospital. He stayed there for two weeks. Disappointed by the whole ordeal, my mother purchased a 1941 Oldsmobile. Mother said that from now on, we were going to be independent and if ever Bo became sick again, he wouldn't have to be humiliated by riding in a police squad car."

Mamie and Alma both felt that the polio illness left Emmett with a speech impediment, which resulted in severe stammering. Whenever he would get excited or nervous, it was particularly bad. It also left him with weak ankles, which meant they had to buy special shoes for him. In later life, his speech defect made him evade long conversations with strangers and they had disciplined him to keep quiet around adults, his grandmother said. They both smiled fondly as Mamie recalled a humorous situation involving her mother and her mother's second husband, "My mother had married for the second time to a Mr. Thomas Gains. He was especially fond of Bo. In fact, he wanted Mama to sign over her property to Bo so he would have some security when he grew up, But Mama tossed her head and said, "Humph, just suppose Bo gets married and his wife decides she doesn't want me and Sister around. She could put us right out in the street." Mamie concluded by saying that Thomas Gains died in 1945.

In 1947, Alma said she married Henry Spearman, her third husband. They moved from Argo to Chicago, but Mamie and Emmett continued to reside in Argo, surrounded by other relatives. Mamie continued to work consistently and as a single mom, she admitted that her whole mindset was on working and saving for Emmett's college education. Mamie started first with the Army Signal Corps and then transferred to the Veteran's administration. Unfortunately, during her employment there, she suffered an acute attack of appendicitis. In 1948, she went to work for Social Security as a clerk-typist.

In 1950, Mamie began contemplating about relocating to a place far from the humdrum existence of small town Argo, Illinois. Her father, John Carthan had moved to Detroit, Michigan after remarriage and he persuaded her that Detroit would be a nice place for her to live and raise his grandson, Emmett. During their residency in Detroit, she obtained employment at the Fort Wayne Induction Center. Mamie recalled that Bo was very unhappy living in Detroit and he became restless and heartbroken. Emmett wanted to get back to his beloved Argo and she did not think it wise to make him stay. She decided to send him back to the care of her uncle, Kid Carthan, her father's youngest brother. During the time Mamie and Emmett lived in Detroit, she met and began dating a man whom she identified as Pink Bradley. She was lonely and because Pink had developed a good relationship with Bo, Mamie said she felt he would be a good second father for him. Mamie and Pink Bradley were married on May 5, 1951 in Detroit and moved back to Chicago in November of the same year.

The same year Mamie assisted her mother, Alma, in purchasing the two-flat at 6427 South Saint Lawrence Avenue. Her mother also had her second home at 1421 West 14th Place on Chicago's West Side. Mamie and her new husband moved into the second floor apartment of the two-flat and Bo came to live with them. In August 1953, she and Pink Bradley separated after a volatile and explosive marriage and she filed for divorce. After her divorce, it was Bo and Mamie. Disappointed in her marriage, she said that she intently set in place to make Bo the kind of man every mother wants her son to be. It is interesting to note that Mamie and Emmett were more like sister and brother than mother and son. Mamie said they had no secrets from each other. They talked and argued everything out. Emmett was mature for his young age. If he did not care for something, she did, he would say so, but she added that he was never a sassy child. Mamie recapitulated that there were times, when Emmett would call his grandmother about something she had done and Alma would bawl her out good. In addition, when Mamie got exasperated with Emmett, she would report to her mother and Alma would scold Emmett. Alma kept both of them in check, Mamie said.

Since Mamie had to maintain their livelihood, they had an arrangement. Emmett had to do all the housework and the laundry.

Mamie did all the cooking but she skilled him in the preparation of simple delicacies as well. Emmett became a good housekeeper, clean and neat, and he very seldom shirked his responsibilities. Like any other child, Emmett loved to play and sometimes he would slip off leaving some of his chores or forgetting the loaf of bread, his mother had sent him to the store to pick up. Mamie reminisced humorously about the episode, "I remember one summer evening when I came home from work, all hot and fatigued. I sent him to the store to pick up some grocery items. He was a baseball hound and there was a sandlot game going on. Emmett put down the bag of items and involved himself in the game. That's where I found him when I came out looking for him, all evil and angry. He was thirteen then and as big as I was. I whipped him all the way home and he never said a word. However, when we got to the house, he tried to tell me what had happened and as he was excited, he was stuttering. "N-N-now, now, just look at yourself," he said. Then getting control of himself, he said very firmly. "Now, how do you feel making a show of yourself out there in the street?" I had to admit that I was ashamed of myself for losing my temper so."

Emmett was a 'normal' youngster, who got into altercations with his playmates, yet he had one outstanding trait; he could not tolerate friction involving those close to him. It completely unsettled him until he could negotiate peace between the warring parties, his mother said. Mamie believed this might have stemmed from his early realization of a broken home and the problems that came with it. Consequently, he wanted harmony surrounding him and anyone close to him. To further illustrate her point about Emmett's inability to deal with friction, Mamie reminisced with fondness about her young female cousin, Thelma Wright, the daughter of Moses and Alma's sister, Elizabeth Wright who had come to live with them in 1953. Shortly after that, Thelma's older sister, Loretta Wright came to reside at her place of residence too. Mamie was proud of the fact that Thelma was attending Northern Illinois University, as Mamie was big on education. Since Loretta had a full-time job, Mamie felt that the extra income would be a much-needed help since she was the sole bread earner. Mamie instructed the two young women that while they resided with her, she expected them to do a certain amount of housework. Tempers rose and this soon developed into a problem. Like most girls, Mamie felt that her two cousins occasionally became careless and left things around the house undone. When Mamie laid down the law of her household, her two cousins moved out. Mamie said she was incensed over the situation and that it caused quite a strain on family relations.

Emmett was very unhappy about it all and kept prodding his mother to go and see the girls and make up. Mamie recalled, "Finally, late one Saturday night, after he had pestered the life out of me, I said irritably, 'all right, let's go'." When she and Bo walked into the apartment where her two cousins were staying, the girls were so surprised to see them. Mamie and her two cousins resolved their differences and then proceeded to have a joyous time laughing, singing and playing the latest records on the phonograph. "Bo, was so happy, his eyes were just shining," she said.

Mamie and Emmett did not return home from visiting her cousins until three o'clock in the morning. When they finally entered the second floor apartment, where she and Emmett resided, they heard the telephone ringing. It was her mother, Alma, frantic to know what had happened to them. Alma said she had been calling since twelve o'clock that night. When Mamie told her what had happened, Alma laughed and called her grandson, "Our little peacemaker."

The Christmas of 1954 was a very memorable and special Christmas for Emmett and his family. This was the Christmas Mamie, her mother and father spared no expense on Emmett. Alma said for some strange reason that Christmas seemed to evolve around Emmett. Emmett received lots of gifts and money from his family. Mamie said she and her fiancé, Gene Mobley even gave Emmett a hundred dollars, but instead of spending the money for his personal needs, he resolved to buy gifts for his less fortunate cousins who lived around the local area.

Crosby Smith

Emmett Louis Till
Mamie Carthan Till (Mobley)

John Nash Carthan

Alma Smith Carthan Spearman

Emmett Louis Till
Age 2

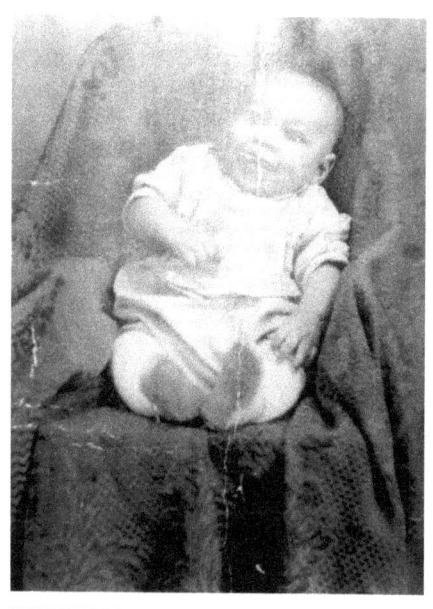

Emmett Louis Till
Age 4-5 months

Emmett Louis Till
Double photo, Age 2 months

Emmett Louis Till
Mamie Carthan Till (Mobley)

Emmett Louis Till
Age 14

Emmett Louis Till
Age 14

CHAPTER ONE:

ARRIVAL

In mid-August 1955, the summer was active and blistering with heat in Chicago, as the city dwellers contended with the onslaught of temperatures in the high nineties for what became consecutive weeks of hot summer days. At 12th Street and Michigan Avenue, the Illinois Central Station stood majestic and erect in downtown Chicago. A hot sticky August summer month, where streetcars and trolley buses rushed here and there on the downtown city streets and around the train station. The Illinois Central Station was a lofty five-story building with large pillars reaching upward toward the height of the colossal structure. The double glass revolving doors dispersed around the four-city-block-building of the Illinois Central gyrated with the constant movement of wayward travelers entering and leaving the edifice.

The City of New Orleans passenger train shuttled its way into the spacious interior walls of the station and came to a slow crawl until it reached its arrival point. Shortly after the passenger train arrived, conductors emerged from the antiquated cars to assist passengers, as they began to leave the train resting on the tracks amid the sound of the train's pulsating engine, which vibrated the interior surroundings.

Moses Wright, the sixty-four year old great uncle of Emmett Till rose from his seat on the train and reached for his suitcase. The comely and country looking, God-fearing, average height, lean and grayish black man of ordinary intelligence emerged from the front car of the passenger train and pushed his way through the busy throng of people in the station. Moses occupation was sharecropping; he was a sanctified minister and the father of twelve children. Four grow siblings from his first wife and eight siblings from his second and present marriage. He and members of his family resided in the small Southern town of Money, Mississippi, which was a one stop, backwoods community in the Delta of Mississippi. There Moses lived with his second wife, Elizabeth, the second oldest sister of Alma who was Emmett Till's grandmother, and three of their young sons of eight siblings. Moses was born in Lexington, Mississippi and he moved to the delta community with his family in 1927. In 1955, he had been a resident of Money since 1946.

It was Thursday afternoon, August eighteenth in the city, when Moses arrived in Chicago, fatigued from the fourteen-hour train ride to attend the funeral of his close friend, Robert Jones who was also the father-in-law of his oldest daughter, Willa Mae Jones from his first marriage. During his stay, he planned to visit other relatives in the surrounding area. Moses carried the full-size suitcase with ease, as he stared with amusing curiosity at the unfamiliar faces rushing to and from in the bustling filled station. Moses was not a stranger to the area, yet each time he traveled by train to the city of Chicago; the fast treading and engaging whirlwind activity of city life seemed to provoke feelings of fascination and interest in him. A gaze made obvious through his amusing stares at the strangers of mixed races, which caused him to reflect on the differences between city life filled with city slickers and the open and slow-paced life of country living in the South.

In the midst of the crowd, Moses eyes dotted around the station searching eagerly for the emergence of the familiar faces scheduled to meet him. The wooden long benches occupied with travelers, some waiting for the arrival of loved ones and others waiting to leave on their long awaited excursions, lured him and he walked with an unhurried stride toward one of the benches to rest. As Moses sat among the inhabitants, he continued to watch the casual activities of the preoccupied faces of the people engaged in their own thoughts of conversation in the spacious station. It was not long before he found himself engaged in a conversation with two friendly elderly male strangers: one a Jewish man and the second a White man as they sat across from him.

Willa Mae Jones, a medium built woman in her late thirties rushed into the Illinois Central Station, accompanied by her son, fifteen -year-old, Curtis Jones and her nephew, sixteen- year-old, Wheeler Parker, Jr. She searched diligently for her father, as Wheeler and Curtis scurried toward the stairs leading to the lower level where trains often arrived and departed. An expression of relief hastened across her receptive face brought on by the coolness of the station. A soothing cool comfort to her body that embraced her it seemed from the sizzling summer heat of the day.

Meanwhile, Wheeler and Curtis arrived at the lower level. They maneuvered themselves strategically through the crowded station, and they soon recognized their grandfather, Moses sitting on a bench nearby. At first, Moses did not perceive his grandsons advancing toward him because of his monopolizing conversation with the two elderly male travelers as the men engaged each other's topic of conversation with interest.

Soon thereafter Willa Mae arrived at the lower level and keeping Wheeler and Curtis in sight, she too noticed her father as the two youngsters raced toward him. Wheeler was unable to contain his excitement and he cried out, "Poppa!" The sound of the familiar voice captivated Moses attention and he rose from his relaxed posture enthusiastically and stretched forth his arms to receive his grandsons, as the two youngsters thrust their bodies into his embrace. His excited mannerism extended to his approaching daughter with a broad smile and out stretched arms, as their arms lovingly clinched around each other with a hearty hug. Willa Mae's joyous expression revealed the admiration she held for her father.

"How's Mama Lizzie and everybody doin'," she asked?

Amid the convergence of activities around them, he informed her that everyone was doing well.

During the conversation between Moses and his daughter, he reached for his suitcase spontaneously resting beside him, but his grandson Curtis moved in quickly and retrieved it; "I got it, grandpa, Curtis said eagerly! Moses watched with amusement as Curtis appeared to struggle with the suitcase and he asked, "You sure that ain't too heavy for you, Curtis?" Curtis felt vigor as he seized the suitcase with a firm grip and said, "Naw grandpa! I'm strong! Wheeler watched his cousin with humor and he could not resist the open opportunity, "Yeah under the arms, he added."

As they walked through the coolness of the station, the realization of his visit struck Moses with a sudden cognizance and his demeanor grew somber as he reflected on the memory of his best friend, a longtime friend whom he had been very close too and now was sadden by his death and impending funeral. Moses asked pensively about the time of the funeral and about his son-in-law, Willie B. and she told him that the service would commence at 10 A.M. the following morning. She also told him that her husband in spite of his grief was relieved that his father would no longer have to suffer with the pains of cancer. With Wheeler assisting his cousin with the suitcase, the four of them departed the train station en route to her apartment on the South Side of Chicago.

CHAPTER TWO:

THE GATHERING

After Moses Wright's arrival to the city of Chicago on the previous day, the following day, Friday, August nineteenth- was another sunny hot day in the city with no relief from the persistent heat. Yet in spite of the heat, the Sixty-four hundred block of South Saint Lawrence Avenue on the Southeast Side of Chicago was bustling with the playful activities of school age children enjoying their summer vacation away from school on the late humid summer morning. The houses on Saint Lawrence stood compressed of two and three-flat buildings nestled among elm-shaped trees, which stretched the length of the block. Saint Lawrence Avenue as well as the surrounding neighborhoods was moderate to middle-class in 1955. It was a family neighborhood predominantly of Americans of African ancestry where many of the families owned the buildings where they lived.

Inside the second floor apartment of the thriving red brick

two-flat in the middle of the block, fourteen-year-old, Emmett Louis (Bobo) Till entered the modern simple tastefully attired kitchen. His eyes found the radio sitting on top of the refrigerator on the opposite end of the kitchen and he walked over to it and turned the portable radio on. The burst of rock and roll music emitted from the radio at a high volume and filled the apartment. Emmett stood attentive for a moment preoccupied listening with enjoyment as "Rock Around the Clock" a song by Bill Haley & His Coments consumed him as the melodic emphatic driving beat emanated and danced off the walls throughout the kitchen. It was not long before he found himself swaying and bobbing in rhythm to the beat as he danced over to the octagon table near the window.

Emmett had grown into a handsome, light-skinned; stocky built youth with curly hair and hazel eyes. Casually dressed in blue jeans, white T-shirt and black and white sneakers, he began to arrange various food items on the table in the order that he had planned to use them. Alone in the apartment, he felt good listening to the radio blaring at high volume without his mother's interruption screaming at him over the loud music, "Bo! Turn that music down!" Emmett approached his task with confidence as he stood over the table pondering his first attempt at baking a cake without his mother's assistance. His thoughts raced back and forth in his head trying to recall the steps from watching his mother as he studied the ingredients scattered on the table. Emmett's concentration shifted over to the clock on the wall in front of him, ticking away the hours before his mother was due to arrive home from her full-time job, later in the afternoon. Emmett's little league game scheduled just hours away the same afternoon made him cognizant of his appointed task.

Emmett began to work without delay by pouring a half a cup of flour into the white mixing bowl then adding half a stick of butter, two caps full of vanilla flavor, two eggs and a full cup from the box of ready mix, which he also added to the compound. He seized the spoon prone nearby and began to stir the mixture with anticipated enthusiasm of his planned endeavor. Emmett whipped the ingredients around in the bowl with confidence as he added the necessary items as needed. Satisfied that he had mixed the contents well enough in the bowl, he placed the bowl under the blades of the mixer and then watched as the compound mixed. The r-r-roaring sound from the motor of the mixer, which filled the apartment, nearly drowned out the sound from the radio, which continued to hold his interest, as he then adjusted the volume to compensate for the noise from the mixer. Emmett's preoccupation centered on his efforts to accomplish his goal, therefore, he kept a watchful eye on his task taking shape in the bowl. At the conclusion of the music, the news report invaded the kitchen and before Emmett knew it, he found himself drawn to the familiar news topic on race.

The radio newscast disclosed information regarding the racial tensions in a far South Side white resident housing project known as Trumbull Park. The report also disclosed information on how the Chicago branch of the NAACP had accused the Trumbull Park housing authority of prolonging racial tension by seeking to sale the project with the sole purpose of forcing Negroes out. Emmett's eyes shifted with interest from the news topic to his appointed undertaking. He engaged the news report with an inquisitive frown as he attempted to relate the subject matter with a sense of familiarity,which to no purpose caused his mind to wonder from the news report back to his mission awaiting him on the table. Nonetheless, the newscaster's voice from the radio continued to permeate throughout the kitchen. *"In national news, the two unsolved murders of Reverend George W. Lee, age fifty-two of Belzoni, Mississippi on May 7 and sixty-three-year-old, Lamar Smith of Brookhaven, Mississippi two weeks ago on August 13 over voter registration, continued to baffle the NAACP and the nation. The two men were apparently murdered for leading voter registration drives in an effort to encourage local Negroes to vote in the upcoming gubernatorial election in Mississippi. Reverend Lee was fatally shot from a passing car while driving, and the gunshot blast caused serious wounds, which caused a contentious disagreement between the local sheriff and medical doctors as the debate was over LED pellets removed from Reverend Lee's head and face, which the local sheriff said were probably dental fillings. Even after the doctors told him that LED pellets were outdated and no longer used, the sheriff concluded without conducting an investigation that Reverend Lee had died from a traffic accident. At the conclusion, a coroner's jury disregarded evidence indicating that Reverend Lee was murdered and ruled his death as unknown causes. In Brookhaven, Mississippi, local witnesses and the local sheriff watched as a white man shot Lamar Smith with a .38 Caliber pistol at close range after several white men who began arguing with him for his efforts in organizing Negroes in the area to vote approached him as he stood on the county courthouse lawn."*

One would get the impression by Emmett's ostensible interest in the news report regarding matters of race, that he had some knowledge and understanding about racial conflicts meted out to people of color. On the contrary, Emmett Till was precocious for his age and he had often impressed his mother and grandmother with his awareness of current topics, topics that one would perceive to be negligible for a fourteen-year-old. Emmett was a typical youth fascinated with radio and television. It was common for him to witness from television news images, incidents involving race violence perpetrated on those of his race as the media reported on an onslaught of images of racial confrontations in the South as well as in parts of the North on a daily bombardment, as violent race matters made headlines daily throughout the nation and parts of the world; visual images, revealing such brutal violence as was reported regarding flagrant and heinous lynchings executed by ultra-conservative white mobs on Americans of African ancestry whom they felt violated social racial etiquette on any level. In spite of any exposure he might have saw or heard from the media. Emmett Till's limited personal knowledge of such race matters only made him a youth aware of his surroundings, yet too young to grasp the seriousness of it. So in the safe confines of his resident, Emmett encountered the news report with enlighten interest.

In the meantime, he continued to focus on the task at hand, as he added more portions of butter, one more cup of ready mix and half a cup of flour to the compound. Subsequently, Emmett watched in harsh disappointment as his efforts to bake a cake began to disintegrate before his eyes. With all the efforts that he had mustered in accomplishing his goal, the ingredients became thick and gooey in the bowl. The realization that his efforts were failing became apparent as his failed endeavor ignited feelings of frustration within him. Emmett struggled with feelings of disappointment and he decided that his only recourse of action was to seek assistance from his next door neighbor who resided on the second floor of the two-flat next door. Emmett turned the radio down, vacated the kitchen, and when he entered the back porch area of his resident, he spotted his neighbor, Maedean who resided in the adjacent building owned by her mother.

Emmett watched Maedean in the next yard walking toward the trash container near the garage to discard the bag of garbage she was carrying. Maedean was a witty, easygoing and temperamental woman in her early thirties. She lived in the second floor apartment with her employed husband, and their three school age children. Emmett leaned against the porch railing and with a hearty burst of excitement; he called out to her, "MAEDEAN!" The excited tone in his voice caused a slight startled expression on her face and she asked, "What is it, Bo? Is somethin' wrong?" Emmett stammered out his explanation, "Well…kind of. Can you come up here? I'm havin' sort of a problem."

Maedean replied, "I'll be right up!" She placed the garbage in the trash container and then she vacated the yard of her residence and entered the adjacent yard where Emmett lived and scurried up the back stairs to the second floor apartment. When she entered the kitchen slightly out of breath, she found him standing at the table staring into the bowl. Maedean could not help noticing the disorderly sight on the table and his untidy appearance, as his clothes and face were spotted to a certain extent with flour. She shook her head in amusement and broke out in hilarious laughter at his unsuccessful attempt at baking. "Lord! Emmett Louis Till what are you doing," she asked?

Emmett struggled to stir the thick adhesive tacky mixture

intensely as he added more water to the mix and then he asserted, "I'm bakin' a pound cake." Maedean examined the mixture closely and she iterated, "A pound cake?" Emmett responded, "Yeah! I wanna surprise Mama when she comes home from work." They both stared indecisively into the bowl. Then he added, "But… I've done something wrong. Look at this, what's the matter with it?" Maedean picked up the box of ready mix and she remarked to him, "You used this?" Emmett stared at her curiously and then he uttered, "Yeah, why?" Maedean replied with humor, "Because, it's ready mix, Bo! You can't bake a cake with ready mix it is only for baking cornbread…it's ruined!" Disappointingly, he asked, "think so?" "I think you better quit and clean up this mess before your mama gets home," she replied. Maedean watched after a disappointed Emmett as he began to clean up his failed attempt at baking and she asked, "Need some help cleanin' up?" Emmett replied, "Thanks, but I can manage." Maedean then uttered with humor, "Wait 'til I tell mama 'bout this." "Just make sure you tell her that I'll be by later to check on her," he replied. Maedean walked toward the door to leave, she turned to him again and said, "You know Mama thinks the world of you." Emmett responded with a broad smile as he watched her desert the kitchen and he resumed his cleaning task.

Later that same evening, Emmett joined his neighborhood friends in a vigorous game of sandlot baseball. He and neighborhood friends were playing on the schoolyard grounds of the McCosh Elementary School. The McCosh Elementary School occupied the entire block of Sixty-Fourth and Champlain Avenue. During the game, Emmett's little League team was leading their opponents by one point. It was the bottom of the ninth and the bases were loaded. All eyes turned to Emmett, as he stepped up to home plate and positioned the bat in his hand. As his teammates watched him with expectation, he peered with confidence at the fifteen-year-old male pitcher. He then brushed the dirt from home plate with the side of his sneaker. Then he carefully wiped the sweat from his brow with the back of his hand, rotated the bat in his hand like a pro and then nodded to the pitcher. The male pitcher seemed to emulate his favorite professional baseball player, Johnny Antonelli of the New York Giants, a baseball team who had won the 1954 World Series Championship, as he whirled his arm around in a circular motion and released the ball in his hand, which moved through the air rapidly toward Emmett. The youngsters' chatter erupted into euphoric excitement, as Emmett smacked the ball out of the park. As Emmett scurried from base to base, his teammates, ranging in age from twelve to sixteen, yelled, "ITS A GRAND SLAM! WAY TO GO, BO!"

When Emmett scurried toward home plate, his focus of attention shifted to his two cousins entering the school grounds. Wheeler Parker Junior who resided in Argo, Illinois and his cousin, Curtis Jones entered the school grounds from Champlain Avenue. When Emmett crossed over home plate, he continued over to greet them as they walked toward him. Emmett and his two cousins began to converse when their conversation was interrupted by a tall, slender-built youth whom they knew, and soon joined in the conversation. The youth was sixteen-year-old Eric, a normal looking, average height and temperamental teenager.

Eric asked, "Hey fellows. How you be?"

"We're cool... Wheeler replied.

Emmett, being the impulsive practical joker who loved playing pranks on friends and relatives alike observed the friendly exchange between Wheeler and Eric and he just could not resist the comical opportunity to seize the moment. He told his cousin, "H-Hey-y-y, Wheeler! You shoulda heard what Eric's been sayin' about you." Eric stared at Emmett in a perplexed manner.

Curtis and Emmett watched the amusing dilemma unfold between Eric and Wheeler with humor. Wheeler obviously became agitated over the implied accusation and he confronted Eric. Wheeler asked him pugnaciously, "What you say about me, man? Eric replied sharply, "Did you hear me say anything about you?" The two youth's behavior led to a verbal confrontation as they exchanged insults with one another. Their signifying caused the two youths to move toward one another in a combatant manner. Emmett perceived that the situation was about to get out of hand and he moved in quickly to alleviate the tension between them. Standing between Wheeler and Eric, he informed them, "Aw, man! I was just joking, don't be mad!" They stared at him through irritating eyes and then they smiled reluctantly at each other. Emmett then took them by their hands and said, "C'mon shake hands." Wheeler and Eric complied with his request and they shook hands indicating that their friendship was still intact. Emmett then asked, "You're cool!" Eric and Wheeler both replied, "We're cool!" Shortly thereafter, Eric remembered that he had an impending errand to make for his mother and he bade them farewell and deserted the school grounds.

Meanwhile, Emmett, Curtis and Wheeler walked over to where the youngsters were celebrating their victory over their opponent. As they watched the mingling between both teams with interest, Wheeler turned to Emmett and said,

"Hey, Bo...me and Curtis is goin' down South, tomorrow."

Emmett asked anxiously, "Tomorrow, with who?"

Curtis replied, "With grandpa, Moses."

Emmett's disappointment came through his expression and he eagerly informed them, "I wanna go!"

"They're over to your house right now," Wheeler replied.

Emmett informed his coach and his neighborhood companions that he would see them later and he and his two cousins abandoned the school grounds en route to his place of residence.

They walked along Champlain Avenue laughing and joking with each other and when they reached the corner of Champlain and Sixty-Fourth Street; Wheeler observed his girlfriend, Paula whom he had been dating since mid-spring. Fifteen-year-old Paula was actively jumping rope with her two closest friends: fourteen-year-old Sharon and Sharon's thirteen-year-old sister, Nancy. Wheeler, Emmett and Curtis came to a grinding halt to watch the three girls jumping rope with other girls near the neighborhood Jewish grocery store. The girls were so preoccupied with their activities that they were unaware that the three male youngsters were watching their playful activities.

Curtis watched with fascination as Sharon flaunted her athletic and artistic routine of double Dutch jumping. He was obviously captivated-by her, but reluctant to ask her to go steady with him for fear of being rejected. Sharon's younger sister, Nancy was infatuated with Emmett, but he felt that she was too young for him. Actually, Emmett had always been rather bashful when it came to dating, because of his embarrassing stammer, which made him avoid long conversations with girls or people he did not know well. His knowledge of girls came by watching older boys around him, especially his best friend and playful cousin, Wheeler Parker from Argo, Illinois.

Wheeler, Curtis and Emmett began to walk toward the girls, who were now pretending not to notice them, as the three male youngsters paused to watch the activities played out among the girls, Wheeler playfully asked, "Hey, Bo. You kiss Nancy, yet? You know she wants you too." Emmett attempted to project a debonair smile for the sake of his image and he replied, "Naw, man. I'll wait 'til she gets a little older." "What! She's just one year younger than you," replied Wheeler with humor. Curtis then asked, "Say, Wheeler…you kiss Paula?" Wheeler replied with assurance, "Yeah, I kissed her and that ain't all." Curtis and Emmett laughed with fascination at the meaning of the emphasis he placed on "and that ain't all."

Curtis whispered to his two cousins, "Man, look at that, they're ignorin' us." Emmett then interjected, "Bet I can get their attention. Watch this!" He wolf-whistled and the girls suspended their activities shortly thereafter, as they stared at the three handsome youngsters with girlish interest. Nancy watched Emmett and when he smiled at her, she dropped her head in a bashful response.

Paula walked over to Wheeler and he took her hand in his as they engaged in small talk. Curtis and Emmett conversed with Sharon and Nancy. Paula then asked, "Where you on your way too? Wheeler replied, "Over to Bo's to see if his mother will let him go down South with us tomorrow." Paula asked disappointingly, "You're leaving, tomorrow?" He reassured her by saying, "I'll see you before I leave." Emmett and his two cousins began to walk away from the girls and they remarked, "See you late Alligator." "After while Crocodile," the girls shouted back flirtatiously.

A short time later, they raced up the stairs to the second floor apartment where Emmett lived. Upon their noisy entrance into the immaculate living room decorated in conservative furnishings, the noise the youngsters made peeved Mamie slightly, as everyone's attention turned to their playful entrance. Mamie an attractive, temperamental, strong self-willed woman of proud middle-class dignity and faith, was entertaining her mother, Alma, her Uncle Moses Wright and his two daughters, Willa Mae Jones and Hallie Mae Parker. Hallie Mae was the youngest of Moses four siblings from his first marriage and the mother of Wheeler. With a slightly ruffled expression on her face, Mamie verbalized to them, "Bo, Wheeler, Curtis. You know I don't allow that!" In unison they replied, "Sorry!" When the youngsters relaxed themselves among the gathering, Moses greeted Emmett with a firm handshake and said, "Reckon dis be Emmett? Boy, you be almost big as a man." Emmett smiled bashfully, as his mother and grandmother beamed with pride. Emmett sat next to his grandmother and Wheeler and Curtis sat next to their mothers, as Alma asked her brother-in-law, "Moses, how long will you be staying?" "Reckon I'll be leavin' tomorrow," he replied to his sister-in-law. "So soon Uncle Mo'…you just got here," Mamie uttered. "Reckon so, but I gotta be git'n' back to Lizzie and the boys. I'm takin' Wheeler and Curtis with me," he intoned lightheartedly. Hallie Mae elucidated gleefully, "Yes, Wheeler will be out of my hair for two weeks. I got five more if you wanna take 'em, Poppa." Moses uttered with a sense of humor, "Reckon not, baby! Two is a powerful nuf." Wheeler threw an amusing frown at his mother and said, "Aw, ma'… I'm not that bad." There is laughter among the family gathering at the comical exchange between Wheeler, his mother and grandfather.

Emmett interjected vigorously, "Mama, can I go with 'em?" Mamie declared firmly, "Now, Bo! You know I'm planning the trip to Omaha next week and I want you to go with me."

Ma' can I please go with you next time?" he asked.

At first Mamie was reluctant to give her consent because of her concerns about racial unrest in the South and her vacation plans, which she had planned for and had every determination to consummate. Although, Emmett was persistent, Mamie unambiguously said no to his request. Alma watched the sadden demeanor of her grandson and she indicated to her daughter, "Sister, you know how close Bo and Wheeler are…" "Yeah you know wherever one goes, the other one wants to go too," Willa Mae added. Mamie suggested, "Bo hasn't been South since he was nine years old. The South is so different from the North. There's always so much racial tension down there." Moses then revealed to Mamie as the others looked on, "We been hearin' 'bout y'all troubles up here in de norf. Mississippi ain't so bad." After considerable thought and family persuasion, she gives her permission predicated only on her son's promise to be obedient. Emmett promised his mother that he would be on his best behavior.

CHAPTER THREE:

DEPARTURE

The day filled with family activities had gracefully made its pilgrimage into night. The second floor apartment was quiet and the visiting guest were long gone to their place of residence and the only interruption to the state of tranquil existence, was the conversation between Emmett and his mother, which they were having in his medium size bedroom embellished in traditional furnishings. Emmett was preparing for bed and Mamie was conversing with him about racial etiquette in the South and how he must adapt himself to a new way of life during the time of his planned visit to Mississippi on vacation for the next two weeks. Emmett was very excited about his excursion, which was to start the following day.

Mamie sat next to him on the side of the bed and she informed him that while he was vacationing in Mississippi that he had to say "Yes Sir" and "Yes Ma'am" at all times and he hearkened intently with wide-eyed enthusiasm, as he hung on her every word. She explained to him that because he was much older now that he had to avoid if possible, getting into any fights as he once did at age nine when he first visited relatives in Mississippi. Mamie further explicated that the South was very pandemic with racism as opposed to the calculating deceptiveness of racism in the North. Emmett watched her with probing eyes, and then he asked, "You mean like Trumbull Park and Cicero?" Emmett's knowledge of Cicero and Trumbull Park came as no surprise to Mamie, as the troubles there made those areas one of the most vehemently preserved bastions of white racism in the Chicago metropolitan area.

An area which exploded into a race riot in 1951 when a Black family attempted to move into the all-white community of Cicero, where the venom of racial hatred and rioting lasted for three days. Until finally at the urging of Alderman Archibald Carey and the Cook County Sheriff who persuaded Governor Adlai Stevenson who was governor of Illinois at the time to order out the National Guard to vanquish the agitation. An agitation that Mamie and Emmett as well as other Blacks who lived in Chicago knew very well as their lives were inundated by one report after another of outbreaks of racial violence around the general Chicago area as well as in the South.

It was not that Mamie had some premonition about her son's trip to Mississippi. She just felt the need to instill in him the importance of adapting himself to a new way of life in the South. Therefore, she continued to enlightened him, "Bo, I want you to understand that just like Cicero and Trumbull Park; there are white people in Mississippi who are just as hostile toward us."

Emmett observed his mother with an inquisitive expression and he asked, "Mama, why do they hate us?" Mamie replied, "Unfortunately, I don't have a logical answer regarding the racial hostility of some white people. And you know…I don't think they really have a sensible answer either." Emmett uttered, "You know Mama, hating somebody because they're a different color than you is, stupid!" Mamie smiled her agreement and then she added, "That's right baby. The good Lord created all people and he did not make one race any better than any other race." Mamie further explained to him, "What I want you to do is make every effort to stay out of fights and away from trouble and if an incident does occur, you should apologize and if necessary, you should go on your knees." Emmett stared at her with probing eyes and then he asked, "Mama, why do they judge people by what color they are instead of what they do? I'm a Negro, but I'm just as good as anybody else, right Mama?" "You are just as good as anyone else and don't you ever let someone make you feel less than that," she replied.

Mamie watched her son with motherly love as Emmett said his prayers and then climbed into bed.

She assisted him as he tucked himself in and she said, "You better get some sleep, we have a busy day, tomorrow."

Emmett smiled at her and said, "Good night, Mama. I love you." She replied, "Sweet dreams, baby. I love you too."

Mamie kissed him on his forehead, turned out the light, left the room, and closed the door behind her.

The following late morning, Saturday, August twentieth, Mamie was again in the medium size bedroom with Emmett and she was vigorously packing his clothing for his departure. Mamie delicately folded his pants and shirts and placed them in the open suitcase on the bed and then closed it. Emmett had his back toward his mother as he searched through his jewelry box on the dresser and retrieved the signet ring with the inscription and date engraved on it. The ring once owned by his late father, Louis Till now belonged to him. Emmett tried the ring on and turned to his mother and said, "Look, Ma' ...it fits!" Mamie smiled and told him that he was getting to be a big boy.

A short time later the same afternoon, Mamie's fiancé, Gene Mobley—a tall, dark easygoing man in his late thirties and her mother entered the living room of the second floor apartment. Emmett asked eagerly, "Gene, you got the ticket?" Gene presented the train ticket for Emmett's inspection and as he looked it over carefully, Gene said, "It's real!" Alma commented with lighthearted humor, "He's so excited; he can't even speak to his favorite Grandma." Emmett looked up slightly embarrassed and smiled and said, "Hi, Grandma'!" He embraced her around the waist and she kissed him on the cheek. Their affection caused light laughter among them, and then Gene, Emmett's barber presented him with a new wallet, which contained several photographs of white female movie stars. The new wallet pleased Emmett exuberantly and he exclaimed, "Wow! Thanks Gene!" He soon removed his personal photos from his old wallet and transferred them to his new one. Shortly thereafter, they left the apartment, to do some last minute shopping before Emmett's departure.

A short time later, the same afternoon, Moses arrived at the Illinois Central Train Station in downtown Chicago with his two daughters, Willa Mae and Hallie Mae; their husbands, Wheeler Parker Senior and W. B. Jones and their sons, Wheeler and Curtis. Wheeler Senior was assistant superintendent of Sunday school at the Argo Temple Church of God in Christ, located in Argo, Illinois; the same Argo church where Emmett rode the Sixty-third Street bus for more than an hour from his Chicago home to attend the church of his childhood. Moses and his two daughters reclined on the bench in the waiting area and conversed, as the two youngsters accompanied their fathers to the ticket booth to purchase the round trip tickets for their departure. All around them travelers were moving about the station with the look of anticipatory eagerness and petulant interest, as they awaited the start of their excursion. The travelers were of mixed races.

During the conversation between Moses and his two daughters, Hallie Mae verbalized, "Poppa, if the boys get to be a handful, just put 'em back on that train and send 'em home." Willa Mae humorously replied, "Child, you know all Poppa gotta do is speak in that stern voice and I guarantee you, he won't have no problems." Moses interjected, "And you know I don't mind usin' my strap." The statement caused laughter among them, as W. B., Wheeler Senior and their sons joined them a short time later.

Shortly thereafter a male voice announced to the waiting passengers that the 'City of New Orleans' train was ready for boarding.' Moses and his family gathered their belongings and proceeded to the lower level where the waiting train was waiting idle on the track. Wheeler glanced around curiously and remarked, "Where's Bo?"

Meanwhile, many blocks away that same afternoon, inside the interior walls of the spacious department store know as, South Town Community Store; with the minutes fast ticking away, Emmett was placing his feet into a pair of high top shoes with crepe soles, as his mother, grandmother, Gene and the female sales person looked on. The special shoes, purchased by his mother were to protect his weak ankles, while he was on vacation in Mississippi. The location of the department store on the corner of Forty-seventh and South Parkway Boulevard, were en messed with busy shoppers who for the most part were mainly of Americans of African ancestry. The shoppers moved about the aisles, scrutinizing the merchandise with unconcerned interest. After Mamie purchased the shoes for Emmett, she began to canvass items, which were of interest to her as Alma, Gene and Emmett followed behind with contentment. Emmett soon discerned the lapse of time from the nearby clock and he pointed out excitedly, "Mama! Look at the time we gotta get to the station before the train leaves." They left the department store immediately and scurried for the downtown station.

Upon their arrival at the train station a short time later, Emmett raced impetuously for the waiting train, as Mamie, Alma and Gene attempted to keep up with him. Willa Mae, Hallie Mae and their husbands were the first to catch sight of Emmett making his way to the lower level, as he bolted toward the 'City of New Orleans' train a short distance away and they raised their voices in sporadic excitement, "Hurry, Bo!" You can make it." Wheeler and

Curtis parents attracted their attention as they peered through the window at them and they watched along with their grandfather, Moses with exhilarated humor as Emmett ran toward the train. Just as he approached the waiting passenger train, it pulled away from the station. Overcome with disappointment, Emmett and Mamie sought assistance from the nearby ticket agent and they were informed that the next scheduled stop for the 'City of New Orleans' was at Sixty-third and Harvard Avenue.

A short time later the same afternoon, Gene, Mamie, Alma and Emmett arrived just as the train was pulling into the Sixty-third Street Station. Gene parked Mamie's gold colored '55 Cadillac with a white top and white interior near the entrance and they climbed the stairs to the waiting train that had come to a complete halt at the station. As they stood on the platform of the station, Mamie and Alma embraced Emmett with strong loving affection and he smiled bashfully and as Gene shook his hand, Moses appeared in the doorway of the train. He gave his sister-in-law, Alma and his niece, Mamie a big hug. The blast of the train's whistle meant the final call for boarding before the train departed. As Emmett prepared to follow Moses into the train he turned to his mother again and uttered, "Mama, look in on Mrs. Johnson for me and don't forget to pick up 'Mike'." Emmett was talking about his golden retriever while loose in the neighborhood had caught the attention of the Chicago City Dog Pound who picked up 'Mike' several days earlier. Just before Emmett boarded the train, he turned to his mother as he took off his watch, "Here ma', keep this 'til I get back. I won't need this where I'm going." After Moses and Emmett boarded the train it pulled away from the station. Mamie and Alma overwhelmed with emotions watched as the train departed and traveled down the iron rail fluctuating from side to side en route to the Delta of Mississippi. Later during the afternoon, Mamie and Gene arrived at the city dog pound to pick up Emmett's golden retriever, Mike.

CHAPTER FOUR:

THE DELTA

The following day arrived all hot and sunny as it was Sunday afternoon, August twenty-first. Luella Johnson a full-bodied, widowed woman in her late fifties and the mother of four; was in the backyard of the two-flat which she owned. It was the same two-flat where her younger daughter, Maedean lived with her family in the second floor apartment above Luella, who lived alone after the death of her husband several years past. Luella was busy saturating a bed of colorful roses near the fence with a half-filled water container. She was so preoccupied tending to her garden that she was unaware of Mamie exiting the garage and entering the backyard next door. Luella was Emmett's special responsibility. Emmett assigned himself as her special guardian to assist her with any needed essentials such as, running errands or assisting with chores like watering or cutting the grass or just providing companionship when he felt she was in need of company.

Mamie had returned home from church and after placing her car in the garage, she stopped to converse with Luella. She complimented Luella on how beautiful her roses were and on her floral arrangements and Luella responded by telling Mamie that she was welcomed to any floral selection of her choice. As their general conversation continued, Luella asked, "Where's Bo, how come he didn't come by yesterday?" Mamie replied, "He left yesterday to visit relatives in Money, Mississippi. But, he told me to make sure that I looked in on you." Luella's admiration burst forth through her smile and she replied, "Bless his heart. Why don't you give him to me?" Mamie smiled with motherly pride, "Honey, he's the joy of my heart...it's hard enough being away from him for two weeks, but thanks for offering, anyway." At the conclusion of their conversation, Mamie bade farewell to Luella and then made her way up the back stairs to her second floor apartment.

Mamie looked forward to the beginning week of her vacation and she was looking with anticipation toward the rest and possible relaxation from her job as a voucher examiner with the United States Air Force. She was still pondering her trip to Omaha during the late part of the week to visit relatives, but first she resolved to do some last minute house cleaning before the start of her excursion. A short time later during the afternoon, her mother Alma came by to visit and she assisted Mamie with some of her household chores.

Meanwhile the same afternoon, the passenger train with the inscription 'City of New Orleans' attached to its side arrived at the Grenada Train Station in Grenada, Mississippi located about thirty miles east of Money, Mississippi. The train finally came to a squeaking halt outside the two connected structures with all the outward grandeur of southern hospitality. The doors slid open, the conductors disembarked placing footstools under the stairs, and at once the passengers began to leave the train. Moses; his two grandsons, Wheeler and Curtis; and his nephew, Emmett emerged from the train into the blazing heat of the Mississippi Delta.

While Moses and his young kinfolk's were waiting outside the station for the arrival of Moses three youngest sons who were scheduled to pick them up, an elderly male friend whom he had known for many years approached him. The two men indulged each other's conversation of interest, thereby, ignoring the restless youngsters standing nearby. The heat in Mississippi was more humid than the heat in summer-time Chicago and it became intolerable for Emmett and his cousins to endure; consequently, they sought refuge in the nearby station. The youngsters ambled in a leisurely pace through the door, paying no attention to the WHITE ONLY sign-hanging overhead.

Inside the segregated station reserved for whites, numerous white occupants of mixed genders and ages were conversing with one another, as children of some of the adults played in view of their parents in the simple yet neatly furnished station. When the Southern inhabitants caught glimpse of the three black youngsters' entrance into the whites' only section, their red faces revealed a state of consternation. There was a sudden stillness, which inundated the area, as they gazed upon the black intruders with hate fill animosity. The youngsters watched the inimical environment with perplexed uncertainty.

Meanwhile, Moses and his companion rushed into the white section just as several adult white males were walking toward the youngsters and one of them uttered harshly, "What y'all niggers doin' in here?" Moses stepped between the agitated white males and his discontented relatives who watched the men in silent anger. In a condescending manner, Moses submissively made supplication for his young relatives' impetuous lack of conformity to racial decorum, and he made every effort not to make eye contact with the hostile whites; then he and his friend hustled the youngsters out of the white section. They entered the colored section adjacent to the white section, which was not as nice as the white only section next door. Inside the station, Moses reprimanded the youngsters concerning racial etiquette in the South. Moses further told his young kinfolk to make certain that they were observant of the two distinct signs and that they were to use only the facilities with the colored only signs. The youngsters convinced Moses of their understanding regarding the matter.

A short time later, Moses youngest sons: Maurice, 16; Robert, 14; and 12 years old, Simeon arrived at the station to pick up their visiting relatives from Chicago. Moses three sons greeted their visiting relatives with an auspicious reception and then they set out in Moses' 1946 gray Ford Sedan en route to the backwoods community of Money, Mississippi. The '46 Ford Sedan rumbled along the dry rural back road trailing funnel-shaped clouds in its wake. Emmett, Wheeler and Curtis watched with fascination at the broad flat fields reaped with cotton and worked by black sharecroppers as the fields reached out evenly toward the far horizon. The automobile passed a countrified Baptist church near the small delta town of Philipp, Mississippi.

Inside the church, an assemblage of Southern white parishioners fanned themselves briskly to escape the boisterous attack of the intense summertime heat inside the one-story structure. Their attention was riveted on a white Minister who was a medium built conservative man in his late forties. The minister was preaching about salvation and he spoke potently, "I won't y'all to hear me church. You know there is room in heaven for all God's people. There is a place for good white people and there is a place for good colored folks. They have their own separate heaven and it is just as good as ours." The congregation ignited into robust "Amen" and thunderous applause as the minister continued his sermon.

Meanwhile amid a sea of broad cotton fields stretching endlessly across the region, the small delta town of Money, Mississippi set nestled abreast a dusty crossroad. The small town consisted of a Post Office, a Filling Station and three stores crammed around a School and a Cotton Gin Mill. One of the general stores was the "Bryant's Grocery and Meat Store." Within the Bryant's general store, Roy Bryant a twenty-four year old, handsome, curly hair and somber man with unchanging traditional values, was painting some long overdue shelves with the aid of two black field hands. The black field hands were LeRoy (Too-Tight) Collins, age twenty-two and Collin's best friend, Henry Lee Loggins age twenty-three. The two field hands worked for Roy's half-brother, John W. Milam who had given them permission to assist his half-brother at the store. Sundays found the store closed, to allow Roy to do necessary work around the general store. Roy's biggest profit was snuff-and-fatback, which he sold to black sharecroppers on credit as well as extending credit to poor white sharecroppers.

Roy's wife, Carolyn, twenty-one; an attractive Irish woman with jet black hair, dark eyes and a shapely small physique; entered the store from the back living quarters, where they resided with their two small boys, ages two and three. Carolyn began to assist around the store by cleaning the counter and the shelves behind the counter as the children played together in view of their parents. Roy and Carolyn's social life was visits to their families and whenever they could borrow a car from a family member, they traveled to the local drive-in for entertainment. For extra money, Carolyn took care of the store when Roy worked away from home, often driving a brother's truck on family related business. Roy's mother, Eula Lee had been married twice and as a result of a previous marriage, she gave birth to eleven children respectively. In her first marriage, she gave birth to five boys all "Milam Children" and in her second, she gave birth to three boys and three girls all "Bryant children".

Neighbors considered the Milam-Bryant family as a lusty and devoted clan, who worked, fought, voted and played together. The Milam-Bryant clan was such a well extended family that the 'half' in their kindred had little or no consideration. For numerous years, the family had operated a chain of cotton field stores as well as leasing trucks and mechanical cotton machinery.

In reference to Americans of concentrated African ancestry, the Milam-Bryant household thinking was like many of their white southern neighbors who used the analogy that blacks would never reach the level of equality to whites, just as it was improbable for peacocks to intermingle with sparrows or for lions to lay down with lambs. For the genealogy of the Anglo-Saxon race was a special breeding pass down from generation to generation of its own kind, a consideration of immense sovereignty to the darker race, whose mindset denoted the opinion of a given superlative breeding, a God given right and superiority over the darker race. Therefore, the reasoning was that it was ordained of God himself that whites were to rule and blacks were to serve and serve they did under the most inhumane conditions from slavery to Jim Crow.

An hour later the same afternoon on the G. C. Frederick plantation, Moses wife, Elizabeth watched from the screened porch waiting for the arrival of her husband and relatives from Chicago. She watched with anticipation as the '46 Ford driven by her son, Maurice turned off the gravel road and pulled in under the low hanging persimmon tree in between the two cedar trees in the front yard. Elizabeth's family called her, Mama Lizzie. Mama Lizzie was an attractive woman in her mid-fifties and a schoolteacher in one of the schools near the town of Money. Mama Lizzie and Moses had eight siblings, six boys and two girls and the three youngest males lived with them in their L-shaped tenant shack on the cotton field plantation. Mama Lizzie was already out the door before the vehicle came to a halt in the front yard and when the occupants vacated the automobile, she gleefully rushed to greet them. Mama Lizzie was surprised to see how much Emmett; her sister's grandson had grown since his last visit to Mississippi. The family members entered the tenant shack where the reception continued. Mama Lizzie had prepared a big dinner for her visiting guest.

Meanwhile at the Bryant's general store, a green and white 1955 Chevrolet pickup truck with a white top arrived and parked outside the store. The occupants in the truck consisted of John Williams Milam, thirty-six, a large bodied man with a receding hairline. He was an ultra-conservative and an extrovert with unchanging southern values. Sitting adjacent to him was his wife, Juanita and their two small boys, ages five and three. Riding in the rear cargo area of the truck was John's brother, L. C. Milam, age thirty-four. L. C. was an overseer who managed the Clint Sheridan plantation near Drew, Mississippi. L. C. was Roy's half-brother. The occupants vacated the pickup truck and entered the general store to visit Roy and Carolyn. During their conversation, Roy and L. C. contemptuously joked about the way; "Big John handled the niggers on his farm." As the two black field hands, Too-Tight and Henry Lee looked on with indifference, J.W. as he was known, arrogantly uttered with a sense of pride, "Y'all talk like I'm a bully. Hell! I ain't no bully; I never hurt a nigger in my life. I just know how to work 'em. Long as niggers stay in their place, they ain't got no trouble with me." His sardonic statement of never hurting blacks in his life prompted a hilarious response from his two brothers. J.W. then turned toward the two black field hands as they were painting the shelf nearest the counter and he asked, "Ain't that right, boys?" Both field hands replied conscientiously, "Yessuh, Mister J.W."

Too-Tight and Henry Lee was painfully aware of J.W. and his sibling's violent reputation toward blacks who did not keep their place so they knew that their safety hinged on their subservient and passive behavior toward their white overseers. As the conversation between Roy and his brothers continued, Roy was informed by his brother, L. C. that he was to take a brother's truck to New Orleans to pick up some packed cartons of shrimps and transport them to San Antonio, Texas and from there he was to proceed on to Brownsville, Texas. While in Brownsville, J.W. told Roy that he was to pick up some machine parts for their brother, J.B. J.W. disclosed that if Roy departed on the early following morning, he could probably conclude his task either, Thursday or Friday of the same week.

Several hours later the same night within the medium size room used for sleeping quarters and outfitted in simple traditional furnishings, Roy and Carolyn were preparing for bed. As they undressed; he removing his shoes, socks and trousers and she removing her dress, their conversation centered on Carolyn and their children's living arrangements with members of his family during his absence. Carolyn suggested that maybe she and the children should stay with members of her family during his absence but Roy insisted that it would be easier for her to stay with his family who lived nearby. They climbed into bed together and they continued their discussion about where she and the children would stay and which family member they would stay with, while he was away. He informed Carolyn that under no circumstances was she ever to stay in the store alone. Roy's tenderness and the fact he would be away from her for a whole week aroused her. Soon they began to play passionately in bed, and their passion led to an intimate moment between them.

CHAPTER FIVE:

BRYANT'S GENERAL STORE

With the sweet smell of morning dew rising early before dawn, Carolyn moved around the living quarters with the same routine like all the other mornings that Roy had to leave on some business function for one of his brothers. She had been up an hour before she awoke Roy and as he dressed in the adjacent room, she was busy preparing breakfast and then wrapping sandwiches and fried chicken that he would eat later while he was on the road.

"Roy, supper's on the table," she said. "Mawnin' honey," he said.

He soon entered the kitchen still tucking his short sleeve shirt in his trousers. Carolyn busied herself packing a few clothes for her husband in his traveling bag while he sat at the table polishing off the hefty breakfast with gratification. The sound of two pickup trucks arriving outside the general store captured Roy's attention and after finishing his meal, he began to prepare for his journey. He gathered his traveling bag, kissed his wife goodbye and his sleeping sons in the next room, vacated the store, and walked with unhurried paces toward the pickup trucks.

J.W. watched him with contentment as Roy approached his truck. Then J.W., his wife, Juanita and their two children left the first vehicle and J.B., the brother of J.W. exited the second truck. J.B., the oldest brother of the Milam clan operated a general store in Minter City, Mississippi. As Roy conversed with his two brothers, Juanita and the children entered the store where they were to stay with Carolyn until she closed the store around nine o'clock the same night. They were to await the arrival of J.W. to transport them back to his place of residence in Glendora, Mississippi. It was no secret between Roy's two half-brothers about Roy's over protective jealous nature he held for his wife against his white male neighbors. Roy was often concerned about his local male neighbors being flirtatious toward his wife, which on occasion led to Roy getting into physical confrontations over the matter and the continued teasing by his male siblings about it. It pleased Roy when J.W. told him that he would come by every night to transport Carolyn and their two young children back to his place in Glendora, during his absence. J.B. humorously suggested, "She show is a right pretty thang, you best keep a close eye on her 'round these here red necks." J.W. broke the tension in Roy's eyes when he uttered, "Now J.B. don't go givin' Roy no worries he ain't need be concerned 'bout. You know how he gits sometimes." Roy uttered with stern confidence, "Don't take much for me to kill some motherfucker come sniffin' 'round here after my wife." At the conclusion of the three men's conversation, Roy drove away in the pickup truck driven by J.B. and J.W. drove J.B. back to his place of business as they departed traveling in opposite directions down the dusty gravel road.

Many hours later during the late part of the morning, amid broad cotton fields stretching toward the far horizon, there were numerous sharecroppers of various ages and genders who were curvilinear in the fields under the hot sun of the day picking cotton. A short distance away, the Wright's family tenant shack was quite busy with the males of the house consisting of Moses; his three younger sons and his three visiting relatives from Chicago who were in the fields not far from the tenant shack working the cotton crop.

Meanwhile inside the L-shape tenant shack, Mama Lizzie was busy with her daily chores around the house while she was preparing supper. A short time later, she walked over to the door and with an energetic yell, she called out to her working kinfolks', "Y'all C'mon and eat now, suppers on the table." The youngsters raced to the tenant shack with Moses following behind, and when they entered the resident Moses uttered, "Mum-Mum, show smells good, Mama." Moses, his three sons and two grandsons left to wash for supper, while Emmett remained behind to converse with his Aunt. During Emmett's conversation with his Aunt, he informed Mama Lizzie that he did not like picking cotton and that he was willing to relinquish the four dollars a day to assist Mama Lizzie with her daily chores around the house. Mama Lizzie reassured him that although she would need to talk it over with Moses, she did not feel that his request was unreasonable.

Emmett's face burst into a warm prosperous smile of engaging delight and he then left to wash his hands in preparation for supper. Later the same afternoon after Emmett and his cousins had finished their chores they migrated to the nearby riverbank where they joined other local black youths and the youngsters indulged their playful activities of fishing and swimming.

Two days later, August twenty-fourth, it was a humid Wednesday evening and the East Money Church of God in Christ was active with excitement, where Moses Wright was the pastor. Inside the church filled to capacity, the mixed adult choir was singing a vigorous rendition of "What a Friend We Have in Jesus" and the black parishioners were clapping and swaying in time to the music. Emmett and his cousins were sitting in the rear of the church and like those in attendance; the spiritual excitement had them caught up as well. After Moses fiery sermon on salvation, he prayed over the congregation and then dismissed the service. In the rear of the church, Emmett sat between his eighteen-year-old cousin, Ruth Mae Crawford and her fifteen-year-old, brother, Roosevelt related to Emmett on his grandfather's side of the family. Sitting on the bench with Emmett was his cousins Wheeler, Curtis, Maurice and Simeon.

Emmett and his cousins were the first out of the church and the younger males scurried toward the '46 Ford Sedan parked near the door entrance to the church. As the youngsters stood around the vehicle, they contemplated whether they should go to Moses and Mama Lizzie's tenant shack or take in the sights by traveling around the countryside. Another older relative, nineteen-year-old, Thelton Parker who was the nephew of Hallie Mae through marriage, soon joined them. Thelton had lingered behind to ask Moses permission for use of his automobile to ride around his visiting relatives from Chicago and Moses consented to his request. The youngsters entered the sedan and while they were deciding where to go next, Emmett asked, "Hey, is there a store around here? I want some candy." Wheeler uttered, "Yeah, I'm thirsty!" Thelton suggested that perhaps they could stop by the Bryant's store, which was close by and pick up the items before moving on with their plans.

A short time later, around 7:30 the same evening, the 1946 Ford sedan pulled up and parked in front of the general store with the inscription, "Bryant's Grocery and Meat Store." There were numerous black youngsters playing checkers and wrestling in front of the store. The occupants fled the vehicle and some of the youngsters soon joined in the playful activities outside the store. Thelton and Ruth stopped to converse with some friends whom they knew. Curtis and Roosevelt ambled over to where several youths and an elderly man in his mid-fifties where playing checkers. Emmett, Wheeler, Maurice and Simeon conversed with some of the local youths. During the youngsters playful conversation, two of the local youth's began talking about girls and Emmett, Wheeler, Maurice and various youths standing nearby participated with willing fascination in the conversation. All the older youngsters boasted and teased one another about alleged intimate relations with girls in the area. As the boasting among the older youths became more intense, Emmett's inexperience caused him to feel excluded; consequently, he became competitive in his efforts to show them up. He took the wallet from his back pocket and made visible to them the pictures inside including two white female students whom he had attended class with. Too Wheeler's amazement, Emmett stated boastfully that they were his girlfriends. Emmett noticed the surprised expression on Wheeler's face and he clandestinely winked to him indicating that he was only joking about the matter.

The youths crowded around Emmett to get a closer look at the photographs and a tall, slender, sixteen-year-old local youth suggested, "You talkin' mighty big Bo! Since you know how to handle white girls, let's see you go in and talk to the pretty white lady in the store there." In unison, several of the youths persuaded, "Yeah, Bo! Let us see you do it. You ain't chicken is ya'?" They stared at him with a taunting look and Emmett knew that he would have either to accept the challenge or acquire the consistent badgering of their sneering contempt.

Reluctantly he entered the store and the youngsters surrounded the door peeking in. Emmett walked nonchalantly over to the counter and asked for two cents worth of candy and a soda pop. Carolyn placed several pieces of candy and a bottle of soda pop on the counter and she acrimoniously asked, "Is that all?" Emmett nodded his head in the affirmative and looked over at the youngsters surrounding the door and Carolyn observed them as well. He retrieved some change from his pocket and she directed him to place them on the counter to avoid any possible contact with his black skin. He collected the numerous pieces of assorted candies and the soda pop for Wheeler and he turned to walk away, but then he turned to her again, smiled and said, "Gooooody-b-b-bye." She followed him to the door to quiet the youngster's noise outside and as the youngsters were laughing at Emmett for not following through on the bet and as he left the store in front of her, he wolf-whistled. Carolyn became enraged at the insult of the young nigger as she naturally assumed that the wolf-whistle was meant for her.

Outside the store, Maurice, Wheeler and Thelton rushed over to him and Maurice uttered sharply, "Boy, you oughtta know better than that!" Carolyn returned quickly to the store to get Roy's .38 Colt automatic under the counter. Several of the local youths screamed, "She's git'n' a gun!" The elderly man spoke to them out of concern and said, "Boy, y'all better git out o' here. Dat lady come out o' dar, blow y'all brains out." During the excitement, Emmett and his cousins fishtailed away from the store speedily in the '46 Ford. In the meantime, a twenty-year-old, black field hand named, Johnny Lee approached the general store. He was a muscular young man who worked at the nearby Cotton Gin Mill during the day. Johnny Lee perceived the frenzy around the store, and he asked one of the local youth's nearby what had transpired and he was informed that a, "Chicago boy got fresh with Miz Bryant."

Meanwhile Carolyn was upset when she returned to the store with the gun in her hand and she told her sister-in-law, Juanita, "Some young nigger just got fresh with me." Juanita was openly concerned, as they conversed about the incident. During their conversation, Juanita informed Carolyn that maybe they should keep it between themselves because of Roy's jealous temperament and violent nature, which sometimes exploded physically toward Carolyn when he felt she was out of line. Meanwhile in the car, the older occupants were scolding Emmett about his behavior at the general store and he was both confused and alarmed about all the hysteria.

CHAPTER SIX:

RUMORS

A short time later the same evening, the '46 Ford driven by Thelton arrived at the Wright's tenant shack and when the occupants entered the resident, Emmett's cousins informed Mama Lizzie about the incident at the Bryant's general store. In Ruthie Mae's flustered conversation with Mama Lizzie she warned, "Mama Lizzie, you know them crazy white folks, they might do somethin' to him." Emmett watched the many faces around him with intensity and he became frightened, accordingly, he wanted to go home the following day. Mama Lizzie moved quickly to alleviate his anxiety and deciding that the implicit danger was being exaggerated far too much, she reassured him by saying, "Ruthie Mae, stop scarin' him with all that nonsense talk. Bo you can stay and finish yo' visit." They agreed not to tell "Poppa Moses" about Emmett's behavior in the general store, because Moses would reprimand them with strict discipline and then he would take a strap to Emmett as well.

Several hours later the same night while Moses and Mama Lizzie were preparing for bed, Emmett, Simeon, Robert and Curtis were playing strenuously in the adjacent room. Moses was irritated by the noise emanating from the next room and he uttered unrelentingly, "y'all better sim'er down in dar' fo' I get my strap!" Robert and Simeon knew from the austere sound in his voice that they had better yield to his command or suffer the consequences and they quickly replied, "Yessuh, Poppa." Within the simple furnished average-sized room, there were two full size beds. Emmett and Simeon shared the same bed and Robert and his nephew, Curtis slept in the adjoining bed. As the four youngsters settled down from their energetic activities, it was not long before they were fast asleep.

Meanwhile in the adjacent room, Moses and Mama Lizzie reclined prostrated in their full size bed. He attempted to have a general conversation with her, merely too find her staring out pensively toward the poorly lit room, buried in thoughts of her own. Her inattentive demeanor caused him concern and he asked, "Is somethin' botherin' you, Mac?" Moses often called her Mac and she called him Elder. Mama Lizzie reacted with guarded apprehension and without thinking she asked with suspicion, "Elder, why you say that?" Moses informed her that he was concerned that she might be ill or something and Mama Lizzie put his mind at ease by telling him that she was preoccupied with thoughts, which were negligible in nature. Content with her explanation, he turned out the light, positioned himself comfortably in bed, and quietly fell asleep. Mama Lizzie reclined restlessly in the dark room concerned about her conversation with her young siblings regarding the incident at the Bryant's general store. She had heard some talk about Roy's reputation concerning his past indiscretions and about his jealous nature pertaining to men who flirted with his wife and there were even rumors that on many occasions his invidious nature caused him to physically attack his wife. However, as far as Mama Lizzie was concern from what she was told my Emmett and his cousins, his boyish prank appeared to be harmless and playful for a child his age. Mama Lizzie soon began to reason out the harmless minutiae of her anxiety and persuaded that she was over reacting, she soon disregarded the matter and like her husband, sleep soon consumed her.

It was Thursday afternoon the following day, August twenty-fifth and Carolyn was busy working in the store alone, when Billy Campbell, a twenty-three-year-old relative of Roy and J.W., entered the store and from his outward behavior, she could see that he was irritated. As they engaged each other's conversation, Billy inquired about the incident which had circulated all over town and he uttered with contempt, "if I hadda' been here, I woulda' shot that nigger!" Like a raging inferno, the rumors continued to spread rapidly about the wolf-whistling incident and many of her concerned neighbors came by the store expressing their indignant opposition over the contemptible act. To her white neighbors they feared that such an act would lead to race mongrelization between the black race and the white race or even worst to social and political progression by the Supreme Court, which had voted in favor of brown verses board of education in May of the previous year. So as far as whites were concerned, the consistent struggle over voter registration only galvanized Southern opposition determined to preclude the progress of racial integration at any cost.

Early the following Friday morning before dawn, August twenty-six, a flash of headlights illuminated the front porch area of the single level house owned by J. W, Milam. Inside the truck, Roy Bryant sat quietly in a state of fatigue and then he finally turned the truck engine off. Roy was returning from his four-day family business journey and all he wanted to do was sleep. His unshaven and bleary-eyed appearance was evident that he had slept little during his expedition. Roy left the pickup truck and upon his entrance into the dimly lit house where everyone was sleeping, he found his way into the familiar room where Carolyn was sleeping and he undressed and climbed into bed beside her. Three hours later, the same morning, Carolyn quietly dressed while Roy slept with ease. Carolyn left the room and joined J.W., Juanita and the children, as they were already sitting at the table having breakfast. Carolyn's conversation with her brother-in-law entailed the return of her husband. J.W. was pleased with his return because it meant another successful venture and much needed money for the small family business.

J.W. told Carolyn that Roy would probably rest all day before returning to his place of residence at the store. She smiled at the comment and continued masticating the breakfast on her plate. J.W. was the first to finish his breakfast and he left the resident to attend some minor auto repairs on his pickup truck. During his brief absence, Carolyn quietly informed Juanita about the concerns her neighbors had expressed to her regarding the episode at the store. Although, Juanita agreed with their wanton opposition, she was relieved that J.W. had not heard about the offensive act inflicted on his sister-in-law by the young dauntless nigger. Juanita knew about her husband's violent nature at times and she was not naïve about racial violence involving her husband and some of his male siblings against blacks and other nonwhites who did not keep their place or conform to racial etiquette. Juanita never engaged her husband openly about his reputation regarding racial matters, because she felt the less she knew the better. When J.W. returned to the kitchen of his residence that morning, he gathered his family and a short time later, he dropped his family and his sister-in-law and her young children at the general store in Money. Carolyn and Juanita entered the store to begin their daily chores, and he pulled away and headed the pickup in the direction of Glendora, where he was to manage one of the large plantations occupied with black sharecroppers.

Later the same afternoon, a '53 blue and white Chevy arrived at the general store in Money. The two occupants in the vehicle were Roy and his younger brother, B.W. Bryant. When Roy left the automobile from the passenger side and as the car drove away, he began to notice several of his white neighbors sitting around on storefront porches staring at him and whispering. He suddenly became troubled in his mind by their behavior toward him and when he approached the store, he observed Johnny Lee, exiting the general store. Roy stared him straight in the eye and asked, "Boy, what's wrong with everybody 'round here?" Johnny Lee avoided any eye contact with him directly and he made every pointless effort to hedge on his question, but Roy was persistent. At some point in Roy's conversation with Johnny Lee outside the store, it did not take long to learn about the rumors circulating around town concerning the wolf-whistle involving his wife and young Emmett Till. Johnny Lee also disclosed that the "Chicago boy" was "visitin' Preacher."

Roy asked aggressively, "Preacher Mose Wright?" Johnny Lee answered regrettably, "Yessuh!"

Roy entered the store furious and he confronted Carolyn who watched him with concern and he made known to her his knowledge of the incident, which had monopolized the interest of their neighbors since the incident had transpired. Carolyn was somewhat surprised about his knowledge of the incident, yet she knew it was just a matter of time before he found out. As they conversed, Juanita listened quietly from the adjacent room, as Carolyn informed Roy of the details that had occurred. She concluded by telling him, "the nigger got fresh and he tried to fondle me." Roy's animosity seared so deep within him that his words became suppressed and ensnared in this throat and his anguished expression revealed the silent utterance seeking, wanting impetuously to force its way out of his month. Carolyn stood by and sadly watched her husband with helpless regret, as he turned and stared out the window at his neighbors sitting on storefront porches. Later during the night, Roy reclined in bed next to his wife and while she slept, he wrestled restlessly with his impregnated thoughts contemplating his plan of action, as he lounged in bed unable to sleep.

CHAPTER SEVEN:

THE KIDNAPPING

The following day-Saturday, August twenty-seventh, it was early in the afternoon and Mamie was still dressed in her bath robe, as she entered the second floor apartment with various pieces of mail in her hand. She fingered through the mail and uncovered a letter from her only child, Emmett. She quickly opened the letter and it read, "Hi, mom! Having fun with my cousins. Please send my motor bike. I'll pay you back. I'm out of money." Mamie's plans were to leave for Omaha on Tuesday of the same week that Emmett left, but she could not seem to escape her state of lassitude. Even after resting a full day in bed, the shackles of her lethargic condition held her captive until Friday of the previous day.

Emmett's absence caused a tremendous emptiness around the apartment and Mamie was missing him so much that she seriously contemplated about traveling to Money, Mississippi with the intention of escorting her son home. She even called around to see if she could find a cousin to accompany her. Mamie pondered the thought that perhaps Emmett's two-week vacation plans would be shorten by his need to be around familiar surroundings. In her mind, she had speculated that conceivably, Emmett would probably be returning home either Saturday or Sunday, the first week of his vacation in Mississippi, because he would be homesick. If he had not arrived home by then, it was her plans to leave for Money the following morning. Mamie had heard from a relative that one of her male cousins' was looking for someone to chaperon him to Mississippi. Ironically, her cousin was away from his home in Argo at the time and he never received the message that she was available. Now that she had relinquished her vacation plans to Omaha, her decision was just to wait for Emmett's return home from Mississippi.

Meanwhile, the same afternoon in Money, Roy and Carolyn were busy in the general store collecting debts from white and black sharecroppers in the area. Saturday was the most industrious time, because it was always collection day. A time when they could collect cash from their poor sharecropper neighbors who had borrowed needed items on credit. Because of the busy activities in the store, Roy had to postpone his plans to pay a visit to Moses Wright until later in the evening.

Several miles away, the same afternoon, Moses and other sharecroppers were assiduously picking cotton as their bent over bodies worked the cotton crop in the fields under the hot sun as they placed the picked cotton in the long white and gray sacks, which they were dragging, strapped to their shoulders. As they worked on the G.C. Frederick plantation, spiritual hymns sung by many of the sharecroppers in the fields submerged the countryside. One of Moses' neighbors, a full-bodied black woman in her mid-fifties made known to him about the wolf-whistle incident at the Bryant's general store involving his nephew from Chicago. Moses glanced over at his nephew Emmett Till with a troubled stare. Emmett and his cousins were near the tenant shack having a good time playing baseball unaware of the conversation that had taken place.

During the late part of the evening of the same day, Moses and his family were sitting around the handmade wooden table having dinner. Moses watched Emmett as he consumed the meal on his plate and then he asked, "Bo, hear tell you got fresh with Miz Bryant at the store." Mama Lizzie, her three younger sons and Wheeler and Curtis were surprised as indicated by the expression on their faces to learn of Moses knowledge of the incident. Emmett stared down into his plate, embarrassed for the trouble he felt he caused and then he uttered, "Y-Y-Yes sir!" Moses spoke with concerned frustration to him, "Boy, what's got'n' into you? You can't do dat down here!" Mama Lizzie interjected softly, "Elder, he ain't mean nothing by it…" "Mac, dem peckerwoods crazy 'nough down here…we ain't need no trouble," he remarked sternly. Emmett observed Moses and Mama Lizzie with wide-eyed regret and his state of compunction moved him to try and ease the tension between them and he asked, "Uncle Mo'…would it help if I apologized?" Moses remarked, "I reckon so…reckon, we go by after church, 'round noon… now finish yo' supper."

Later the same night, J.W. arrived at the general store alone and he conversed with Roy. Their conversation evolved from general topics of chitchat to the most serious discussion troubling Roy's mind. He pulled J.W. close to him in almost a whispered tone and informed him, "I won't you to come over early in the mawnin', 'cause I need li'l transportation." J.W. objected aggressively, "Gaddamn, Roy! Sunday's the only mawnin' I can sleep. Can't we make it 'round noon? Roy bellowed angrily, "Hell, Naw! Some Chicago nigger visitin' Preacher done insulted my wife… and by golly, that nigger's gonna pay!"

J.W stared at him for a moment as if searching for some humorous revelation to his statement and then he briskly replied, "I'll be here, Early!" He remembered an errand that awaited him and he informed Roy, that he would return later to complete their discussion of the matter. He then left the store and drove his pickup truck to J.B.'s store, several miles away in Minter City; too undertake some miscellaneous chores for his older brother. Several hours later during the same night, he completed his task and then closed the store around 12:30 a.m., and then drove to his home in Glendora, Mississippi, a few miles to the north off Highway 45.

Early Sunday morning, August twenty-eighth, it was near 1 a.m. and J.W. was sitting on his front porch alone, drinking a bottle of beer and staring out into the darkness, contemplating his conversation with his half-brother, Roy. His wife, Juanita and the children were away visiting her relatives in Greenville, Mississippi. He decided that it would be useless to bed down for the night, therefore, he soon left the porch, filled the pickup full of gas and made a few stops before heading to Money.

Meanwhile the same morning, it was 1 a.m., when Moses and his family arrived at the tenant shack from visiting Mama Lizzie's younger brother, Crosby Smith and his family. The Smith family was residents of Sumner, Mississippi, which was about forty miles north of Money. The automobile came to a halt in the front yard of the tenant shack. Mama Lizzie awakened the five young occupants sleeping in the back seat. Moses awakened Simeon sitting between the two of them. They guided the sleepy youngsters from the vehicle and entered the tenant shack to put the youngsters to bed. Before Mama Lizzie and Moses entered their tenant shack, they looked around for any signs of unexpected visitors.

Sometime later, the green and white pickup truck driven by J.W. and a '54 Oldsmobile arrived at the general store. Riding in the cab with J.W. was Roy's cousin, Billy Campbell and riding in the rear of the pickup were Too Tight and Henry Lee. L. C. Milam was the driver of the Oldsmobile and he was to transport Carolyn to a sister's home nearby for the night and then meet them later at their planned rendezvous destination. It was after 2 a.m., and Roy and Carolyn alone in the store were asleep. The children were staying with her mother for the weekend. The store was dark except for a night light over the door. J.W. walked over to the door and pounded on it several times, before Roy, who was half-dressed, opened it. J.W. spoke to him aggressively, "C'mon! Let's go git that nigger, now!" Roy awoke Carolyn from a hard sleep and they got dressed in the poorly lit room. She watched Roy as he soon exited the room and entered the general store where he retrieved his gun, the .38 Colt automatic from under the counter. Carolyn was escorting the men to identify the youth. It was a dark moonless still night, when Roy and Carolyn entered the car and the seven occupants traveled in the two vehicles toward Moses' tenant shack, which was three miles East of Money, Mississippi.

It was past 2:30 a.m., when the party of seven arrived at the L-shaped tenant shack. J.W. and his brother, L.C. drove their vehicles with no headlights in under the low hanging branches of the two cedar trees between the low hanging branches of the persimmon tree in the front yard near the edge of the road. The house was dark and the occupants in the resident were asleep. Under the dark moonless, chilled night, the three burly men: Roy, J.W. and their cousin, Billy who was carrying a bat, moved toward the tenant shack in an ominous stealthy manner. Too Tight and Henry Lee watched the men from the rear of the pickup truck with uncertainty and fear.

J.W. was carrying a .45 Colt automatic in his left hand and a five-cell flashlight in his right hand. He stopped and gave a hard look then motioned for the two field hands to come toward the house. They were there to catch Emmett if he tried to escape. The three men approached and entered a screened porch that ran the full thirty-foot width of the tenant shack. Too Tight and Henry Lee remained outside, while the three men entered into the porch area. There were two doors leading to front bedrooms within the enclosed porch area. The bedroom on the right was the company room, where Wheeler and Maurice slept in the same full sized bed. The door to the left entered the bedroom where Moses and Mama Lizzie were sleeping.

Roy pounded on the door to the left with intense hostility. The pounding noise on the door startled Moses and Mama Lizzie from their sleep. Moses rose from the bed and walked over to the door and asked, "Who dat?" Roy uttered, "This is Mister Bryant, from Money, Preacher." Mama Lizzie reacted quickly upon hearing the name Bryant and she rushed to the dark room directly behind the room where she and Moses slept and she began to arouse Emmett from his sleep, but she was having a hard time attempting to arouse him from a hard sleep. Emmett and Simeon were sharing the same bed.

Moses remarked, "All right, suh…Just a minute." He hesitated before opening the door, as he made sure that Mama Lizzie was out of sight, he then opened the door and went out on the enclosed porch; Roy asked, "Preacher, you got three boys from Chicago, here?"

Moses replied, "Yessuh!"

J.W. said, "We wanna talk to that boy who done the talkin' at Money."

Moses uttered, "Yessuh…I'll git him."

It was Moses intentions to have the men wait on the enclosed porch, and as he tried to close the door behind him, the three men forced their way in and followed him into the house, through the door to the right. The sound of the three white men talking in the room awakened Wheeler and Maurice. The intruders vacated the company room and walked through to another room that was empty, then they turned left and entered into the connecting back bedroom where four youths were sleeping in two full size beds. Robert and Curtis remained asleep during the ordeal.

Emmett was now sitting on the side of the bed, drowse from lack of sleep. Mama Lizzie's efforts to awaken Emmett from sleep aroused Simeon as well.

J.W. audaciously asked, "Turn on the light!" Moses attempted to flip the light switch, but for some unknown reason the light would not come on. J.W. then shined the light from the flashlight into Emmett's face. He then spoke harshly, "You the nigger who done the talkin'?" Emmett squashed his eyes to relieve the pain from the harsh light in his face, and at first, as he was confused and sleepy, he did not respond to the question asked by J.W. It was only when J.W. had asked him again did he stammered out his answer, "Y-Y-Yeah!" J.W. pressed the cold steel barrow of the Colt 45 against his head and he menacingly uttered, "Don't say 'Yeah' to me, nigger. I'll blow your fuckin' head off. Get your clothes on." Emmett hoisted himself up from the size of the bed and began to put on his shirt and trousers, and then he reached for his socks. As the occupants in the room looked on in fear, J.W. said, "Just the shoes, mind you?" Emmett, whose young eyes were quickly filling with water, yet desperately fighting back tears as he was trying to understand what was happening around him disclosed to J.W., "I don't wear shoes without socks?" J.W., Roy and Billy stood there staring at him with racial venom flowing through their veins, as Emmett made them wait as he put on his socks and then his shoes.

Mama Lizzie and Moses were frightened and feeling powerless as they tried two arguments on their nephews behalf to appeal the white intruder's sense of rationalism. Moses pleaded, "Don't take him, suh. He's just a child; he didn't know what he was doin'. Just take him out in the yard and whip him and I'll be satisfied." Mama Lizzie was standing over Emmett now lacing up his shoes on the side of the bed and she entreated, "I'll pay you gentlemen for the damages. Please, don't take him, he's just a child." Billy barked bitterly to Mama Lizzie in an aggressive and threatening manner, "Shut up…and get back in bed, and I wanna hear those springs, you hear or I'll beat hell out of you!" Wheeler and Maurice listened in horror to the ordeal from the concealed empty room.

The three white men marched Emmett out into the yard through Moses and Mama Lizzie's bedroom. When J.W. walked passed Moses, he impulsively asked, "Preacher, how old is you?" Moses replied curiously, "I'm sixty-four." J.W. stared at him with eyes void of compassion and he stared him sternly in the eyes and said, "If you say somethin' 'bout this, you won't see sixty-five." The men with Emmett walked toward the car, Moses walking behind them glanced over at the two field hands who tried to hide their faces from him and he continued his focus on his nephew and the three white men and he asked, "Where you takin' him?" Roy turned and replied, "Nowhere, if he ain't the right one." Moses and his family watched the lamentable ordeal unfold before their eyes as J.W. shouted to them, "You niggers go back to bed, you hear!" When they approached the '54 Oldsmobile, Roy asked Carolyn, "Is this the nigger?" Mama Lizzie and Moses watched petrified as they heard her say from the window of the car, "Yes, he's the one."

J.W. directed Too Tight and Henry Lee to…"fetch that boy and plant 'em in the back." Too Tight and Henry Lee escorted

Emmett to the rear of the pickup truck and positioned themselves on either side of him. Roy entered the truck with Billy and J.W. and shortly thereafter, the men drove their vehicle with no headlights away from the tenant shack, as Moses and Mama Lizzie watched helplessly in remorse, discontent and horrified.

The pickup truck and the car drove quietly away from the tenant shack and faded down the road into the night. Mama Lizzie and Moses frantic with excitement rushed to the home of their white neighbor, Wilford Morris, a stocky middle-aged man who resided nearby. Inside the sitting room of the single level resident, Mama Lizzie sobbed out the details of the abduction of her nephew to Wilford and his wife, Francis. In a sympathetic gesture she urged him, "Will, see if you can find him." Wilford threw on some clothes and he and Moses left to search for Emmett at the Bryant's general store. When they arrived at the general store, they look for any sign of the kidnapping party with his nephew and Wilford remarked to Moses, "Reckon they didn't come here… this here a big place 'round here…wouldn't know where to start lookin'." After deciding that he could do nothing more, Wilford convinced Moses to return him to his place of resident.

Mama Lizzie and Moses quickly returned to their place of residence, then they left immediately in the '46 Ford en route to the home of her younger brother, Crosby who resided miles away in Sumner, Mississippi. Maurice, Wheeler and Simeon watched pensively from the window of the tenant shack, as they watched the vehicle fade down the dusty road in the opposite direction, en route to Sumner, Mississippi.

CHAPTER EIGHT:

THE SEARCH

It was 3 a.m., that early Sunday morning of August twenty-eighth. Inside the second floor apartment in Chicago, Mamie was hosting friends and relatives who had arrived five hours earlier. The two visiting friends were her best friend, Ollie who had moved from Argo to Chicago and Ollie's male love interest. Ollie and her male friend were around Mamie's age and she had known Ollie since her high school days in Argo. The second couple sitting on the sofa with Mamie was her cousin and his wife and they were in their mid-thirties and residence of Argo, Illinois. Ollie had called Mamie earlier on Saturday evening around 7 p.m., and she persuaded Mamie to go out with her to a new dinner lounge on Seventy-First Street, where they stayed until nine o'clock the same night. Mamie had been expecting her relatives from Argo to drop by the apartment and she wanted to make sure she was there when they arrived. As Mamie and her guest laughed and talked with one another, she decided to make an early breakfast of ham, eggs and sausages for them. They soon joined Mamie in the kitchen, where the lighthearted conversation continued.

As their conversation progressed, Mamie informed them of the letter she had received from Emmett earlier during the day and as she found herself just bragging on her kid, she uttered to them, "If Bo Till could get his feet on Chicago soil, he would be one happy kid." There was a moment of strange silence in the room, as Mamie was at once bewildered, which caused her to examine her reasoning for making such a statement. Just as unexpectedly, everyone in the kitchen resumed talking and laughing again and Mamie continued preparing the breakfast and none of them said anything further about the statement.

Meanwhile, many miles away from Chicago, the '55 Chevrolet pickup truck traveled west on Highway Eight, en route to a secluded area somewhere near Rosedale, Mississippi, some forty-five miles away. Riding inside the cab was J.W., Billy and Roy. The riders in the rear of the truck were Too Tight, Emmett and Henry Lee. The three men in the cab were discussing where they might want to take "the young nigger" first. Emmett sitting with his back against the cab could hear their conversations about him. As the men conversed, Emmett's first instinct was to jump off the truck, but where would he hide in the unfamiliar territory, who could he go too for help, as he stared out at the dark mysterious surroundings fleeting by swiftly. J.W. suggested a secluded area where he once hunted wild geese just outside of Rosedale. He indicated that it would be just the place to, "whip the nigger and scare some sense into him." Billy and Roy laughed at the thought of J.W. describing his intentions to just whip Emmett with his

.45 and then stand him up on the bridge, shine the light from the flashlight on the water which was a hundred feet down and make Emmett think they were going to push him in. He continued, "Brother ain't nuthin' like a scare nigger staring death in the face."

Meanwhile in the rear of the truck, Too Tight stared at Emmett curiously and he asked, "What you done, done?" Emmett stammered out the words in fear and uncertainty, "I-I didn't do nothing." Henry Lee watched Emmett with heartfelt pity and then he added, "Here tell you sass, Miz Bryant." Emmett continued to plead his case in the hopes that the men in the cab would soon realize their mistake and set him free as he replied, "But, I-I-I didn't." Too Tight asked him, "You be from the norf?" Emmett replied, "Yeah!" Henry Lee asked, "You to young be sassin' somebody, boy. How old you?" Emmett replied, "Fourteen!" J.W. drove nearly seventy-five miles in search of the bluff. For two hours, they drove, yet they were unable to locate the bluff in the darkness.

Meanwhile the same early morning, within an uncluttered living room, Moses and Mama Lizzie were in the home of her younger brother, Crosby Smith, a handsome, light complexion and temperamental man of religious faith. He was forty-seven and the youngest brother of Alma and Mama Lizzie through their late mother. Mama Lizzie was being comforted by her sister-in-law, Lillian, forty-five, while Moses was discussing the details of the kidnapping ordeal with Crosby. Crosby was in the process of putting on his shirt and shoes and he conversed with Moses about contacting Sheriff George Smith (no relations) of Greenwood, Mississippi, in the event, they were unable to locate their nephew,

Emmett Till. Mama Lizzie was emotionally distraught, as she sobbingly explained, "Oh, Lord! I didn't think they would take a child. Crosby, you gotta find him!" Moses, Mama Lizzie and Lillian watched as Crosby walked to the corner of the room. He stared at the shotgun-resting upright against the wall. Crosby then lifted the shotgun into his hand to examine whether the chamber was loaded and closing the loaded chamber, he informed them, "I'll do what I havta do." Moses and Mama Lizzie were concerned about their children's safety, as the children were alone in the tenant shack and they decided that Moses should return to be with them. Moses and Crosby soon left the resident in search of Emmett, while Mama Lizzie and Lillian watched after them with helpless anguish for waited news of their missing nephew.

A short time later, the pickup truck arrived at the Progressive Ginning Company near Doddsville, Mississippi, which was about thirty-five miles west of Money. The area was dark and desolate, as J.W. brought the vehicle to a stop in front of the plant. The three white men left the cab of the pickup truck and they reconnoitered the remote area in a stealthy manner in an effort to ensure themselves that the area was secluded. J.W. and Roy stumbled upon the cotton gin fan machinery prone nearby. They looked at each other as if thinking the same thoughts, and then with curious glances, they stared at the contraption prostrated on the ground. By this time Emmett's eye lids were so heavy from lack of sleep that he fell asleep in the back of the pickup truck and it would take Roy's harsh voice and his violent shaking to arouse him from sleep. As Too Tight and Henry Lee watched in uncertainty, Roy called out to Emmett to get out of the truck and come over to where they were standing. Emmett was frightened and disoriented; therefore, his reaction was slow and reluctant to obey him. Roy reiterated with bitter animosity, "Boy, I said git over here, ya' here?"

Too Tight and Henry Lee told Emmett that he had better obey or they would harm him. Emmett slowly vacated the rear of the truck, watery eyed and ambled over to Roy as the others looked on. Roy grabbed him by his shirt and shoved him toward the heavy device and he ordered him to carry it over to the pickup truck. Emmett struggled with the device to hoist it from the ground, nonetheless, he could not lift the heavy gin fan machinery and he stumbled under its' weight.

J.W. then ordered Too Tight and Henry Lee to assist Emmett in carrying the heavy machinery over to the truck and they struggled with the eighty pound weight of the fan. After they finally loaded the heavy apparatus on the truck, J.W. drove away from the agribusiness area quickly, as he headed north on Highway forty-nine and the pickup truck traveled down the dusty gravel road and faded into the early morning night.

CHAPTER NINE:

CLINT SHERIDAN

It was minutes past 5 a.m., Sunday morning, August twenty-eighth. There were numerous black sharecroppers of mixed genders moving about upon the vast grounds of the Clint Sheridan plantation during the early morning hours. The location of the Clint Sheridan was about three point five miles west of Drew, Mississippi. Drew was about twenty-two miles northwest of Money. On the Clint Sheridan plantation like many plantations in the delta, Sunday morning's were special times for black sharecroppers to enjoy their own personal leisure times from six days of working the cotton crop. This was their time off to enjoy their own countryside pleasures. Sunday morning was a time when many looked forward to Sunday worship at the nearby Baptist church off the plantation. One look at this place was reminiscing of the old South where reconstruction after the civil war gave birth to Jim-Crow.

Not far from the cotton fields, a black youth whom everyone knew as, Willie Reed was leaving his tenant shack, which was one of many tenant shacks dispersed throughout the plantation. Willie Reed, an eighteen year old youth, tall and slender with handsome youthful features and a youth of average intelligence, whom many described as easygoing and shy by many plantation neighbors who knew him for many years. Willie walked with unhurried pace down the gravel road leisurely to his neighbor friend's dilapidated tenant shack, which was a short distance from his place of residence on the plantation, an elderly friend who was very close to his grandparents. He ambled over to the door and firmly knocked on it. Inside a vigorous female voice uttered, "C'mon!" Willie opened the door and entered the kitchen to greet his two neighbors. They were Mandy Bradley and her husband, Alonzo. Mandy was a full-bodied woman in her early fifties. Her husband, Alonzo was a stocky man in his mid-fifties. Although, Alonzo's last name was Bradley he was not related to Mamie Bradley or her ex-husband. Mandy was busy preparing breakfast for her husband who was sitting at the table with anticipation of consuming the meal prepared by his wife. Mandy invited Willie to join them, but he courteously declined her invitation. During the small talk between Mandy and Willie he asked, "I'm fixin' ta go to the store, Miz Mandy. Do you need somethin'?"

Mandy had preoccupied herself as she was removing the country sausages, bacon and eggs from the iron skillets and placing them in the plates on the handmade table nearby and she turned to him and replied, "That's mighty nice on you, Willie. I reckon I need some fatback and five pounds of flour." After placing the filled plates of breakfast items on the table, she then removed numerous pieces of currency from the glass container and placed the coins in his hand. Willie smiled graciously, waved goodbye and abandoned the residence.

Willie Reed walked along the dusty gravel road en route to the general store some distance away. When he approached the dilapidated unpainted capacious shed nearby, his attention as well as those moving about in the fields was riveted on the green and white pickup truck with a white top approaching. The pickup truck, which the sharecroppers were familiar with because of the occupants frequented visits to the plantation, was now turning into the road leading to the shed. The truck passed directly in front of Willie Reed and he observed J.W., Billy and Roy riding in the cab. Willie knew J.W. and Roy after seeing them many times, because of their numerous visits to see their brother, L. C., who also lived on the Clint Sheridan plantation and was hired by the owner to be overseer and manager. When the pickup truck passed by and proceeded toward the shed large enough for two vehicles and other supplies, Willie came face to face with Emmett Till sitting on the floor of the truck with his back against the cab. Also sitting on either side of Emmett were Too Tight and Henry Lee whom Willie was also acquainted with. He stared inquisitively at the three occupants in the cargo area of the truck entering the shed and then he continued down the road toward his destination.

Inside the dilapidated shed, L. C. was waiting with two of his white male companions, as they were conversing and drinking beer. The sound of the approaching truck with its occupants alerted their attention and the two slender built men in their early thirties moved quickly to open the doors of the shed. Upon the truck's entrance into the interior of the shed, J.W. pulled the vehicle to a squeaking halt and L. C. ambled toward the truck as J.W., Billy and Roy vacated the cab area of the pickup. The two male companions closed the shed doors behind the truck's entrance and they joined their comrades standing near the vehicle.

Roy cast an antipathetic glance at Emmett and he harshly demanded him to get out of the truck. Emmett watched the men with terrifying wonder, as they stared at him with wide-eyed repugnance. Emmett began to slowly climb out of the rear cargo area of the truck, as Too Tight and Henry Lee watched him with sympathetic concern. The six white men surrounded him, and the two field hands, frightened and confused, vacated the rear of the pickup and retreated to the opposite side of the shed in an effort to put distance between them and the white mob. J.W. pulled Emmett close to him and he stared menacingly into his eyes stained with tears and uttered, "Chicago boy, I'm tired of 'em sendin' yo' kind down here to stir up trouble. Gaddamn you, we gonna make an example of you…just so everybody can know where me and my folks stand." Emmett tried to plead his case, but the words would not come because he was frightened and stammering badly. Roy stared at him with hate-filled eyes and then he said, "Li'l nigger! I'll teach you 'bout sassin' my wife." He then threw right and left punches to Emmett's abdomen, which caused him. to lose his balance and fall to the gravel floor. L. C. lifted him from the floor and as Emmett began to cry, J.W. pounded him once across the head with the .45 Colt while L. C. and Billy held his arms firmly. J.W., Roy, L. C. and Billy began to beat him with more intensity, as Emmett sobbed uncontrollably.

The adult blows struck hard against Emmett's young body. The thrashing blows grew more intense as Emmett struggled against the pain, as blood flowed from his facial wounds and his swollen head caused by the blows. The two white companions urged them on with vituperative utterance of racial profanities. The two black field hands watched the savage beating in dreaded fear, and their passive demeanor to years of consistent social oppression caused an inner resentment toward the men whom they once regarded as paternal companions.

Meanwhile, Alonzo and Mandy deserted their tenant shack. She was carrying a pail and walking with a limp because of arthritis in one leg. Alonzo was walking with slow paces by her side; the sound of the brutal beating from the shed and what appeared to be a child sobbing caused them concerned. Mandy walked slowly to the nearby artesian well a short distance away. Alonzo walked toward the cotton fields to join his neighbors who were showing concerns about the sound coming from the shed. Just as Alonzo arrived at his destination among his sharecropper neighbors, they began to converse about the situation with nervous glances and then they stared peevishly at the shed which was not far from the artesian well, as the sound of the savage beating and the painful cries of a child sobbing echoed through the surrounding area. Some of the male and female sharecroppers stood around with their eyes transfixed on the shed. In spite of their inner hostility toward the ordeal, their powerless fear caused them to walk away from the structure, fearing that they were powerless to change the situation.

When Mandy arrived at the well, she commenced to pump

water from it. As the ice-cold water filled the pail, she irritably viewed the shed again and said under her breath, "Damn red neck peckerwoods!" She carried the pail filled with water back to her tenant shack. Upon her arrival, she stopped in the doorway and stared at the shed again before entering and closing the door behind her.

Alonzo listened as two of his male friends discussed the arrival of the pickup truck owned by J.W. One of his friends was Frank King who was struggling to restrain his anger and irritation after listening to the sound emerging from the shed and they conversed about the situation that was far too familiar to them. A situation shaped in their eyes by powerful evil forces, which rendered capricious cruelty and oppression on those who violated racial etiquette. Frank suggested to Alonzo and the other male sharecroppers that perhaps if they gathered enough weapons that they could storm the shed and stop the brutal beating. However, all the sharecroppers around him felt that the outcome would be deadly for them. Frank's anger stirred deep within him like a volcano ready to explode and as he focused his attention on the shed, his conversation with Alonzo and the others about the ordeal only made him realize how powerless he was to affect the outcome. Yet, like many of his black and indigent sharecropper neighbors, Frank longed for change from his oppressive and savage environment. He and Alonzo as well as black sharecroppers throughout the State of Mississippi knew that their very survival was contingent upon social change to free them from their racist and downtrodden existence.

A short time later, Willie returned with two bags of grocery, which he was carrying. He walked along the gravel road en route to the tenant shack of Mandy. His route took him near the shed again and his troubled expression consumed his focus of hearing the sound of a merciless beating and the desperate cries emanating from the shed. When Willie approached directly in front of the shed again, his attention was soon diverted to J.W. exiting the structure and moving with an unhurried pace toward the artesian well nearby. Willie stared suspiciously at the gun and holster that J.W. was wearing. J.W. reached for the handle of the protruding utensil and he began pumping the ice-cold stream from the well into the cup he was carrying. As J.W. lifted the filled cup to his mouth, his eyes came upon Willie watching him with prying curiosity. J.W. guzzled down the water, wiped his mouth with the back of his hand and then he remarked grimacing, "Boy, if you don't won't no trouble, you git!" Willie moved quickly, as he replied, "Yessuh!" He continued down the road to the domicile of Mandy as J.W. drank two more cups of water and then he returned to the shed, where the vicious beating and the painful cries were continuing.

When Willie entered the tenant shack of Mandy, he informed her about the pickup truck's arrival with Too Tight and Henry Lee, and some other unknown young person sitting in the rear of the truck as it entered the shed. He also told Mandy about the troublesome noise emerging from the shed. Willie placed the bag containing items he had purchased for Mandy on the wooden handmade table. She watched his troubled demeanor and he turned to her and he asked, "Who dat, they be givin' a whippin' to in the shed, Miz Mandy?" Mandy looked toward the window with anxiety, "Reckon, I don't know child," she said. Willie's concern for the three black occupants on the truck prompted him to ask, "You reckon dey killin' 'em out there?" Mandy began to remove her grocery items from the bag and placing the food items on the table she replied, "It show ain't look right." They both stared out the window at the shed again. Her anger began to rise deep within her and she uttered, "Reckon, I'll never know how them lowdown, ornery, peckerwoods live with they meanness." Willie replied, "Dey ain't fit to be blessed."

Subsequently, Willie left her tenant shack and as he walked the short distance to his place of residence down the road from Mandy's he could still hear the beating and a weak voice crying repeatedly, "Lord have mercy." Willie's observation of the shed allowed him to see white men going in and out of the side door of the shed. He walked over to the well as if he was about to get a drink of water as blacks were not allowed to drink from the cup reserved only for whites, but he continued to watch the shed where the sound of the savage beating continued. In the emerging daylight hours, Willie soon pressed on toward the shabby three room tenant shack where he resided with his grandparents and as they were preparing to attend church later that morning, he conversed with them about the beating episode, which was taken place in the shed.

CHAPTER TEN:

DILAPIDATED SHED

Inside the tenant shack that Willie Reed shared with his grandparents, Ed Reed and his wife, Mattie, he anxiously disclosed to them about what was going on in the shed not far from their residence. Willie Reed's grandparents had raised him from a very young age after his mother, Willa Thomas moved away to Chicago after abandoning him. After placing the bag of grocery items on the table as he continued to conversed with them he uttered, "The Milam brothers be beatin' somebody out there in the shed." Ed stared at him curiously and he asked, "What ya' talkin', boy?" His grandmother Mattie opened the door of the tenant shack and the three of them stood surrounding the door entrance, listening to the disturbing noise coming from inside the shed a distance down the road adjacent to the barn.

Meanwhile inside the shed, J.W., Roy, Billy and L. C. pounded their fisticuffs hard against the young powerless body of Emmett causing him to collapse to the floor and while lying on the gravel floor, they continued striking his young defenseless body by kicking him with force. During the blows, Emmett struggled to live as blood filled the floor from his open wounds. As their white companions watched from the side, the men withdrew briefly from beating him and they stared at him laid out on the floor barely alive, swollen and bleeding from his wounds; Emmett's agony and pain had caused his crying to become very muttered and Roy gazed upon him with eyes of hatred and he said acrimoniously, "Git up nigger!"

Billy reached down and seized Emmett's weak body by the back of his trousers in an effort to lift him from the floor and in the process; Emmett's pocket was torn, freeing the wallet, which had fallen to the gravel surface. Emmett's weak body slumped to the floor again and Billy retrieved the wallet prone near his feet. Billy began to search through the wallet and he perceived the white female pictures inside. This caused him to become furious and he declared angrily, "Look here, y'all-dis here nigger got a pocket book full o' white gals." All the white men in the shed surrounded Billy to get a closer look and they too became tempestuous at the implication conveyed by the female pictures in the possession of the young black nigger and in their minds, they reasoned that Emmett had a connection to them. The resolution to the outcome in their minds unanimously was death to the young violator of racial etiquette. Roy took out his gun and aimed toward Emmett's head, but his half-brother, J.W. stopped him by pushing the gun away and warned, "No, not here! Reckon somebody will hear it."

The white men looked on angrily at the young black child still barely clinging to life with eyes devoid of mercy. The eyes of J.W. moved around the large shed like a wandering camera, then they came upon a brace, and a bit apparatus used to drill holes occupying a small corner space of the shed. He ordered Too Tight and Henry Lee, who were frightened with uncertain terror to carry Emmett's lifeless body over to the device near the wall. J.W. and Billy placed Emmett's swollen bloody face into the steel plates and they tighten the plates against his head. Roy started the motor and the whirling metal drill of the sharp pointed object penetrated Emmett's cranium near his right ear.

Outside of the shed on the plantation standing nearby were Alonzo, Frank and other sharecroppers conversing on the plantation and eyeing the dilapidated structure. Another man, Walter Bullup who was milking a cow in the barn adjacent to the shed on the plantation abandoned his task and listened as a sudden, piercing cry emanated from the shed, then ceased. During the savage beating, Walter continued with his chores attempting to distance himself from the danger that he had no control over. The sharecroppers in the fields focused their attention on each other and then at the shed with uneasy glances.

Daybreak was fast approaching the area and the four white men inside the shed began to struggle with their jitters of the possibility of being identified by sharecroppers in the early morning night. As their white companions fled the shed, J.W., Roy, L. C. and Billy threw nervous glances at each other and then at the dead body of Emmett Till lying face down on the gravel floor. Too Tight and Henry Lee withdrew to the opposite side of the roomy shed, nauseated and stricken with horror and their grief caused them to hide their faces in shame. J.W. contemplated a plan of escape and he discussed his intentions with his three white relatives. He instructed the two field hands to remove Emmett's clothing. Roy and J.W. perceived a portion of barbed wire prone in proximity and the four white men gazed upon the naked body of young Emmett as they eyed at each other with uncompromising glimpses. J.W. further instructed Too Tight and Henry Lee to place Emmett's corpse and his personal belonging in the rear of the pickup truck. Roy carefully transported a portion of barbed wire and placed it in the rear of the truck on top of the exhaust cotton gin fan. L. C. and Billy then threw an old tarpaulin over the back of the truck.

The four white men conversed about the situation and they decided that the two field hands should stay behind to clean up the scene of the murder and that L. C. should supervise the operation. A short time later, J.W., Billy and Roy departed the shed and as it was daylight, every sharecropper in the fields had diverted their attention to the pickup truck leaving the area, including Willie and his grandparents, as they watched from their tenant shack.

In the meantime, L. C. directed Too Tight and Henry Lee to clean the blood stains from the tool apparatus. He then ordered them to pour a bag of cottonseeds all over the gravel floor of the shed to hide the bloodstains. Upon their completion, L. C. after backing his Chevy into the shed transported them back to their place of residence in Glendora shortly thereafter. They fled the area inconspicuously as sharecroppers watched the vehicle leave the region, because L. C. told the two field hands to stay down in the car until they were clear of the plantation. It is interesting to note that sharecroppers living on the plantation during the savage beating and murder of Emmett Till said they heard no gunshot during and after the pickup truck departed from the plantation during the morning of August twenty-eighth.

Many miles away, the same morning, Moses arrived at his tenant shack, exasperated from searching for his nephew to no avail. Fear gripped the youths in the tenant shack as they peered out the window and observed Moses '46 Ford Sedan approaching their secluded resident. When they recognized the automobile, they rushed out to greet Moses, excitedly in sporadic unison, "Poppa, Poppa, did you find, Bo?" Moses sadly stated that neither he nor his brother-in-law, Crosby Smith was able to locate Emmett. Upon their entrance into the tenant shack from the enclosed screen area, he urged them; "Y'all git your clothes!" As the sorrowful youths began to gather some of their belonging, Simeon sadly asked inquisitively, "Where we goin' Poppa?" Moses informed them that he was transporting them to the home of his son, Moses Junior until the location of Emmett was accomplished. Moses Junior, the eldest son of Moses and Mama Lizzie resided in nearby Philipp, Mississippi with his wife and children, and Philipp was roughly about eight miles north of Money. Moses decided that it would be better if the children stayed with relatives during the ordeal for their protection. Afterwards, they left in the automobile en route to their destination.

In the meantime, the same morning, Crosby arrived at the sheriff's office in Greenwood, Mississippi. He parked his '53 Ford pickup truck in front of the two-story structure. Amid the early morning daylight sky, he sat in his truck for a while, wrestling with his state of anxiety and grief. Crosby turned his attention to the building and he gazed upon the unwelcome sight and then at the shotgun on the seat next to him. He concealed the weapon by placing it under the seat, and then he vacated his pickup truck. He mounted the few steps and entered the building. Inside the building, Crosby walked over to the desk where Deputy Sheriff John Cothran, a slender white man in his mid-forties was sitting behind a desk and talking on the telephone. Cothran diverted his attention to Crosby advancing toward him and he placed his hand over the mouthpiece and asked, "Can I help you?" Crosby informed the deputy that he needed to see the sheriff. The deputy inquired about the details of his business with the sheriff and Crosby uttered audaciously, "Some white folks kidnap my nephew."

His directness and courage to bring charges of a crime against white men surprised the deputy and he quickly excused himself from the phone conversation and ended the call. As he turned his attention toward Crosby, and after learning his name he then announced his presence to the sheriff. Cothran escorted Crosby to the sheriff's office and returned to his desk for some unfinished business. Crosby entered the normal-sized office and met Sheriff George W. Smith, a large bodied man in his early fifties and a white southern moderate who pointed him to the empty chair and they began to converse. During their informative conversation, Crosby filed charges against Roy Bryant and his three accomplices whom he could not identify in the abduction of his nephew, Emmett Louis Till. Crosby recapitulated, "They claim he got fresh with the white woman. But, he's only fourteen!" Sheriff Smith glanced up at him in a distasteful manner and he uttered, "Reckon, he ain't from down here?" As the sheriff resumed writing down the information, Crosby replied, "No sur! He's from Chicago."

Sheriff Smith's sympathy and his legal conviction over the situation compelled him into action, accordingly, he promised to investigate and make an arrest as soon as he and his deputy could file their reports. The sheriff also informed Crosby that once those involved were apprehended, that by law, he could not charge the accomplices with anything other than kidnapping and he asserted, "Both murder and kidnapping is punishable by death in this state." The sheriff rose from his chair walked over to the open door to summon his deputy sheriff.

Deputy Cothran entered the office and as Crosby looked on, he and Sheriff Smith discussed the facts of the case. They talked over plans to investigate Roy and to locate his accomplices and they arranged to question Moses and his family to ascertain more facts. Subsequently, Crosby drove his pickup truck back to his home in Sumner and the sheriff and his deputy set out in search of Emmett Till and his kidnappers.

A short time later the same morning, the pickup truck transporting, J.W., Billy and Roy were traveling east and then it turned and traveled northeast on Highway Eight. J.W. drove calmly along the highway, and then his eyes spotted an approaching patrol car behind them some distance away through the rear view mirror. His nervous behavior attracted the attention of Billy and Roy and they noticed the speeding car gaining fast behind them.

The sound of the distant blaring siren converging from the rear caused the men to become openly jittery and their fear caused a panic reaction as Roy uttered, "Damn! Reckon they got us now." As they sat petrified by the approaching patrol car, J.W. slowly impeded his acceleration; he pulled the truck to the side of the road. The men eyed each other with troubled glances and then at the covered cargo in the rear of the truck.

The patrol car converged alongside of the truck resting on the side of the road; however, it did not stop, but continued traveling down the highway incessantly. There was an expression of relief, which burst across their faces. J.W. decided that it was too risky to travel with three and he said, "Reckon, I'll be droppin' you by your place, Billy. Ain't no need involving you no further in this thing?"

Meanwhile the same morning, Sunday, August twenty-eighth, in the home of Moses Junior, Moses conversed with his son; a medium built man in his early thirties. As the youngsters looked on, he informed Junior about the kidnapping ordeal and his plans to have the children stay with family members, because of his fear that the Milam-Bryant clan might try to harm them. Moses Junior agreed with his concerns regarding the situation and he remarked, "what about you, Poppa...what about yo' safety?" Moses replied, "I ain't worried 'bout myself, I just want my family safe." Since the youngsters had slept little because of Emmett's abduction, he ordered them to try to get some sleep. Subsequently, Wheeler and Curtis were unable to sleep and they, later the same morning, placed a call to their mother's in Chicago informing them about Emmett's disappearance.

It was an hour and half later the same morning. The '55 Chevy pickup truck driven by J.W. arrived at an isolated steep riverbank near the L. W. Boyce plantation not far from Swan Lake. He brought his pickup to a halt several yards from the riverbank of the Tallahatchie River. J.W. and Roy left the cab and moved quickly to the rear of the truck. They looked around at the lonely surroundings in a furtive manner. The two men felt confident that their concealment was safe. Then they removed the tarpaulin, which covered the rear of the truck. They worked feverishly- first by removing the cotton gin fan, then the barbed wire and finally, Emmett's body. The two white men cut and tied the barbed wire around the dead body of Emmett's neck and head and then attached it to the gin fan machinery. Afterwards, they lugged the apparatus down the steep riverbank into the brown muddy waters of the Tallahatchie River. They watched the device slowly sink the corpse into twenty feet of water, too which J.W. uttered sarcastically, "Reckon, it'll be a cold day in hell 'fore somebody find that nigger!" The statement caused a hilarious response from the men and then they departed the scene quickly in the pickup truck.

CHAPTER ELEVEN:

THE CALL

Several hours had elapsed since Roy and J.W. had discarded the body of young Emmett Till in the muddy waters of the Tallahatchie River on the Sunday morning of August twenty-eighth. J.W. was alone in the tool shed in the back of his home in Glendora, Mississippi. In the tool shed, there was a fire burning, J.W. was watching it intently, and as the flames annihilated Emmett's clothing; he took sips of beer from the bottle he was holding in his hand. As the flames completely devoured the clothing of Emmett Till, he added Emmett's crepe soled shoes to the blaze. The burning process was long and laborious, because Emmett's crepe sole shoes were difficult to burn.

Later that morning around 9:30 a.m., the morning of August twenty-eighth, inside the second floor apartment in Chicago, Mamie was asleep in bed. Suddenly, the sound of the telephone ringing on her night table startled her from sleep. In her state of somnolent, she reached aimlessly for the receiver and picked it up firmly and she said in a raspy voice, "Hello…Hello?" The caller's troubled voice replied, "Hello…?" Then there was a moment of silence and finally the distraught female voice came through the receiver, "This is Willa Mae. I don't know how to tell you…Bo; they came and got him last night." Mamie immediately sprang up in the bed startled, "What! Who came and got him?" Willa Mae broke down crying and hung up the telephone. Mamie immediately phoned her mother about the distressful news and her mother ordered Mamie over to her home at once. Mamie quickly concluded the phone conversation with her mother and then she started getting dressed and mechanically began making the bed. The thought occurred to her, "Why are you making the bed? That's not important. Bo's missing." Mamie then called her fiancé, Gene and he told her that he would be right over.

Meanwhile the same morning inside the general store in Money, Mississippi, Carolyn was in the store area alone. She was behind the counter, preoccupied glancing through a clothing magazine with interest and she took puffs from the cigarette she was smoking. Carolyn raised her head to stare toward the window consumed by her own thoughts of interest when she noticed a vehicle approaching the store. Carolyn watched the approaching vehicle with thought-provoking interest; she stared curiously at the familiar auto parking outside the store, and realized it was Moses '46 Ford Sedan. Outside the store, Moses vacated the automobile alone, and on his face, he had a troubled look as he walked toward the Bryant's general store. Moses paused on the porch and stared at the 'store closed' sign hanging in the door window before he decided to enter the store.

In the meantime, Carolyn rushed to the back living quarters to awaken her husband, Roy from a hard sleep. After awaking Roy, she returned to the store area once again. When she entered the store, Carolyn was surprised to find Moses standing at the counter, he stared relentlessly at her, she watched him uncomfortably, and then Moses asked aggressively, "I wanna see Roy Bryant." She replied to him, "Wait here. I'll get him!" Carolyn deserted the store only to return once again from the back living quarters a short time later with her husband, Roy. Roy gazed surprisingly at Moses and then he asked, "What you want, Preacher?" Moses replied assertively, "I come for my nephew…" Roy replied in a defiant manner, "He ain't here!" Moses continued, "Where you take him?" Roy declared, "We ain't taken him nowhere…when we found he was not the one, we turned him loose." Moses stood his ground and stared back at him with uncertain anguish and then he uttered, "I don't won't no trouble, alls I want is my boy back." Moses then left the store en route to his place of residence, as Roy and Carolyn looked on. As they watched him drive away, Carolyn asked, "Roy y'all did turn him loose, didn't you?" Roy smiled callously at her and then he withdrew to the back living quarters to bed down again.

In the meantime, Gene and Mamie arrived at Alma's single-level home on the near West Side in a middle-class neighborhood in Chicago. The location of Alma's home was at 1426 West Fourteenth Place and the neighborhood consisted of single-level homes and two-flat buildings. The inhabitants of the area were of mixed races, mainly blacks and a few whites. Mamie said while she was en route to her mother's home and in her state of anguish that Gene offered to drive her car and when she gave in to his request, she soon felt he was driving too slowly and when they approached Sixty-third and Halstead Street, she slid under the wheel and stepped on the gas. She sped away breaking numerous traffic laws and Mamie did not stop until she arrived at her mother's home. It was her intention to seek police escort if the police had stopped her. Inside the modestly furnished living room of her mother's home, Alma, Mamie and Gene were discussing the situation over and deciding what legal action to take. Mamie was grief stricken and she said to them, "I have to keep hoping that he is still alive. I can't give up hope." Alma watched Mamie with anxiety and uncertainty and she attempted to be optimistic in the face of such dreaded distress, which prompted her to respond to her daughter's fear by attempting to reassure her, "Now, sister! Don't go worrying unnecessarily…we don't know anything, yet!" Gene held Mamie's hand in his and then he offered, "She's right, Mamie. He's probably alright."

Since Moses had no telephone, it was impossible for family members in Chicago to contact him. Therefore, Alma called her younger brother, Crosby to ascertain any information that he might have about Emmett's disappearance. During Alma's conversation with Crosby, there was a knock at the front door and Willa Mae soon entered the home to converse with the family. Between tears, she sobbed out more details about the events leading up to Emmett's abduction. As they watched her with intense anguish, she informed them that, "Curtis said Bo whistled at a white woman in a store."

Mamie replied curiously, "That doesn't make sense…I can't imagine, Bo doing anything like that." Alma interrupted, "Are you sure, Willa Mae?" Willa Mae nodded her assurance. Mamie asked impatiently, "When did this happen?" Willa Mae said woefully, "Last Wednesday and some white folks came and got him this morning." The revelation intensified their agony and all day Sunday, they called other relatives in Mississippi and stayed by the telephone, hoping and waiting for Moses or Mama Lizzie to call them with more information about Emmett's disappearance and whereabouts.

CHAPTER TWELVE:

ARREST

Sometime later the same Sunday afternoon of August twenty-eighth, Sheriff Smith drove his patrol car over the graveled road to the Wright's tenant shack, which bordered three miles outside of Money. Mama Lizzie and Moses were in a somber mood as they sat on the enclosed porch staring out at the surroundings active with black sharecroppers moving about under the humid summer heat. Soon their attention focused on the approaching patrol automobile and they vacated the enclosed porch area to await the vehicle's arrival. They watched the driver with fearful anxiety, fearing the sheriff's arrival could only mean bad news and so they watched as the sheriff abandoned the black and white alone and ambled toward them.

Maurice, Robert, Simeon, Wheeler and Curtis mingling about in the cotton fields, raced toward the tenant shack upon observing the arrival of the local sheriff. As the youths raced toward the house, sharecroppers mingling about in the fields looked on in curiosity at the excitement around the tenant shack of the Wright family. Meanwhile, Moses dialogued with the sheriff and he acknowledged with curious anticipation, "Afternoon, Sheriff." Sheriff Smith replied, "Afternoon, Preacher, Lizzie." Mama Lizzie asked intolerantly, "Sheriff, you come with news 'bout my nephew?" Sheriff Smith responded with remorse, "Naw, ma'am…but, I got my deputies out lookin' for him. I'm here to question, y'all." As the youngsters, Mama Lizzie and Moses listened unflinchingly, the sheriff asked, "Now, I won't y'all to tell me one by one, just what happened?" During Sheriff Smith's interrogation, he learned that two vehicles had arrived during the early morning hours at the Wright's residence. Moses revealed to the sheriff that Roy Bryant had identified himself when he arrived at the tenant shack with several other men including Roy's brother, the 'big bald headed one.' Maurice knew Roy and his half-brother and he informed his father, "That was Mister J.W., Poppa!"

Mama Lizzie informed the sheriff about her skirmish with the third man who was also in their tenant resident that morning. She also informed the sheriff that neither she nor Moses was able to identify him by name. At some point in her conversation with the sheriff, Mama Lizzie remembered that during the ordeal, she did get a glimpse of the man from the flashlight that J.W. was carrying. She described him as a young slender built man whom she thought resembled Roy Bryant as the man who threaten to beat hell out of her if she did not get back in bed. Moses and Mama Lizzie stated that a man and woman whom they identified as Miz Bryant never abandoned the car.

Sheriff Smith wrote down the information and then he asked, "Did you hear anybody, identify the boy?" Moses replied, "Yessuh…Miz Bryant!" The sheriff looked puzzled at them and then he remarked, "Reckon, I need to pay Mister Bryant a li'l visit." As they looked on in anguish, the sheriff drove away from the area in his patrol car. As the vehicle traveled down the dirt road, Moses turned to his wife and said, "Lizzie, reckon we be git'n' de boys back home ta Chicago, right away." She agreed and he followed her into the tenant shack to assist her, as she prepared to pack Wheeler and Curtis suitcase for their journey home to Chicago. As the adults entered the tenant shack, the youngsters watched after them melancholy.

A short time later, the sheriff arrived at the general store in Money, Mississippi. Inside the store, Roy was looking out the window, when he perceived the patrol car approaching from a short distance. He reacted quickly and after informing Carolyn of the sheriff's arrival, he ordered her to hide in the back living quarters and he vacated the store to converse with the sheriff. Roy walked toward the patrol car as Sheriff Smith vacated the vehicle, and Carolyn returned to the store area in a clandestine manner and watched from the window, as her husband conversed with the sheriff outside the store near the patrol car.

Outside the store, Roy spoke directly, "Afternoon, sheriff! What brings you out this way?" Sheriff Smith replied austerely, "I'm here 'bout that little Negro boy, y'all took from Preacher Mose place this mawnin'," Roy tried to conceal his surprised expression, as he replied, "Like I done told Preacher, he ain't here… I turned him loose." Sheriff Smith asked with open frustration,

"You tellin' me y'all went and got that boy?" Roy became affronted to the implied allegation by the sheriff concerning the possible involvement of accomplices and he aggressively replied, "Yeah, I went and got the nigger, but…I turned him loose!" Sheriff Smith removed a legal document from his shirt pocket and he said, "I got here a warrant for your arrest." Roy countered contentiously, "A warrant! What's the charge?" "Kidnapping," the sheriff bristled.

He ordered Roy to get into the sedan patrol car and Roy consented to his request under protest. Meanwhile, inside the store, Carolyn watched the exchange between her husband and the sheriff. Observing from her concealed location, she watched the arrest in a state of panic. Upon Roy's entrance into the back seat of the vehicle, the sheriff glanced at the store again, then he entered the car and drove away toward Greenwood, Mississippi as Carolyn and her neighbors looked on in anger. As the patrol car faded down the gravel road, she rushed to a nearby neighbor to seek assistance in transporting her to Roy's sister, Irene, who resided nearby. Upon her arrival at her sister-in-law's residence, she excitedly informed Irene who was a small built attractive woman about Roy's arrest by Sheriff Smith and they immediately set out in the family auto to notify other family members.

Meanwhile later the same afternoon, the '46 Ford sedan arrived at a farmhouse in Duck Hill, Mississippi. The town's location rest about twenty-two miles east of Money. Moses and his family vacated the vehicle and a middle-aged man in his mid-fifties greeted them. The man, William Parker, was the older brother of Wheeler Parker Senior. During their conversation concerning the present crisis, William agreed to drive Wheeler and Curtis to Memphis,

Tennessee, for their trip home to Chicago. Mama Lizzie and Moses wistfully embraced their grandchildren and afterward, the youngsters departed in the automobile en route to Memphis. Several hours later, the same evening, Wheeler and Curtis peered through the window of the 'City of New Orleans' train in the Memphis station. As the train pulled away from the station en route to Chicago, Wheeler buried his face in his hands and wept quietly as Curtis stared out the window with heartfelt sorrow.

Sunday evening had overspread the Mississippi Delta area and in the town of Greenwood, Mississippi, Sheriff Smith was busy in his office. The sheriff was busy interrogating Roy Bryant. Roy inquired about his impending release and the sheriff divulged to him that due to the serious charges against him, that his bond was being withheld as a result of the abduction of Emmett Till. During his questioning, Roy reiterated with irritation, "I done told you, I went and got him. But, after I talked to him at the store, I turned him loose."

Sheriff Smith replied curiously, "Came by your place this mawnin'...wasn't nobody in?"

Roy replied convincingly, "I was at my folks all night, playin' cards."

Sheriff Smith suggested with slight exasperation, "Reckon, this whole thing could've been solved, if y'all had taken the boy back to Mose place."

Roy replied bitterly, "Ain't my concern where he goes. You ain't got no right to keep me here!"

"I best be keeping you here 'til we clear this thing up," the Sheriff replied. The sheriff then asked him about the whereabouts of his half-brother, J.W. and the third man described by Moses and Mama Lizzie. Without hesitation, Roy adamantly denied his half-brother's involvement or the involvement of anyone else. Roy then added with frustration, "I take care of my own affairs!" A short time later, Deputy Cothran entered the office area where the sheriff was conversing with Roy. Cothran informed the sheriff that he was unable to locate, J.W. during the search. As the two officers conversed at length, Deputy Cothran stated that he would continue the search while the sheriff was away attending a law enforcement meeting in Jackson, Mississippi, the following day.

The following day, Monday morning, August twenty-ninth, in the town of Glendora, Mississippi, J.W. arrived at the two-room tenant shack in the black section of town. The tenant shack is the resident where Henry Lee resided with his common-law wife and his three small children. J.W. was openly distraught because of his concern about Roy's arrest and he relinquished his occupancy in the vehicle loaned to him by Roy's brother-in-law. He walked to the tenant shack near the Reid's Cafe' and pounded on the door. An unkempt woman who looked much older than her sixteen years opened the door. J.W. inquired as to the whereabouts of Henry Lee and Clara, the common-law wife of Henry Lee told him that Henry Lee was out back of the house. She then withdrew to get him as J.W. entered the resident uninvited. While he waited the arrival of Henry Lee, he looked around at the disheveled living conditions and then at the three small children sleeping crammed in a single bed. Shortly thereafter, Henry Lee entered the two-room tenant shack obviously on edge after seeing J.W. again so soon after the brutal murder of the young child and as Clara looked on with suspicious interest, the two men abandoned the resident. Outside the rented resident, they stopped near the car and J.W. inquired, "I need to find, Too Tight." Henry Lee glanced at him inquisitively and then he said, "I'll take you to him." They walked across the road to another tenant shack and there they found Too Tight with his girlfriend. As the three men walked toward the parked vehicle again, J.W. told them that Roy had been arrested and that there was a strong possibility that his arrest was imminent.

During the conversation between J.W. and the two field's hands, the conversation was mostly from J.W. who did all the talking, he threatened them by stating that they had better keep quiet about the young nigger's death. J.W. further stated to them that if they conversed with anyone about the details of the murder, he would personally see to it that the two field hands were killed and not just them but members of their families too. The two field hands glanced at him uncomfortably and with mistrust and as he glared back at them, Too Tight replied, "I swear we won't say nuthin'-Mister J.W. The eyes of J.W. ricocheted from Too Tight to Henry Lee who responded with a reluctant nod. J.W. seemed satisfied with their response and before he entered the car loaned to him, he said to them, "Reckon, I'll be seeing you boys." He closed the door of the vehicle and drove away toward his home a short distance away. As the Chevy traveled down the gravel road, the two field hands stared at the driver with intense antipathy.

When J.W. arrived at his home a short time later, he observed Deputy Sheriff John Cothran conversing with his wife, Juanita. The deputy's arrival came as no surprise to him and J.W. soon deserted the automobile he was driving and walked toward Cothran with steadfast composure. Cothran asked, "You, J.W. Milam?" J.W. replied, "I am!" Cothran opened the back door to his patrol car and he said, "I'm a-arrestin' you for kidnappin'." J.W. did not protest the arrest. Instead, he complied with the deputy's orders by getting into the back seat of the patrol car. As the deputy prepared to get into the patrol car, Juanita called out in helpless anxiety, "Where you takin' him, deputy?" Cothran replied, "To the county jail in Greenwood, Ma'am!" Juanita looked on in anguish, as the deputy sheriff drove away toward Greenwood, Mississippi.

CHAPTER THIRTEEN:

STORMY NIGHT

Later the same morning, Monday, August twenty-ninth, Mamie was again in the home of her mother's and they were conversing about the call she had made to the National Association for the Advancement of Colored People (NAACP). A NAACP assistant referred Mamie to William Henry Huff, their Chicago Branch Attorney whom they considered an authority on extradition and civil rights cases. At times, Alma watched her daughter with a distant stare of anguish as her inner torment and fears regarding the disappearance of her only grandchild appeared too much for her to bear. Inside her own troubled anxiety, Alma struggled with the longing, napping, and throbbing pain of grief as she ached desperately for any hope of information leading to the whereabouts of her missing grandson. In her state of solicitude, she inquired about the calls that her daughter had made to the local FBI office and to various Chicago newspapers. Mamie told her mother of the promises made by the FBI to ascertain the facts surrounding her only child's abduction in Mississippi. She also informed her mother about the willingness of the Chicago Tribune, the Chicago Defender and various other Chicago newspapers to enlighten the general public on the developing events involving the race hate-crime of her missing child by printing the story.

Mamie was irritable and stymied by the lack of information concerning her son's disappearance and she told her mother of her determination and plans to get the 'fastest thing out of Chicago to Mississippi…" to personally search for her son and ascertain any information regarding his disappearance. In her state of alarm, Mamie rushed to the telephone in an attempt to call for reservations and as she reached for the receiver, the telephone began to ring. Mamie stared at the ringing telephone and she just could not force herself to pick up the receiver. Alma perceived her frightened hesitancy and she quickly answered the telephone. The caller was Alma's younger brother; Crosby and she informed him of their intention to leave for Mississippi as soon as possible. Crosby asked Alma to allow him more time to locate Bo before any of them traveled to Mississippi. Alma agreed reluctantly with his request and at the end of their conversation, she told her brother to keep them informed of any developments in the case.

Later the same evening Alma and Mamie were sitting together on the sofa in the living room of Alma's single level home watching the late evening news on the television set, when their attention focused on the local news topic. They watched as the newscaster reported, "Local authorities deep in the delta of Mississippi are still searching for fourteen year old, Emmett Louis (Bobo) Till, believed kidnapped from the home of his uncle early Sunday morning." The story of Emmett Till's abduction also began to appear in the late edition of various newspapers around the general area and parts of the country.

Meanwhile earlier the same afternoon of Monday, August twenty-ninth, B. W. Bryant arrived at the county jail in Greenwood, Mississippi in the company of his brother-in-law, Elroy Campbell. Elroy was an average looking man in his early thirties with southern sectarian behavior. He was a slender built man who was married to B. W. and Roy Bryant's sister, Irene. The men had arrived at the county jail to visit and converse with Roy and J.W.

Roy and J.W. were in isolated cells on separate floors. Roy found himself housed on the first floor and J.W. was one floor above him. When the two men arrived at the county jail, B. W. visited with his older brother, Roy while Elroy visited with J.W. who requested his visit. During the visit between J.W. and Elroy, they clandestinely conversed about the murder of the 'young nigger' and the involvement of the three family members. J.W. was troubled as he informed his brother-in-law about the talk he had overheard from the deputy sheriff concerning the search for his pickup truck. Elroy disclosed to J.W. that he should not concern himself about the pickup truck because family members including L. C. was taking every meticulous effort in assisting one another in moving the truck from various secluded locations in an attempt to conceal its location from local law enforcement officers.

J.W. had misgivings about their strategy and he enlightened his brother-in-law to the fact that he did not think it wise to continue transporting the pickup truck from place to place, because of the endangerment of being intercepted by the local sheriff or his deputies. He suggested that Elroy locate Too Tight and Henry Lee and have them clean the evidence of the murder from the pickup truck. At the conclusion of their conversation, Elroy leaned close to J.W. and in an amusing manner, he asked, "Where y'all put that nigger?"

J.W. smiled callously and then he remarked, "Someplace, where the hound dogs can't git at him."

The statement caused laughter between the two men and then Elroy concluded his visit with J.W. Shortly thereafter, Elroy and B.W. deserted the jail and set out in the automobile of B.W. and they drove 3.5 miles outside of Drew, Mississippi to converse with L. C. about the conversation Elroy had had with J.W.

It was near midnight in Chicago and Mamie was restless and unable to sleep, as she struggled with her anxiety in the refurbished attic of her mother's home. Mamie was sharing the room with her young twelve year old female cousin who was spending the night with the family. She watched her young cousin with concern, as her cousin scuffled in the next bed as if she was having a bad dream. Mamie's grief and agony only intensified by the sound of the neighborhood dogs howling mournfully and she pleaded quietly for them to stop. In her state of distress, Mamie prayed softly, "Please Lord…don't let anything happen to Bo. He's all I have in this world." Many hours later around 5 o'clock the following morning of Tuesday, August thirtieth inside the refurbished attic, the little cousin of Mamie's woke up screaming, crying uncontrollably, and moaning. Mamie was roused from sleep and she jumped out of bed and went to aid and consoled her cousin, who had turned completely around in bed. Mamie ultimately calmed her cousin's fears and afterwards, she asked the young child what was disturbing her. Mamie's little cousin told her that she had a horrible dream about Bo and that in her dream; Bo had blood all over him. Mamie's anguish and misery increased with every detail of her cousin's description of the nightmare she had had.

Sometime later the same Tuesday morning of August thirtieth, inside a modestly outfitted office on Chicago's South Side, Mamie was having a conversation with her Attorney, William Henry Huff, an average looking, astute, forceful and proud black man in his late forties about her son's kidnapping. Mamie also inquired about the legal violation of her son's civil rights. At some point in their conversation, Huff reassured Mamie of the NAACP's determination to do a complete and comprehensive investigation in the case as well as the full cooperation of his office to assist in her fight for justice. Mamie informed him about the call she and her mother had received from her Uncle Moses Wright earlier the same morning, she disclosed that during their dialogue with Moses, he had told them about the four white men, a white woman and two Negroes who had come to his tenant shack and abducted Emmett at gunpoint. She further disclosed to him about her uncle's visit to the general store and how Roy Bryant had told him that he and his brother had released Bo unharmed and that the storeowner was unaware of Emmett's location. Mamie searched the attorney's face for any sign of encouragement, as she listened attentively to his consultation and in her desperate need for some kind of hope, she speculated, "I think Bo is probably hiding afraid in the home of some colored people." Attorney Huff watched her with contrition and then he added, "It is my sincere hope that he is, Mrs. Bradley." As they continued their conversation, he presented to her copies of telegrams, which he had sent to Illinois Governor William G. Stratton, the United States Attorney General Herbert Brownell and also to Governor Hugh White of Mississippi demanding a complete and impartial investigation into the kidnapping and possible harm of young Emmett Till.

Meanwhile, a short time later, the same day in Sheriff Smith's office in Greenwood, he was on the telephone talking to Alma in Chicago. While they were conversing, he apologized for the circumstances surrounding her grandson's disappearance. The sheriff briefed her on the arrest of Roy Bryant and his half-brother, J.W. Milam. Furthermore, he described Roy Bryant as, "a mean, cruel man who was implicated in the death of a young Negro man badly beaten and left in a ditch last year." The sheriff sadly informed her that he believed that her grandson had met a similar fate. When Sheriff Smith concluded his conversation with Alma over the telephone, he diverted his attention to an official looking man who was white, tall, medium built and in his early fifties, as the man entered the sheriff's office. The man introduced himself as Special Agent James Hartsfield from the Federal Bureau of Investigation. He told the sheriff that he had come in a non-official capacity to ascertain facts surrounding the abduction of the young boy, Emmett Till. Hartsfield further explained that although his office was located in Memphis, the Greenwood office was part of his jurisdiction. During the FBI agent's conversation with the Sheriff, he learned more about the case.

Sheriff Smith disclosed that Roy stated during the interrogation of ugly remarks allegedly made by young Emmett Till to his wife, while the youth was in the store. He reassured the agent regarding the strong kidnapping charges his office had against the men including their tentative confessions to abduction charges.

Special Agent Hartsfield inquired whether the sheriff had any information concerning the whereabouts of Carolyn Bryant, the wife of the store owner and the missing third man and the sheriff replied, "We got a warrant for her arrest and we're still searching to learn the identity of the third suspect."

Hartsfield asked, "Do you know if interstate transportation were involved?"

Sheriff Smith responded with confidence to his question and then the sheriff replied, "Not to my knowledge. They claim they released him at the store."

"The FBI is monitoring this case very closely. Our sources tell us-there are indications that civil rights groups are planning to dramatize the case as a lynching. This may prove to be embarrassing to the Administration and the Country," the Agent said.

Sheriff Smith responded with patriotic concern, "Well now… we'll just have to make sure that don't happen." The FBI agent smiled his assurance and he remarked, "very well, we'll stay in touch." They shook hands and then the agent vacated the office.

Meanwhile a short time later the same afternoon in Chicago, Mamie had arrived at her mother's home once again and she was fatigued from her busy activities during the day. Just as she reclined on the first chair she came too, Alma rushed into the living room and excitedly asked, "Sister, did you hear the news?"

"What news," Mamie asked?

"Bo's on his way home," Alma said.

Mamie's somber mood ignited into joyous elation and she began to question her mother to determine the source of the information. Her mother told her that she had received several calls from people who said they were calling from the Chicago Police Department. Mamie became apprehensive and suspicious about the alleged information from the mysterious callers and desperately seeking more details, she called the news services to ascertain whether they had any information about her son's whereabouts. Unable to find the answers to her question, she became frustrated and she clamored, "WON'T SOMEBODY TELL ME SOMETHING?" Finally, she called the police department to trace the messages. Someone at the department directed her to the Criminal Division and the Missing Person's Bureau of which neither had any information of any calls. She discovered that those calls had been a hoax on the part of someone, they had not known.

Later that afternoon hundreds of miles away from Chicago in the sovereign state of Mississippi, Too Tight and Henry Lee were driving mechanical tractors on a plantation farm in Glendora, the plantation that J.W. managed prior to his arrest. Shortly thereafter, Elroy and L. C. arrived on the plantation in the pickup truck belonging to J.W. They conversed with Too Tight and Henry Lee and L. C. reminded them of their conversation with J.W.

concerning their involvement in the murder as accomplices. As the two field hands watched them with suspicious glances, Elroy instructed them, "You boys come with us. We got a job for y'all."

Too Tight and Henry Lee relinquished their chores and accompanied the two white men without hesitation, because they knew the dangers of not doing what they were told, again, anxiety and uncertainty plagued the two field hands, as they entered the rear cargo area of the pickup truck. Henry Lee stared in anguish at the bloodstains of Emmett Till on the floor of the pickup, as L. C. drove the truck away from the plantation. The two white men transported the two field hands to an isolated farm some distance away and upon their arrival at the secluded destination, Elroy ordered them to clean the dried bloodstains from the cargo area of the truck, while L. C. scanned the area to intercept any possible unwelcome visitors. It was a task that Henry Lee wanted nothing to do with as the images of that ordeal continued to torment him.

Sometime later during the night of August thirtieth, a thunderous rainstorm was pummeling the town of Glendora as well as the surrounding area, as the storm drenched the Delta region throughout the night. Inside the tenant shack of Henry Lee's, he and Clara were asleep in bed. The lightning flashed violently and the rain thrashed hard against the tenant shack. Henry Lee struggled restlessly in his sleep as Clara slept next to him undisturbed. Suddenly, his subconscious eidetic memory caused him to relive the savage beating and brutal murder of young Emmett Till in his dream. The nightmare caused him to struggle vehemently in bed, as if trying desperately to escape the hideous crime and his torment caused him to cry out in agony. The ordeal awakened Clara and she inquired about his distress, but he was reluctant to confide in her. Clara was persistent in her probe and she asked again, "What is it, Henry Lee?" Henry Lee refused to respond to her request and she continued to watch him with curiosity, while her anxiety over his strange behavior caused her much grief. As sweat moistened his forehead, she asked persuasively, "Whatever it is… it's eaten you up inside, Henry Lee. On a count of…you gotta tell somebody." Clara finally convinced Henry Lee to break his silence and he revealed the shocking details of the brutal murder of the young black child in the shed at L. C.'s place involving Roy Bryant, J.W. Milam, Billy Campbell and L. C. and afterwards, he sobbed in her arms. Clara cradled her distraught man in her arms and as tears began to fall from her eyes, she spoke with quiet anguish, "Reckon, it's all in the hands of the Lord, now!"

Later that same night as the hard rain continued to fall on the region. There in the wooded river area where Emmett's corpse lay buried in twenty feet of water, the thunderstorm saturated the region with such intensity that the high winds caused the Tallahatchie River to gyrate with tempestuous motion. The river's rotation caused the movement of the current to begin hauling the exhaust gin fan attached to Emmett's corpse twenty-five miles downstream.

CHAPTER FOURTEEN:

THE RIVER'S EDGE

A late sunny morning hours before noon, Wednesday, August thirty-first; and it had been three days since Emmett Till's abduction. Mamie and Alma were restless and unsettled by the lack of information from family members in Mississippi. They were especially concerned about the scarcity of information regarding Emmett's whereabouts or facts pertaining to the arrest of other people involved in his disappearance, so they decided their only recourse was to get to Mississippi as fast as they could make reservations in an effort to join in the search for Emmett. Mamie and Alma entered the living room of Alma's home with packed suitcases, they moved about the home indiscriminately wearing an expression of anxiety and distress on their faces. The sound of the ringing telephone startled them. The ringing phone caused a feeling of agony within them and they postponed their activities and watched the telephone in dreaded anguish. Mamie as well as her mother struggled with the thought that the caller was about to bring them the news they prayed would never come, as they stood frozen and watching each other with panic and fear by the ringing sound of the phone. Alma had had an uneasy feeling all day; therefore, she just could not bring herself to answer the call and she turned to Mamie and said, "Sister, I think you better get it."

Mamie walked over and forced her hand to pick up the receiver from the telephone cradle resting on the end table, and slowly said, "Hello!" There was an expression of relief on her face, when she discovered that the caller was her fiancé, Gene. Through their phone conversation, Gene told her that he would arrive shortly to her mother's place to transport Alma who needed to get some last minute errands done before their planned departure to Mississippi.

Meanwhile, a short time later, the same late morning in the quiet saturated delta grounds of the Tallahatchie River submerged in heavy tree lined shores soaked from the rainstorm the previous night. Amid the sweet smell of morning dew hanging heavy in the air, the river was calm. Natural country sounds augmented the region and the sound of crickets chirping briskly seemed to announce the onslaught of heat threatening to invade the area and dry out the soaked region.

Floyd Hodges, seventeen, slender built and an unassuming adolescent who wore overalls and carried a fishing pole to partake in his favorite avocation, made his way through the damp swampy grass en route to the trout line outboard location nearby. Floyd treaded through the damp swampy territory, trying to avoid too much of the ground's muddiness under his feet as he carried his shoes and walked carefree toward his destination. Upon his arrival, he greeted B. L. Mims, the owner. B. L., a somewhat stocky man in his late forties greeted his familiar neighbor with a hand shake. Shortly thereafter, Floyd boarded a small rented motor boat and sailed out to catch the big catfish, whose popularity throughout the area was renowned. As the boat pulled away from shore, B. L. bade him good fortune. Floyd steered the boat in the area where the big catfish was located. The slow moving current caused the boat to drift to the middle of the river. Amid the splendor of the country setting, he gracefully tossed his line into the light brown colored murky water of the Tallahatchie River. Suddenly, his eyes became transfixed on human feet and legs protruding from the water a short distance away. He guided the boat in closer to get a better look at the obscure sight. When he peered through the shallow watery grave, he perceived the corpse of Emmett Till, which was entangled in driftwood and floating upside down. He immediately steered the boat in the direction of the nearby riverbank as he scurried toward the trout line, a short distance away. When Floyd arrived at the trout line outboard, he notified B. L. about his discovery. As they conversed about the situation, Floyd asked, "You reckon that's the niggra boy, dey's a-lookin' for?" B. L. replied, "I reckon…better get the sheriff!" B. L. telephoned Sheriff H. C. Strider of Tallahatchie County and Strider contacted Sheriff Smith about the discovery of the body. B. L. notified Sheriff Strider because Emmett Till's body was uncovered in his jurisdiction.

Several hours later during the quiet lazy afternoon of the same day, Moses, Mama Lizzie, Crosby and Lillian were sitting on chairs within the enclosed porch area of Moses and Mama Lizzie's tenant shack. Their conversation centered on their nephew's disappearance and the vast publicity surrounding the case. Moses made known to Crosby that he had contacted Mamie and told her about the four white men, two blacks and the wife of one of the men who had arrived at his place in a car and a pickup truck during the night of Emmett's abduction. Their point of concentration became transfixed on the familiar patrol car approaching the tenant shack off the dusty gravel road. They abandoned the porch area with a foreboding stare to meet the oncoming automobile.

Sheriff Smith vacated the black and white '51 sedan and walked with heartfelt regret to where they were waiting abreast. The four adults watched Sheriff Smith apprehensively, somehow dreading his presence. He looked into their troubled, grief-stricken faces. He cleared his throat and with contrition, the sheriff informed them that a body, possibly that of their nephew, Emmett Till, had been located in the Tallahatchie River near Philipp, Mississippi.

Soon Maurice, Robert and Simeon arrived at the tenant shack upon observing the patrol car's arrival and they watched the tense tragic event unfold with inquiring eyes as Mama Lizzie reached for her face and sobbed, "Oh, God!" Moses reached out to comfort his wife and as he embraced her, he stared at the sheriff with grief-stricken remorse. The three youngsters reacted to the tragic news upon learning that their young cousin's body had been found as they listened to the sheriff conversing with their loved ones. Simeon ran away in tears, Robert chased after him to protect his little brother and Maurice entered the tenant shack in tearful grief. Crosby held his wife as she sobbed in his arms and he struggled with his own grief, as the four family members reacted to the devastating news, which had forced its reality into their lives. The sheriff asked Moses and Crosby to accompany him to the site to possibly identify the body. While Mama Lizzie and Lillian looked on, the two grieving men left the area in the patrol car with Sheriff Smith.

A short time later, the police car driven by Sheriff Smith arrived with Moses and Crosby to the location amid a crush of spectators, law enforcement officers and news reporters of mixed races from various areas of the country. The men vacated the vehicle, pushed their way through the crowd, and watched with an unfaltering stare, as Deputy Cothran assisted in guiding the boat carrying the nude and savagely beaten and decomposed body of young Emmett Till to shore. At once, numerous news photographers including police photographer, A.W. Strickland from Greenwood, Mississippi, a man in his late twenties besieged upon the boat and joined other news photographers photographing the mutilated face and body of fourteen year old, Emmett Louis (Bobo) Till.

A black mortician named Chester Miller examined the body; the hole in the temple of Emmett's corpse baffled him, because it exhibited no apparent signs of power burns. The mortician also performed a preliminary examination of the recovered skull piece which had detached itself from the back of Emmett's swollen head during the recovery of his body from the Tallahatchie River. Chester asked Moses and Crosby to identify the signet ring, which he had removed from the finger of Emmett's body in the presence of Moses, Crosby and Sheriff Smith; it was Crosby who identified the ring, which he knew belonged to Emmett's late father, Louis Till. Crosby and Moses were stricken with uncontrollable grief at the hideous sight of their nephew's corpse prostrated in the boat. Shortly thereafter, Emmett's body is placed in the waiting hearse and then driven to a nearby funeral home in Greenwood. As deputies searched the area for evidence, Sheriff Smith drove Moses and Crosby back to Moses tenant shack near Money, Mississippi where other family members and friends had gathered.

Shortly thereafter many miles away in Chicago the same afternoon, Mamie was alone in the home of her mother's and she was talking on the telephone to a reporter from the Chicago Tribune. As she conversed with the reporter, he inquired if she had any information on the disappearance of her son and she in turn asked him if he had any knowledge, as the news agency was keeping the wire service on the case. Inside the cluttered news office of Bob, the white reporter conversing with Mamie on the telephone, he is shown to be a slender built man in his late thirties. Bob continued his conversation with Mamie, when he diverted his attention to his white female assistant who was also a reporter as she entered his office briefly and interrupted their conversation. The female assistant handed him a news dispatch sheet. The information on the sheet disclosed the fact that a body, identified as Emmett Till had been removed from the Tallahatchie River near the town of Philipp, Mississippi. She watched him with regret and quietly uttered, "It just came in, Bob." The female reporter quietly vacated the office, as he stared speechless at the Teletype sheet in his hand. Bob became so engrossed in the information regarding the recovery and especially about the description of Emmett's body that he forgot about Mamie on the other end of the telephone.

Mamie soon became suspicious about Bob's sudden silence over the phone and before she could ascertain the reason, he informed her that he had an urgent matter that demanded his resolve and that he would call her later and then he excused himself and hung up the telephone. Because of the nature of the tragic revelation, he felt that the news about Emmett's death should come from a close member of the family. Shortly thereafter, Gene and Alma returned from their errands and Mamie told them about the engaging conversation with the reporter from the Chicago Tribune and his sudden silence at one point during their conversation.

Meanwhile in the news office, Bob sat at his desk staring at the sheet and dealing with his anguish, which was deep and troublesome. He soon regained his composure and his professional instinct caused him to separate his emotions from his responsibilities. He seized hold of the telephone on his desk and dialed one of several numbers given to him by Mamie. He placed a call to the Inland Steel Corporation, where Mamie's best friend, Ollie and her stepfather, Henry Spearman were employed. At the Inland Steel business, which was located in South Chicago, a white female receptionist answered the company telephone and after the reporter identified himself, she connected him to speak with Mamie's friend, Ollie. During the conversation between the reporter and Ollie, he informed her that Mississippi authorities had found the body of Emmett Till. He expressed his commiseration and he explained to her why he felt that the heartbreaking news should come from a family member or close friend. At the conclusion of their conversation over the telephone, Ollie received the news with grief and heartfelt regret.

Inside Alma's home, Mamie, Gene and her mother began collecting packed suitcases in preparation for their planned journey; again, their efforts were interrupted by the ringing telephone on the end table and Mamie quickly picked up the receiver. During her brief conversation with Ollie, Mamie informed her best friend that she could not hold a conversation because she and her mother was on their way to the train station to travel to Mississippi to help in the search for Emmett. Ollie interrupted her and proceeded to undertake what seemed to be the hardest assignment of her life, and she said finally, "They found him!" With Alma and Gene watching Mamie's reaction, which appeared to reveal shock, her voice was at first held captive by her inability to speak, as she struggled through her silence and then finally she asked, "Is he…?" Ollie uttered softly through her tears, "He's dead!" Mamie screamed and then she dropped the phone and sobbed uncontrollably repeating over and over, "NO! NOT MY BABY!" Gene and Alma rushed to her aid as they too were grief-stricken as they attempted to keep Mamie from collapsing to the floor.

CHAPTER FIFTEEN:

REVELATION

Several hours later, the same day, during the afternoon of August thirty-first, inside the office of Sheriff Smith, a Southern white male reporter in his late forties was interviewing the sheriff. The reporter worked for the influential Jackson Daily Times newspaper. During the interview, the reporter voiced his opposition to the enormous publicity that Emmett Till's murder had received around the country and the irreparable harm to Mississippi's reputation as a whole. As they conversed, the reporter asked the sheriff whether it was his intention to arrest Miz Bryant and he inquired whether the sheriff had located the missing third man. Sheriff Smith stared at him with a reassured look and he replied, "We're satisfied, there were only two men involved." The reporter found no problem with the sheriff's supposition, although, the sheriff's response was contrary to what Sheriff Smith was told by members of the Wright family who had stated that there were actually four white men who had abducted Emmett Till. The reporter then asked, "what about those civil rights groups making a fuss over Miz Bryant and you not arresting her?" "We ain't gonna bother the woman, she's got two small boys to take care of, "the sheriff replied. The reporter smiled his support reassuring the sheriff that he bolstered his decision not to arrest Carolyn Bryant. Sheriff Smith in his effort to elude any misunderstanding about his concern over the tragic death of the young black child added, "But, sympathies are still with the boy."

"How you plan to handle the investigation? Especially with all the outside agitation from those civil rights groups, stirring up trouble down here, "asked the reporter. Sheriff Smith replied with some concern, "We're doin' all we possibly can to investigate the murder. We have made a complete investigation and we expect to go as far as possible in prosecuting the case." Contrary to the sheriff's statement, time would reveal that law enforcement officers never questioned any of the relatives of the accused men nor did reporters seek them out. In addition, the store where the alleged wolf-whistled incident had occurred was never searched either to possibly locate the clothes Roy Bryant was wearing during the early morning of Emmett Till's abduction.

Meanwhile, the mood inside of the tenant shack of Moses and Mama Lizzie was an enigma of sorrow, guilt and silent anger. Family members and friends gathered to console one another. Thelton, Ruth Mae and Roosevelt were conversing with relatives and friends and they soon entered the bedroom where their cousin last slept. Maurice, Robert and Simeon were already in the bedroom and their attention was focused on the bed, which seemed to draw their pensive thoughts to the night Emmett was kidnapped. They dolefully expressed their anger and distress over the tragic murder of their young cousin, Emmett Till. Simeon tearfully asked, "Why dem white folks kill Bo, he ain't done nothin'?"

Maurice eyed him sternly and then replied, "They kill 'em, cause they evil!"

Thelton exasperatingly responded, "Yeah and I'm damn well tired of bein' their whippin' boy, too!"

Subsequently, Moses took his wife to one side, they separated themselves from those gathered at their place of residence, and he informed her that he needed to be alone for a while to somehow make sense of this senseless tragedy, which had engulfed them. Moses soon vacated the tenant shack, as Crosby, Lillian, Mama Lizzie and other family members looked on. He drove away and headed his '46 Ford sedan in the direction of his church in East Money. A short time later, Moses sat alone in his freshly painted wooden white church on the front wooden bench of many arranged in a rectilinear formation, one set of benches in front of another throughout the church. Moses stared at the empty elevated pulpit and then at the empty surroundings which seemed to be closing in on him. His thoughts were deep within him, as he struggled with his anger and guilt of not being able to save his nephew from the white racist mob. Shame began to rise up in him as his thoughts reflected on his passive behavior in conforming to years of unjust racial etiquette which placed an unseen insignia of inferiority complexities and limitations on his destiny as well as those of his race. Moses raised his head toward the ceiling as if reaching into the depths of heaven and as his eyes filled with water and crawled without interruption down his withered grief-stricken face, he began to pray aloud, "Lord Jesus, I need to understand this thing…I need you to help me understand, Lord. Dey kill Reverend Lee and Lamar Smith 'cause dey was just tryin' to git Negroes to vote and now dey done went and killed my nephew 'cause of dey evil ways. Lord Jesus, there's a lot of hate stirrin' inside me toward dem white folks for killin' my nephew, but you said we is supposed to love our enemies. I call on you, right now, Lord Jesus to strengthen me and my family to love and forgive dem even as you love and forgive all of us." He picked up the Holy Bible dormant next to him on the bench where he was sitting and he opened the book and turned to Proverbs 3, verses 25-26. He then read the verse aloud, "Be not afraid of sudden fear, neither of the desolation of the wicked, when it cometh. For the Lord shall be thy confidence, and shall keep thy foot from being taken."

In the Tallahatchie County jail in Charleston, Mississippi, Sheriff H. C. Strider contacted Ed, the white funeral director in Greenwood and Strider instructed Ed that Mississippi authorities wanted the body of Emmett Till buried immediately. Ed was at first perplexed by his request, but since it was coming from the authorities of Mississippi; he informed the sheriff that he would see to it that the order from Mississippi authorities were carried out. At the conclusion of his conversation with the sheriff over the telephone, he summoned Chester Miller, the black mortician to his office and upon his arrival; he informed Chester about the directive given him by the sheriff. Chester enlightened Ed that he had not finished embalming the corpse of Emmett Till. Ed disclosed to him that he should not concern himself with the procedure because their orders were to get the body ready for burial. Chester did not openly protest his request, although, he was unsettled about the situation. While Ed was on the telephone arranging to have Emmett Till's body transferred, Chester abandoned the office of the director, entered the empty office adjacent to the funeral director's office, and placed a call to Sheriff Smith.

A short time later, the same day Sheriff Smith arrived at the tenant shack of Moses once again. Sheriff Smith stood outside of his vehicle, as he was reluctant to intrude on the family during their time of sorrow. The sheriff turned his attention to an elderly black woman whom he knew as, Hattie. She was a medium built woman in her mid-sixties and a neighbor of Moses and Mama Lizzie. He watched her as she walked toward the tenant shack with a tray of covered fried chicken. She also eyed him with uneasy glances. As she approached the tenant shack Sheriff Smith uttered to her, "Afternoon, Hattie. You mine git'n' Crosby for me… its urgent!" She glimpsed at him with a slight hostile glance and as she entered through the enclosed screen door, she replied reluctantly, "Yessuh!" She entered the resident and shortly thereafter, Crosby soon deserted the tenant shack to converse with the sheriff. As they conversed near the patrol car, the sheriff informed Crosby that he had received word that Mississippi authorities had ordered the entombment of his nephew and that he could locate the funeral party at the East Money cemetery. The cemetery was not far from Moses church. By the time the funeral party had arrived at the cemetery with Emmett's body, Moses was no longer at the church.

Crosby bolted away in his pickup truck angry and alone as

Sheriff Smith ensued behind in his patrol car. When they arrived at the cemetery which was an old unkempt graveyard dating back to the civil war, Crosby focus his attention on about a dozen men working feverishly as some of them were black men who were hired to assist some of the white men in shoveling open an empty grave. The old graves, some without markings, were those of slaves and impoverished black sharecroppers. It was a place where no whites poor or otherwise, would dare bury their kinfolks. Sheriff Smith kept a close watch on the situation as Crosby walked toward the men of mixed races hastily digging a five foot five inch hole whose length was the size of the large pine wooden box, bearing the body of Emmett Till, which rested nearby. Crosby angrily confronted one of the white attendants and he demanded that they stop the burial proceedings at once. The white attendant aggressively opposed, "Looka here, boy! We got orders…" Crosby fired back, "I don't give a damn what orders you got. You ain't buryin' my nephew here!" The two men stared at each other with a defiant stand. Crosby's aggressive stand surprised the slender built Southern white man whose flustered red face soon revealed his embarrassment and he glanced at his white companions for their reaction and support. Crosby's inner courage grew with more intensity, which ignited a sense of pride deep within him, because for the first time he was taking a stand against racial oppression in his own small way. Ed introduced himself as the funeral director and moved between the two men to avert any confrontation, which he felt would add to the already tense situation. Ed then attempted to reason with Crosby regarding the reason for the immediate entombment, which he stated was due to the body's decomposition. Crosby aggressively told Ed with exasperation, "I don't won't my nephew buried here…I got some rights."

Although, Ed attempted to convince Crosby that he was sympathetic with his efforts to prevent the ordered entombment, he consistently rationalized the necessity for burying the body of his nephew forthwith. Yet the opposition did not intimidate nor lessen Crosby's determination, as he was adamant about his decision, therefore, he insisted that if they did not return his nephew's body back to the funeral home, he would take it there in his pickup truck. Ed, fearing bad publicity from the already embarrassing situation, complied with his request unenthusiastically and he had the men load up the pine wood box and transport it back to the funeral home in Greenwood. Later during the evening, Crosby made provisions with the local railroad and with a funeral home in Tutwiler, Mississippi to have the body transported to Chicago for burial.

Meanwhile, in Chicago that same afternoon, lying on her mother's bed in the front part of the house, Mamie was wide-awake. Alma, her husband Henry Spearman, Gene and other family members gathered in the rear of the house as not to disturb Mamie who wanted to be alone to deal with her grief. Feeling helpless, angry and alone, Mamie reclined paralyzed on the bed, staring out aimlessly in a daze of contemplation. Impetuously, she began to speak aloud, "Lord, what have I done to deserve this? Why are you so cruel that you would let this happen to Bo? Why do you allow this kind of persecution?" At that moment one of the strangest experiences occurred in her life. It was just as though someone had entered the room and began to carry on a conversation with her. It was as real to her as though she was carrying on a conversation with a person of flesh and blood. A light broke upon her vision and it filled the room around her. The vision seemed to take on bodily form and then a divine voice was heard with a message of comfort and hope, "Mamie, be not dismayed for it was ordained from the beginning of time that Emmett Louis Till would die a violent death. Know this that through your sorrow and the innocent death of your son…Emmett Till shall never be forgotten. There is a job for you to do now." She promptly sat erect in bed and stretched out her hands and she began praying hard that no one would come in and disturb her before the conversation was completed, because she wanted the answers and she wanted to finish the conversation taking place before her. Mamie knew that if anyone came in the room where she was and heard her talking, they would instantly have thought she had gone out of her mind with grief. She asked sobbingly, "What shall I do, Lord?" The voice responded, "Have courage and faith that through his death shall come forth redemption for the suffering of my people and his death is the instrument of this purpose. Labor yourself unceasingly to tell the story so that the truth shall arouse man's conscience and righteousness shall at last prevail." At the conclusion of her spiritual revelation, she reclined upon the bed and slept peacefully for the first time since Emmett's abduction and subsequent murder.

CHAPTER SIXTEEN:

GOING HOME

Sometime later the same late afternoon of August thirty-first, Sheriff Smith arrived at the county jail in Greenwood accompanied by Deputy Cothran. They proceeded with much anxiety to the cellblock area, which housed the two accused men. The two law enforcement officers notified J.W. and Roy separately about the fact that local authorities had located the body of Emmett Till, whom the two white men said they had abducted from Preacher Mose tenant shack and then later released. The sheriff and the deputy had informed the two accused men that the body was pulled from the Tallahatchie River near Philipp, Mississippi and J.W. and Roy received the news like a heavy albatross too big to escape the validity of its exposure. Now Roy and J.W. knew where they had placed Emmett's body on a secluded plantation near Swan Lake according to Milam. Therefore, the information given to them caused a perplexed expression on their faces and open anxiety as they contemplated how the body settled twenty-five miles downstream to Philipp, Mississippi. Sheriff Smith was direct and petulant as he informed J.W. that they were now facing an impending murder charge. J.W. stared back at him with strong displeasure and he uttered to the sheriff, "We ain't kill nobody!"

Meanwhile, a white Northern reporter on staff at the Chicago Daily News, a daily Chicago circulated newspaper, arrived in Greenwood, Mississippi to interview the Mayor of Greenwood and then later visit Moses Wright at his residence in Money, Mississippi. The reporter, John Marshfield an average looking, medium built man in his early forties walked toward the Mayor's office across the street from the County Jail. His attention became transfixed on three black men walking toward him abreast and stepping completely off the sidewalk to let him pass. When he approached outside the office of the Mayor, he paused momentarily and watched as the three black men continued to step off the sidewalk each time they approached whites on the street. The subservient behavior of the men caused the reporter some concern and then he finally entered the office to converse with the Mayor.

Inside the neatly furnished office, the reporter extended his hand to shake hands with the stocky Mayor with a receding hairline. The Mayor introduced himself as Allen Stafford. He was a full term Mayor in his late forties. At some point during the interview between the mayor and the Chicago reporter, the mayor seized the opportunity to inform the reporter who listened with interest about the advances the city of Greenwood had made toward blacks of the community. He spoke with a neighborly tone as he enlightened the reporter about the new elementary school recently built and how they allowed blacks to use the white football field, when whites were not using it. He also stated statistically that blacks outnumbered whites by fifty-one percent in Greenwood and about sixty percent in the county as a whole. He stated further to the reporter that racial difficulties between whites and blacks had been at a minimum in the area for some time. Reporter John watched the mayor with a perfunctory humorous expression as the mayor elucidated about the good relationships among black and white residents of his town and the reporter resisted the challenge to debate the mayor on the open display of segregation, which were ubiquitously throughout the South.

The reporter then asked, "How are relations between Negroes and the police down here?" Mayor Safford answered eagerly, "In this city we will not tolerate police brutality toward Negroes." The mayor added that he felt that blacks in Mississippi and particularly in Greenwood were happy with adequate facilities provided them. The mayor concluded by saying, "The citizens here consider the crime of that Negro boy, deplorable." John the reporter replied with a sense of curiosity, "Deputy Sheriff Cothran used almost the same words."

Later that night of Wednesday, August thirty-first, amid the uncanny stillness of the moonless night, three silhouette figures moved in a clandestine manner toward the one story structure of the Love Hope Baptist Church. The three people were Clara, Henry Lee and his father, George. They arrived at the countryside parish, located in the black section of Glendora where Henry Lee and Clara lived and she and his father came to converse with her minister about the situation involving Henry Lee. It was at the urging of Clara who felt that her local pastor could provide advice in the matter. Earlier during that afternoon of the same day, Henry Lee's father had dropped by to visit his son. During his visit, it did not take long for him to learn about Henry Lee's involvement in the murder of the young black child found in the river not far from where Henry Lee's father lived. Though Henry Lee's father found the information stunning, he earnestly disputed with his son at length to disclose the tragic details about the murder to someone they felt they could trust. Therefore, Henry Lee stood hours later outside of the church staring at the objectionable sight, which bore the unwelcome task before him. They entered the empty church where they greeted Reverend Eddie Ware who escorted them to his private office where they could talk with one another without interruption. Inside the minister's small office, Clara and George urged Henry Lee to speak with the minister regarding his knowledge of the murder, but Henry Lee refused their suggestion and the minister watched the situation unfolding in front of him with inquisitive interest. Finally, his father uttered with frustration, "Tell him what you told me 'bout de murder of dat li'l boy, Henry Lee!" Clara advised him persuasively, "Tell Reverend Ware about it, Henry Lee. He'll know what to do."

In spite of the agonizing struggle within himself to keep quiet about the crime, he ultimately broke his silence and he began to divulge the details concerning the brutal murder of little Emmett Till found in the river earlier the same day. The minister sat shocked by what he was hearing and as he stared at them with sympathetic agony and concern, he then suggested, "We got to get in touch with Doctor T.R.M. Howard and Medger Evers." Henry Lee stopped him and remarked with uncertain fear, "No disrespect to you, Reverend, but, you can't tell nobody 'bout this…dem white folk's kill me and Too Tight." The minister tried to ease his fear by telling Henry Lee that two white men involved in the crime were already in jail and with the revealed information could possibly lead to others being incarcerated. Henry Lee replied, "You know how it is down here, dey ain't gonna do nothin' to dem white folks for killin' that li'l Negro boy." The minister watched Henry Lee with heartfelt pity as he contemplated his statement. And deep down inside of him, Reverend Ware knew full well from past experience, especially with the death of his own brother who was shot and killed allegedly by J.W. during his brother's residency in Glendora in 1949 over a wage dispute. Reverend Ware knew just as every black man and black woman living in the South knew that Henry Lee's statement had a validity of truth.

The following morning, Thursday, September first found sharecroppers hard at work on the Clint Sheridan plantation bent over in the hot sun working the cotton crop. Willie Reed; his grandfather, Ed, Mandy Bradley; and her husband, Alonzo and Frank King were working among other sharecroppers in the fields as they too were dragging the long white and gray ten foot long sacks, which they had strapped to their shoulders. While they were working, they conversed among themselves as they permeated their curious appetite with the latest gossip concerning the death of the little child and the recovery of the child's body from the river the day before. Mandy told them, "Here tell the body was so messed up, dey ain't hardly know what he was." Alonzo inquired to those around him, "You ain't reckon dat body got somethin' to do with that beatin' we heard, do you?" His assertiveness ignited their interest and they gave serious thought to his statement. Frank informed them about the newspaper article he had found with a picture of the little boy found in the river. They all surrounded Frank to examine the photograph from the local newspaper. Then Willie aroused their stinging interest when he informed them that he recognized the picture as that of the little boy he saw on the pickup truck of J.W., the morning of the beating. Willie also informed them that he observed Roy and Roy's cousin whom he did not know by name riding in the cab and Henry Lee and Too Tight in the rear of the pickup truck with Emmett as it entered the shed. Willie Reed remembered seeing Roy's cousin when they visited the plantation several weeks prior to the savage beating.

The revelation caused much anger, shame and distressed in them that a mere child so young could be the object of such race hatred right in the mist of them and Mandy spoke through her anguish, "Lord, how could dey do dat to a li'l child." Their huddling together soon attracted the attention of L. C. who was watching them from a distance and he was both inquisitive and concerned about what they were doing. As he watched them curiously, he asked aggressively, "what y'all niggards doin' over there? Git back to work, ya' hear!" As he stared at them, they stared back at him with hostile defiance and for the first time, he watched them in silent fear as they slowly dispersed and returned to their chores.

Meanwhile, a short time later, the same morning of September first, District Attorney, Gerald W. Chatham, a stocky man in his early fifties and a resident of Hernando, Mississippi arrived at the county jail in Greenwood to converse with Sheriff Smith. He casually entered the sheriff's office with a stern look and then he introduced himself to the sheriff and informed the sheriff that he was assign to the case as prosecuting attorney by Governor Hugh White. As they conversed about the murder case of Emmett Till, he asked Sheriff Smith about the available evidence in the case against J.W. Milam and his half-brother, Roy Bryant. Sheriff Smith replied, "At the moment, we really don't have much right now. What we do have is their confessions about taking the boy."

Attorney Chatham asked him to outline where they were apparently lacking crucial evidence in the case and the sheriff disclosed that his deputies were searching the banks of the snake-like Tallahatchie River for the boy's clothes. The sheriff confessed that they had no actual location where the child was killed, nor were they able to locate the pickup truck, which had carried the child away from the Wright's resident. Sheriff Smith also confessed that they could not locate Miz Bryant to question her and that they did not have the slug allegedly fired into the boy's head. It was the assumption of both Sheriff Strider and Sheriff Smith that a gunshot blast caused the hole in Emmett's temple. The attorney could not hide his frustration over the lack of strong evidence in the case and he seriously contemplated whether he could win a murder case lacking the necessary hard evidence needed to get a guilty verdict. Sheriff Smith perceiving his frustration convinced him that in spite of the lack of evidence presently available, he still believed there was a strong enough case against the two half-brothers and that it was just a matter of time before new evidence would be procurable. Chatham concluded his visit by saying, "Very well, keep me posted on any new developments." The district attorney then abandoned the sheriff's office en route to his place of business at his law firm.

A short time later, the same morning, Moses and Mama Lizzie arrived at the Grenade Train Station with their eight siblings, other family members including Crosby, his wife and children. Family members had assembled at the station to await the arrival of Emmett's body to accompany its final journey home to Chicago. As family members conversed with one another, Moses and Mama Lizzie were having a lengthy discussion about her decision to leave Mississippi permanently and he was determined to change her mind. They had apparently been conversing about the matter for some time, since she had announced her plans to him during the same early morning of their planned trip to the train station to meet the body. Moses persistence to alter her decision came to no avail and he pleaded, "Dis is yo' home, Lizzie." She replied with exasperation, "This is not my home…I just can't live with the hate no more." Mama Lizzie's determination to leave Mississippi did not mean that she was deserting her husband and family, whom she loved very much; it was just the agony of losing her nephew to such senseless race hatred and violence, caused her to abandon the state where she was born.

Deep down inside Moses understood her reasons for leaving, although, it was hard for him to accept and he sadly remarked, "What 'bout me?" Mama Lizzie took him into her embrace and she whispered to him, "Come with us…you are my life, you know that!" He pulled away reluctantly and replied, "Dis is my home…I can't leave." Although Moses and Mama Lizzie's eight siblings were accompanying their mother to Chicago to attend the funeral of their cousin, Emmett Till, they planned to return with family members to Mississippi so that the younger siblings would be available to assist their father with his harvest cotton crop during the fall.

Shortly thereafter, the funeral hearse arrived bearing the body of Emmett Louis Till. The family members watched with grief as the pine wood casket was placed on the Illinois Central R&R Panama Limited and the family members began to board the train shortly afterwards. Mama Lizzie and their youngsters embraced Moses and then they boarded the train as well. As the train pulled away from the station bound for Chicago, Moses watched after it alone and full of anguished.

CHAPTER SEVENTEEN:

NATIONAL INTEREST

Several hours later, the same Thursday afternoon, September first, Mamie and Alma were sitting together on the sofa, as the two were alone in Alma's West Side home. Mamie stared at a photograph of her only child in life, Emmett and she sobbed as she told her mother, "He never harmed anyone. Someone is going to pay for this." Alma struggled with her own heavy suffering that somehow prevented her from speaking as she watched her daughter with anguish and grief. Concern for her daughter's well-being caused Alma to stay close by her side, she watched Mamie gently touch the face of her now deceased son on the picture, and then Mamie verbalized once again, "The entire state of Mississippi is going to pay for this. He didn't do anything to deserve that." Mamie laid her head on her mother's shoulder and her mother embraced her in an attempt to ease the overwhelming grief between them. As they sat quietly staring at the photograph, Mamie told her mother about the spiritual visitation she had experienced on the previous day and how the revelation had revealed to her that the death of her son had a purpose. Alma's grief was so heavy within her that it was difficult for her to comprehend what Mamie was explaining to her because of the enormous burden, which felt like a monstrous weight forcing itself against her. Through Alma's struggling grief, she informed Mamie that she and Gene had arranged for A.A. Rayner and Sons funeral home, to meet the body when it arrived the following morning at the Illinois Central Train Station in downtown Chicago. Soon their attention became inadvertently drawn to the afternoon newscast that they had disregarded up until that moment as the news anchor reported, "The wolf-whistle murder of fourteen-year-old, Emmett Louis Till. A Chicago Negro boy deep in the delta plantation of Mississippi has prompted a bitter statement from the National Association for the Advancement of Colored People, today." The white male newscaster reported the story of Emmett's murder while Mamie and her mother sat mesmerized by the visual images of the snake-like Tallahatchie River and seeing the area where Mississippi authorities had pulled the body of her only child from the murky waters of the river.

The news anchor, a neatly attired man in his early thirties continued his report, "Roy Wilkins, executive secretary for the National Association for the Advancement of Colored People, called the child's murder a straight out lynching which hits all Americans between the eyes." Mamie and Alma watched the television set with engrossed interest as the image of Roy Wilkins, a tall, lean and handsome man in his mid-fifties filled the television screen as many reporters interviewed him at the NAACP headquarters in New York. Roy Wilkins informed the press, "There are some in Mississippi who will maintain white supremacy at any price…even if it means the murder of an innocent child."

The news anchor's image filled the screen again and he reported, "When asked to comment on the statement, Mississippi Governor Hugh White at first disregarded the statement."

However, as Mamie and Alma continued watching the newscast, the television screen manifested a news image, which was that of Governor Hugh White, a stocky and southern aristocratic looking man with a good humored conservative demeanor as he was leaving the State Capital building in Jackson, Mississippi. Once again, when asked to comment on the statement by Roy Wilkins, Governor White remarked humorously about the NAACP, "They're in the press all the time, that gang."

Mamie commented to her mother, "I'll fight to the end to see that justice is done."

Meanwhile, in downtown Chicago, newly elected Mayor Richard J. Daily, a stocky man in his early fifties arrived at his City Hall office. Upon his entrance into the building's lobby, three reporters representing various Chicago newspapers encircled him and they asked him for his comments regarding the brutal murder of the Chicago teenager in Mississippi. The mayor sadly remarked, "It was a brutal, terrible crime…I hope and believe that the full force of our country's law enforcement agencies both State and Federal…will see to it that whoever committed this terrible crime is brought to justice." After his comments about the brutal murder of young Emmett Till, the conversation turned to city politics as reporters asked him about his agenda for the city of Chicago.

Sometime later during the evening of the same day of September first, many miles away from Chicago in the capital city of Washington, D. C., two distinguished looking white men dressed in three-piece suits and sitting at an official looking desk were engaged in conversation. The two men were conversing in a well-groomed outfitted office of the Federal Bureau of Investigation. One of the men was James Barnett who was an average looking; medium built man in his early fifties, whose occupation was a White House Aide to President Eisenhower. His attention was riveted on the other man who was Vincent Santali, a handsome, average height man in his late forties. Santali was a Special Agent for the Federal Bureau of Investigation (FBI). They were conversing about the numerous letters addressed to the White House and the FBI agency concerning Emmett Till's brutal murder in Mississippi. In spite of the strong opposition expressed in the letters mailed to the FBI, the White House and the Department of Justice, their topic of interest centered on a telegram from the "Chicago Defender" denouncing the crime and inquiring what plan of action, the bureau and the government were planning in solving the crime.

Agent Santali reassured Barnett that due to his inquiry within the bureau, his sources had revealed that the telegram came from a black known newspaper publication in Chicago. He further stated that the material was presently in the hands of the Crime Records section for the purpose of surveillance. They conversed about the continued publicity surrounding the case and its continued interest around the country. Barnett did not hide his indifference toward the enormous increasing awareness of the incident and he asked inquisitively, "What is all the commotion about?"

Agent Santali examined the information on his desk and then he replied, "This young Negro boy, Emmett Till from Chicago… became involved in an altercation with a Caucasian woman (looking at the name on the paper)…a Mrs. Bryant, while vacationing in Money, Mississippi."

"An altercation," asked Barnett?

"According to the local sheriff, he got fresh and made ugly remarks to her in the store owned by one…Roy Bryant," countered Santali.

Barnett asked, "I take it, this Roy Bryant committed the murder?"

Agent Santali smiled reassuringly and he responded with confidence, "I am sure he had accomplices, rumor has it there were two or three who entered the resident where the victim was staying at his uncle's place."

"And this boy was only fourteen," Barnett asked?

"That is our understanding," Agent Santali replied.

Barnett suggested, "The facts here seem to indicate a local matter."

Agent Santali concurred, "This is our conclusion as well, the two half-brothers are held on kidnapping charges and a local press release indicated, they will in all probability…be charged with murder."

Barnett contemplated a moment and then he added, "According to White House sources, Negro civil rights organizations are planning to protest on the grounds of a violation of civil rights."

Agent Santali replied, "The bureau has also anticipated a move in this area, therefore, we presented the facts to the Criminal Division of the Justice Department…"

Barnett eyed him with curiosity and then he asked, "And there conclusion?"

"No violation of federal civil rights statue," Santali replied.

Barnett asked, "What about the crossing of state lines?"

Agent Santali replied, "As far as we know, there were 'No State lines crossed'…indicating no violation of federal kidnapping statue."

Agent Santali also informed Barnett about the latest intelligence data on how the foreign press was handling the story of the murder of Emmett Till as the story had began to appear in foreign newspapers abroad and how newspapers often referred to the State of Mississippi as the place 'where the little Negro boy was killed'.

It did not surprise Barnett concerning the revelation of the tragic American story capturing the interest of the foreign press as the White House had knowledge of the same information. He also expressed his concern that the image of the country continued to suffer a damaged image abroad; at the aftermath of what he felt was continued negative publicity. Barnett pondered his thoughts for a moment and then he suggested to Agent Santali that the best way to handle the vast publicity nationwide would be to ignore the case by perhaps censoring the media coverage in the hopes of eliminating the public's interest as well.

Although, Santali agreed with his proposition, he interjected a psychological angle which he felt would be achieved by pacifying the immense complaints by emphasizing that the case was a local matter and reassuring civil rights organizations that the government and the FBI would continue to monitor the case and that local authorities were proceeding with efforts to see that justice was accomplished. At the conclusion of their conversation, Barnett vacated the FBI office.

CHAPTER EIGHTEEN:

A MOTHER'S TASK

Mamie and her father, John Carthan a comely looking and average height man in his late fifties awoke early on Friday morning, September second in her second floor apartment in the Sixty-four hundred block of Saint Lawrence Avenue. They awoke to the same anxiety and trepidation, which had impregnated them when they had arrived Thursday evening, September first to the second floor apartment she shared with her late beloved son. It was Mamie's first time in her apartment after picking up her father from the train station after he had arrived from his home in Detroit, Michigan on the previous afternoon. Mamie and her father had found it difficult returning to the familiar surroundings knowing full well that what awaited them were the embattled, incomprehensible agony of Emmett's absence from the apartment and the assault of his memories throughout every inch of the two-flat tenement. Mamie convinced herself to sleep in her own bed and her father decided to sleep with much sorrow in his grandson's room, during the night he wept quietly as he laid in his grandson's bed. She slept restless in her own bed for the first time since the news of Emmett's abduction and subsequent brutal murder in Mississippi. The train bearing her son's body was due to arrive at the Illinois Central Station at 9 A.M., the same morning and Mamie insisted that family members be on time at the station to meet the arriving train.

John watched his grief-stricken daughter with concerned as she moved around the apartment with fretful anxiety, because in spite of the abstruse circumstances she struggled in her mind to select the most appropriate outfit to wear because she knew the press would be there to cover the grievous event. Mamie answered the ringing telephone with a hastily firm grip of the receiver and she conversed with her mother on the other end of the receiver. Alma informed Mamie of her plans to ride with family members who had opt to meet them at the station to wait for the arrival of the train transporting Emmett's body home from Mississippi.

Several hours later the same morning of September second at the train station that had filled quickly with people who had gathered inside the interior of the Illinois Central Station to quench their inquisitive appetite for the anticipated unfolding spectacle. Eager travelers watched with curiosity as many onlookers continued to arrive at the station waiting like those who had come to witness the arrival of the little Chicago boy's body from Mississippi. In the mist of the crowd, news reporters from around the country came to cover the story. Mamie and her family had also arrived at the station and they were surprised to gaze upon a large outpouring of sympathies from the crowd of people whom they had never met. In the midst of the crowd, Mamie complained of becoming lightheaded as she awaited the train's arrival and a station attendant provided a wheelchair for her. She was obviously the center of attention as the throng of people gazed upon her with commiseration as family members walked slowly beside and behind her as Gene wheeled her through the crowd to the front of the throng. John and Alma watched their daughter with heartfelt contrition as they struggled with their own inner torment and grief. Wheeler and Curtis were also waiting with their parents. In addition, the ministers of Alma and Mamie had also arrived at the station to be of assistance to the family in what Mamie called her darkest hour. The two ministers were Bishop Louis Ford of the Saint Paul Church of God in Christ where Mamie was a faithful member and Bishop Isaiah Roberts of Roberts Temple Church of God in Christ where Alma maintained her membership.

The surging onlookers continued watching the ordeal with sympathetic curiosity as they waited with baited breathe for the anticipated uneasy appearance of the train's arrival as they listened to the ever-expanding sound of the blast from the train's whistle and the swelling vibration of the approaching train from a distance. Soon the train's entrance rumbled though the interior structure of the Illinois Central Station as the Panama Limited passenger train soon came to a slow halt amid the onlookers. When Mamie caught sight of the train's entrance into the station, she bolted from the wheel chair and scurried across three sets of tracks to the baggage car where the encased pine wood box held the body of her only child, Emmett Louis Till. The funeral attendants from A.A. Rayner and Sons who were also on hand to retrieve the body quickly entered the baggage car after the train had come to a complete stop, which enabled the six men to remove the large box from the train. Mamie's eyes became transfixed on the large box like a magnetic force. As the six men placed the casket on the funeral cart and slowly wheeled it toward her, she fell on her knees and sobbed hysterically, "My son, my son! I would have gone through a world of fire to get to you."

Mamie's father and her fiancé, Gene and the two ministers responded quickly to her toil worn grief as they reached out to aid her. Meanwhile weeping relatives including family members arriving from Mississippi formed a ring around the large box and afterwards, the hearse backed into the scene. Above the loud sobbing, Mamie's voice echoed through the station again, "My darling, I know I was on your mind when you died. Oh, my baby…!"

The crowd of onlookers and news reporters from various major news agencies from around the country watched the scene with extreme commiseration and regret. Bob, the white reporter from the Chicago Tribune spoke quietly through his microphone, "This is how a fourteen-year-old, Negro boy vacationing in Mississippi returned home to his mother in Chicago."

The six attendants placed the large pine wood box containing Emmett Till's body into the hearse, Mamie placed her hand gently upon it, and she spoke softly, "You didn't die in vain. Your life was sacrificed for something." As family members and friends watched the hearse slowly leave the station, they began to disperse slowly to waiting cars en route to Alma's home.

A black female reporter representing a national newspaper agency caught focus of Crosby whom she knew was part of the family, as he was about to leave the station with his family. She had recognized him as having arrived with the body from Mississippi. She also had some knowledge of the significant role he had played in postponing the hasty burial of Emmett's body in Mississippi. The reporter rushed over to Crosby to request an interview for the newspaper she worked for. The reporter introduced herself and Crosby yielded to the interview. The reporter asked him to comment on how he had interrupted the planned burial of his nephew. Crosby explained to the female reporter that after being contacted by the local sheriff who had told him where he could locate his nephew's corpse, he hurried to that location. After informing her how audaciously he had suspended their efforts, he remarked, "They were getting ready to spill the body into a hole 'bout four feet deep. He hadn't even been embalmed." The reporter asked, "And your immediate reaction?" Crosby uttered, "To get the body to Chicago, even if I had to stuff it with ice and take it in my pickup truck." Considerate of the moment, the reporter graciously concluded the interview and he abandoned the station with his family.

Several hours later, the same late afternoon, Mamie, Gene and her father, John and a black photographer from Jet Magazine whom we will come to know as David Jackson and another reporter arrived at the two-story structure with the inscription: A.A RAYNER & SONS FUNERAL HOMES located at 4141 South Cottage Grove Avenue. Inside the modestly attired office, Mamie, her fiancé and her father conversed with the funeral director, Mister Rayner, who was an average height man in his mid-forties. While they conversed about the planned funeral arrangement, Mamie suddenly announced that she would like to see the body of her only child. Mister Rayner was surprised at Mamie's request as Gene and John watched her with perplexed anxiety. Rayner then responded to her plea and he said, "Mrs. Bradley due to the massive wounds inflicted on your son's body and severe decomposition, I would strongly advise against you viewing the body at this time…" her father took her by the hand and he spoke softly, "I think it'll be too hard on you, daughter!" Gene stared at her with compassion and then added, "He's right, honey." Mamie watched the three male faces of commiseration as they stared back at her and she replied, "I need to know if it is really, Bo. Don't you understand!" "Mrs. Bradley…if that is your only concern, you have my word, it is being taken care of," Mister Rayner said with certainty.

"It is useless to argue with me…I want to see my son," Mamie replied firmly. The men tried once again to change her mind, but she was adamant about her decision. David Jackson loaded his camera as he prepared to take the most important photographs of Emmett Till's brutal beaten face unaware that his photos will become the most viewed photographs of his journalistic career. He and the other reporter waiting outside the funeral director's office now accompanied them to the back room morgue and Mamie gave Jackson permission to take photos of her son's corpse. Outside the morgue, the funeral director tried again to reason with her too spare her vision of the monstrosity of her son's body covered under the sheet and again she was inflexible in her determination. Before they entered the room, Mamie turned to her father, "Daddy, wait for me out here, Okay?" John took her suggestion as a sign of relief because deep down inside he did not want to see his grandson that way. Mamie took a deep breath and then she and Gene who was feeling uneasy about the whole thing, but wanting to be supportive followed the funeral director into the gloomy colored room along with the two reporters. They watched with guarded uneasiness as Mister Rayner walked over to the covered stretcher and turned down the sheet to reveal the corpse of Emmett Till. Mamie struggled to stay focus as she suddenly became light on her feet, Gene held her at the waist to maintain her balance as they along with the photographer and the reporter observed the horror-stricken sight of the mutilated face of Emmett's corpse. The reporters regain their composures after seeing the shocking sight of the young child's face and David began photographing what would become the famous photograph of Emmett Till's face that would shock a nation, as it appeared in Jet Magazine nationally. As David photographed the face from all angles, Mamie and the others looked on. The reporter as well as Mamie and Gene perceived that the condition of the child's face revealed a beating much more brutal than she or any of the other occupants had envisioned.

Mamie began what she called the most agonizing task of her life as she began carefully examining the corpse to ascertain whether the body was really that of her only child, Emmett Louis Till. Mamie and Gene as well as the two reporters with them scrutinized that several of her slain son's teeth were missing apparently knocked out because of the savage beating. In addition, she perceived upon observing the entire right side of his crushed face that the right eye and right ear was missing. Further ascertainment from Mamie revealed that her son's left eye was bulged and there were barbed wire marks visible on his face and neck and Mamie said there was a hole in his right temple which she said she could see clear through to the other side, a hole which authorities presumed to be a bullet hole, and the funeral director said he was concerned because there were no signs of powder burns around the wound in Emmett Till's temple. Mamie wanted to preclude any doubt by Mississippi authorities and their preposterous claim that the body found in the Tallahatchie River was not her son. Gene closely examined the hairline of the corpse since he was Emmett's barber. Mamie studied her son's body very carefully starting at his feet then working her way up to his hands, the shape of the body, the one remaining eye and the nose and finally his hairline. At the conclusion of their examination, Mamie and Gene were convinced of the identity of her son's corpse. They soon left the morgue to arrange for Emmett's wake and funeral.

CHAPTER NINETEEN:

OPEN IT UP!

Many hours later after Mamie had identified her son's corpse in the morgue of the funeral home now preparing for his wake; early nightfall had fallen over the city of Chicago. On the city's South Side a steady orderly gathering of people continued to congregate on the street outside the A.A Rayner and Sons funeral chapel. Men, women and children who were mainly of American black city dwellers had come from around the city to convene where Emmett Till's wake was about to get underway. There were also law enforcement officers of mixed races assembled to avert any possible violence. Yet, the police officer's observation revealed that the crowd was orderly and somber. The crowd of people had come to pay homage to the little boy whom many of them had never met. Whose tragic death had somehow drawn them like a forbearing and reverent force to a child who had become to many adults in the crowd, as their own personal child, and each of them was touched by a brutal death they felt was based merely on the race of the young child and nothing else. Surely, no white child would ever have endured such racial brutality.

Shortly thereafter, the attention of the crowd became mesmerized on the entourage of vehicles transporting Mamie and her family as they arrived for the wake service of her son, Emmett Till. Mamie, Gene, her mother; Alma, her stepfather; Henry and her father, John were riding in the first car and when they vacated the vehicle, they were overwhelmed by the large crowd of people still waiting outside the funeral home. Again, the outpouring of attention from the numerous people gathered was on Mamie and her family as many in the crowd watched after them with eyes of remorse and sadness. Luella Johnson and her daughter, Maedean and other neighborhood companions were among the many friends invited by Mamie to attend the wake service as they all followed behind Mamie and her family into the two-story building.

During the service, weeping relatives and friends concentrated their attention on the closed metal casket in the center of the chapel and surrounded by floral arrangements. Through it all Mamie seemed to be distant from what was happening around her. Then her eyes slowly came upon the close coffin, she gazed upon the prevailing spectacle, and at first glance, she viewed it as an unwelcome intruder who had forced its miserable display into her existence. Her silent agony soon provoked a hostile reality deep within her and she rose from her reclined posture and walked over to the coffin and made a futile attempt to open the sealed casket, to no avail.

Mister Rayner, Alma and John reached out to prevent her

from succeeding in her attempt, as relatives and friends looked on in heartfelt grief. Yet Mamie's overwhelming grief caused her to react with uncontrollable persistence and she uttered, "Open it up…let the people see what they did to my boy!" Alma and John voiced their strong opposition to their daughter's demand to have the casket open, thereby having an open casket funeral, but Mamie refused to relinquish her demand to have the casket open. Considering what Mamie had told her parent's regarding the horrible condition of their grandson's body and in spite of their daughter's determination to display the horror-stricken sight openly, which was contrary to their wishes, they vehemently protested against her demands. Other family members and friends also voiced opposition to her request, but her tenacity prevailed. Mister Rayner become concerned for her emotional wellbeing; therefore, he consented reluctantly to her demands in an effort to avoid any further hostile outburst from her. As the spectators looked on in dreaded anticipation, he directed one of his assistants to break the seal and open the metal casket. As Emmett's body was viewed by many of the mourners for the first time, for those who dared to look, their facial expression revealed intense anguish, shock and dismay upon viewing the mutilated face of the corpse.

Wheeler, Curtis, Maurice, Robert and Simeon sat near the rear of the chapel and as they watched the outward emotions of grief-stricken commiseration toward the viewing of the body, they sat reluctant to gaze upon the remains of their cousin, because of fear. The death of Emmett Till had been extremely hard on Wheeler and he struggled to maintain the appearance of being an adolescent of gallantry in the present of his cousins and uncles.

Nevertheless, he was unable to contain his emotions and his grief and tears caused those of his young uncles and cousins around him, to allow their tears to flow as well. Twelve-year-old, Simeon was the first to rise from among his brethren and they watched him as he slowly walked toward the open casket as the sadness and grief continued to increase all around him. Shortly thereafter, Simeon's two older brothers, Maurice and Robert and his two nephews, Wheeler and Curtis, followed him to the front of the chapel with the intention of sheltering and protecting young Simeon. When the five youngsters reached the open casket, they gazed in horror at the corpse and then shielded their eyes in uncontrollable grief. When Simeon (who was reluctant to peek) looked upon the horribly mangled monstrosity that was once his loving cousin, Emmett Till, the shock of the image caused him to lose consciousness and Mama Lizzie and others rushed to his aid. The youngsters' grief became so overpowering that the older males had to usher them out of the chapel to aid them in comfort.

During the emotional scene, Mamie abandoned the funeral chapel and she began to mingle among the throng outside, thanking them and showing her appreciation by shaking their hands and conversing with them. She began to invite them into the chapel, as she told them, "Come see what they did to my son." Throughout the night, the crowds of onlookers numbering in the high hundreds continued to file pass the open coffin and as they viewed the brutal and disfigured face of the young child's corpse, they reacted in horror and shock. Many screamed out in grief and others including some young men and women fainted at the sight. The large numbers of mourners increasing to nearly a thousand continued their procession into the funeral home from

8 p.m. until the attendants closed the doors at 2 a.m. Meanwhile, there were many reporters both black and white among the crowd and they were amazed at the large throng of people gathered outside the funeral home with dreaded anticipation of entering as they listened to the mourners reaction inside the chapel. One of the white reporters in his mid-forties turned to a black reporter from the Chicago Defender and said, "I have never witness such an outpouring of sympathy like this." "Neither have I," replied the black reporter.

Several hours later, the same night of Friday, September second, before Rayner ordered the funeral doors closed at 2 a.m., the crowd continued to swell in number and file through the funeral home making their way into the chapel to view Emmett Till's body. Rayner watched the continued gathering of people, and it caused him much uneasiness and concerned about possible structural damage to his property because of the large ensemble of people and he conversed with Alma and John about his concerns. He then asked them if they would accompany him to his office where they could speak privately. Inside the modestly furnished office, he assisted them as they sat in the two chairs in front of his desk. After assuring himself of their comfort, he walked behind his desk and sat in the high back swivel chair. Observing the grief-laden faces in front of him, he then informed them with remorse, "I must apologize for what I'm about to discuss with you."

John and Alma were already feeling embarrassed by the public display of their grandson's mutilation and yet the outpouring of sympathy had somehow given them that inner strength that they so desperately needed at that moment. John and Alma's attention was engrossed on Rayner and John acted with slight irritation toward Rayner because he felt that the funeral director's timing was an intrusion on his family's grief. John pondered why the funeral director needed to conversed with him and his ex-wife since he had received the insurance documents paying for the funeral. John asked slightly annoyed, "What's the problem?" "The problem is the crowd outside," replied the funeral director.

Alma asked curiously, "The crowd?"

"Yes. Our chapel is not equipped to handle crowds of this magnitude," Rayner continued.

"What are you suggesting," Alma asked?

"I suggest we move the body to a larger facility," he replied.

They watched him with a stare almost cantankerous at first glance, as he pleaded his case, "Please, understand my position… we had not anticipated such an outpouring like this!"

Alma's sensitivity soon replaced her somewhat unfriendly demeanor to his dilemma and she offered, "I understand!"

John positioned himself from his uncomfortable posture in his chair, as he struggled with his inner anger and grief over the senseless killing of his only grandchild. John's animosity through his grief was not meant for Rayner; unfortunately, the funeral director just happened to be in his path of hostility.

John asked Rayner, "What do you have in mind?"

"Well, I do know of one large facility which may be available," replied Rayner.

Since Alma was never content with having her only grandchild's service in a funeral chapel, she suggested, "Before you make any arrangements, let me contact my pastor."

"Very well, Mrs. Spearman, I will wait for your decision," Rayner replied.

Later during the night, Alma and Mama Lizzie were conversing alone in the living room of Alma's home. After Alma had placed a call to her pastor, Bishop Roberts, she and Mamie decided to postpone the burial scheduled for the following day and made arrangements to continue the funeral service at Roberts Temple Church of God in Christ. Alma was pleased that her minister, Isaiah Roberts had consented to her request to have her grandson's funeral at his church. Alma further informed her sister that her pastor assured her that she could have the service at the church as long as they needed it. Mama Lizzie looked at her with an inquisitive frown and she asked, "Do you think she'll ever forgive me?" Alma stared at her sister in a perplexed manner and she asked, "Who?"

"Mamie," Mama Lizzie remarked!

"Now Lizzie, don't start blaming yourself over this," Alma said.

"I didn't know they would hurt a child…I just didn't think they would do that," Mama Lizzie said.

Alma stared at her sister looking for words that at the moment eluded her, as Mama Lizzie commented more to herself, "I'll never get over this."

Mama Lizzie turned away from her sister embarrassed for allowing such thoughts to invade on her personal grief. Alma was sensitive to her older sister's uneasiness and she attempted to alleviate Mama Lizzie's misgivings by mentioning to her that she was relieved after talking to her ex-husband who had told her that he had checked on Mamie and that she was finally able to get some sleep. Alma told her how difficult the death of her grandson had been on the entire family and that they just needed to continue to pray and asked the Lord for strength in getting through the tragic moment, especially for her daughter who was under a doctor's care.

"After what's she been through, rest is what she needs," said Mama Lizzie. Alma looked on in agreement.

They decided due to the lateness of the night to try and get some sleep themselves in preparation for the funeral service the following day.

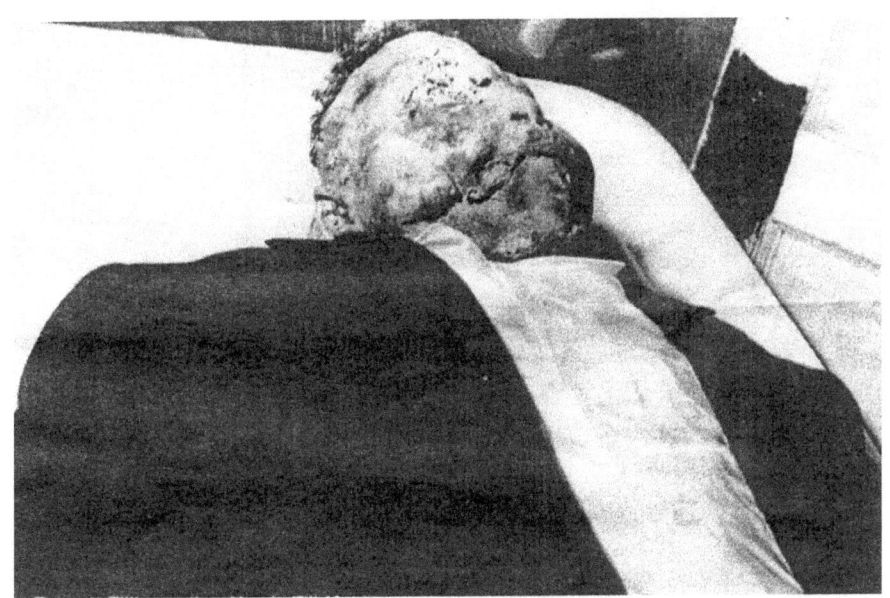

Emmett Louis Till
At death in casket

CHAPTER TWENTY:

UNIVERSAL CHILD

The following morning, Saturday, September third, miles away in Argo, Illinois in the single level home where Wheeler lived with his family. Wheeler was sitting on the side of his bed in the bedroom that he shared with his younger brother, William. He was having a difficult time getting dress to attend the late morning funeral service for his cousin, Emmett Till, which had been moved to Roberts Temple Church of God in Christ located at 4021 South State Street on Chicago's South Side. Wheeler sat on the bed with one leg in his dress slacks and his other leg out. The photograph of he and Emmett together sitting on the dresser held his total concentration.

Halle Mae stuck her head into the bedroom and she became annoyed by her observance that Wheeler had not dressed himself and she inquired, "Wheeler, you're not dressed yet, we gotta leave for the funeral in an hour?" Wheeler turned to stare with blank sadness at his mother and she looked into his grief stricken eyes, which caused Hale Mae to regret her outward exposure of irritation, as she reflected helplessly on her son's grief. She watched him for a moment and then she walked back to the dining room to converse with her husband, Wheeler Senior about her concerns for their son. Both Hale Mae and her husband had been concerned about Wheeler's emotional state since he had viewed Emmett's body for the first time during the wake service the previous night.

Wheeler Senior suggested that he should have a talk with his son and he abandon his wife alone sitting at the table in the dining room. He entered the bedroom, where he found his son sitting on the side of the bed with his head down staring at the floor with both legs in his slacks. Wheeler Senior sat down on the side of the bed next to him and he began to minister to his son with comfort and hope. He put his arm around his son's shoulder and uttered, "Son, I want you to know that I understand how you feel right now. I know what a terrible lost Bo's death is…but, I want you to know that the Lord is our perfect strength even in times of sorrow and pain."

Wheeler looked up from the floor at his father with tear-stained eyes and he said, "Daddy, I don't wanna go to the funeral, but I don't wanna disappoint, Bo." His father replied, "I'm sure you won't be disappointing, Bo. He knew how much you loved him." His father looked him straight in the eyes and said, "Son, as hard as it is right now, there will come a time when it won't hurt as much." Wheeler embraced his father with affection and they sat together quietly dealing with their own personal grief.

Meanwhile, back in Chicago in the Sixty-four hundred block of South Saint Lawrence in the first floor apartment of the two-flat adjacent to the two-flat where Mamie lived, Luella and her youngest daughter, Maedean were also conversing about the brutal condition of Emmett's body on display the night before. Maedean made every effort to persuade her mother not to attend the funeral, since the difficult time her mother had had at the wake viewing the hideous face of the corpse of what remained of her beloved, Emmett. Luella sat staring out of her big bay windows and she began to reminisce on how she would see Emmett walking home from school or watching Emmett and Wheeler playing with neighborhood friends. Luella then asked, "I just find it hard to believe that human beings could do something so terrible to a child so young, I just don't understand." Her daughter replied irritably, "I don't call people like that human!"

Meanwhile in Charleston, Mississippi, hundreds of miles away from Chicago where the outpouring of mourners continued to file pass the remains of Emmett Till; a white northern reporter was interviewing Sheriff H.C. Strider in his office in the Tallahatchie county jail in Charleston. Sheriff H. C. Strider who weighed two-hundred and ninety pounds and a man in his early sixties seat in a chair behind his desk in the simple modestly furnished office as the reporter asked him questions. Sheriff Strider- an ultra-conservative man with dogmatic traditional values engaged the interview with interest with the Northern reporter whose name was Robert Ratcliff, a medium built white man in his early fifties and a news editor of the Pittsburgh Courier News in Pittsburgh, Pennsylvania. As Strider puffed on his cigar and rocked back and forth in his swivel wooden chair, he indicated boastfully, "I'm chasin' down some leads now that looks like that killin' might have been planned and plotted."

The reporter watched him curiously and then he asked, "Plotted by whom?" Sheriff Strider uttered with pride as he remarked, "The NAACP and outside agitators." Ratcliff expressed surprised at his statement and he replied, "Are you saying the Till boy was murdered by the NAACP?"

"Naw, I say they hide that boy somewhere to cause trouble down her," the sheriff replied.

"So you believe the boy is still alive," asked the reporter?

"I been hearin' rumors 'bout that boy livin' somewhere in Detroit," the sheriff communicated.

Ratcliff responded to Sheriff Strider with condescending humor and he remarked, "In Detroit, Michigan?"

"Yes suree! In addition, those two burly niggers who accompanied that boy down here seem to be connected somehow," replied H. C. Strider with confidence.

During the interview process, the reporter continued to take notes during his conversation with the sheriff and he asked, "Can you substantiate this?"

Sheriff Strider asked inquisitively, "Substantiate?"

Reporter Ratcliff explained, "Do you have proof?"

"Well…as far as knowin' anything definite, I don't know it. What I do know is…that body found in the river didn't look like a boy's body," replied the sheriff reassuringly. The reporter watched him with tenacious sarcasm, as the sheriff continued his theoretical speculations. Sheriff Strider continued, "It was the size of a man's body and the face didn't look like the face of the boy published in newspapers down here."

Reporter Ratcliff asked, "What about the charges against the men?"

"I don't see how they can be indicted on the slim evidence now available," the sheriff replied smiling.

A short time later early in the afternoon of the same day in Chicago, a continued throng of people gathered in large numbers outside of the Roberts Temple Church of God in Christ. The crowd of black mourners as well as Jewish and many white sympathizers stood outside the church in a very orderly manner as they waited their turn to view Emmett Till's body inside the church as the open casket service continued. As on previous days, children were again intersperse among the men and woman, and the crowd expanded four deep around three city blocks, stretching from 39th Street to 41st Street. Many young schoolmates of Emmett Till viewed his brutal death as a personal attack against every black child in America. The ensemble gathered outside the church riveted their attention on the attached loud speakers on the outside of the building high above the street. There were also thirty law enforcement officers on hand to avert any possible outbreak of violence from the crowd.

Inside the church, the funeral service for Emmett Till was already in progress, as a twenty-five-voice woman's choir sang, "I Don't Know Why I have To Cry Sometimes." During the musical rendition, there were shouts of "Yes, Lord...praises his holy name" and "Thank you, Jesus." The female choir members were attired in blue and white robes and they clapped their hands and swayed in time to the gospel music as well as some of those in attendance. The church auditorium which seated 1800 easily left no seats empty. Again, Mamie and her entire family were in attendance in the service except for the younger members of the family, because it was agreed that the service would be too hard on them. Also in attendance were local dignitaries and national black leaders from various sections of the country. At the conclusion of the musical selection, a medium built man in his early forties; stepped up to the microphone to address the gathering as he spoke from the pulpit. The man was Archibald Carey, a former Alderman in Chicago politics before becoming a minister. His eyes of remorse moved around the filled capacity of the convocation, and then he spoke with energetic force, "There has been much talk of retaliation since the brutal and cruel murder of this young lad." He pounded his fist on the top of the pulpit, as he continued his eulogy, "Rumors that Negroes should rise up in Chicago and storm the State of Mississippi. But, it is not for us to avenge evil for evil. A mob in Chicago is no better than a mob in Mississippi." During his eulogy and speech, there were sporadic shouts of "Amans" and polite applauses from numerous members of the assemblage.

During his speech, Mamie rose from her seat where she was sitting in the second row behind her father, mother and stepfather,

Henry Spearman as well as other members of her family, as they were sitting on the left side of the church. She walked over to the open casket, which had a glass cover over it, to view her son's body. The metal casket stood in the middle of the aisle directly under the raised platform. Floral arrangements adorn the casket on either side and extended the length of the raised alter. There were three photographs of Emmett in life, which were pinned to the open casket lid, a request made by Mamie. The photographs were in mark contrast to the mutilated remains in the coffin. She viewed the distasteful remains that were once her handsome loving son and cried out in agony, "Lord, Jesus…please help me!" Gene and John moved to her side to assist and aid her. As stain eyes watched the ordeal in torment, including the ministers and the choir members, as all eyes were on Mamie, Gene and John as both men wrapped their arms around her and the onlookers continued to watch them as Gene and John led her back to her seat and she continued to sob uncontrollably. Minister Carey regained his composure and he continued, "In spite of this tragedy, there are good people in the South. There are people in the south who do not condone this sort of thing anymore than we do. What we need now is calmness and reason. What we need to do is let the Lord handle this thing." He concluded his speech and took his seat on the alter platform, as the congregation ignited into polite applause.

The next minster to speak was Mamie's pastor, Bishop Louis H. Ford- a handsome, amicable and discipline man of faith. He was in his early to mid-forties. He observed the family members and the many spectators with heartfelt compassion and then he verbalized, "It is ironic how our country can spend millions of dollars trying to win the good will of colored people in Africa and India. President Eisenhower, Vice President Nixon and Secretary of State Dulls oughtta be seeking the good will of colored people in Mississippi, Alabama and Georgia. I think it's time we start to clean up our own backyard, before we try to clean the backyard of the world." The stillness of the auditorium explored into thunderous applause and shouts of, "Say that preacher" and "halleluiah, Jesus" echoed through the assembly. Even on the street outside of the church, people applauded, as they listened attentively to the service from the loud speakers. Bishop Ford continued, "It is written in Romans chapter twelve, verse nineteen, "Dearly beloved, avenge not yourself, but leave the way open for God's wrath; it is written, vengeance is mine; I will repay, saith the Lord. The Lord and the law will take care of this."

Several hours later during the evening of the same day, after the ninety-minute funeral service had ended and Mamie and her family had vacated to Alma's home where the family had gathered. Yet, the crowd continued the long visitation outside the church, stretching three city blocks and growing with the arrival of more people waiting to enter the church. The line of mourners continued to pour into the church four abreast, as they filed pass the remains of young Emmett Louis Till. The line of grief-stricken faces viewed the body and strong young men wept openly without shame; some were shaken with uncontrollable cries of grief. Others including women and several children fainted when they viewed the mute evidence of the unspeakable barbarity of race hatred and rage which had been inflicted on the young child's body. For many American blacks, both young and old, they knew the racist climate which had produced the conditions that led to

Emmett Till's death had to be terminated and they knew those conditions had to change if people of color and especially black Americans were to survive in their native land where Jim Crow racism ruled in the South and parts of the North.

Meanwhile many miles away in New York City during the same evening, executive secretary, Roy Wilkins of the NAACP was holding a press conference in his New York office. He was asked by a reporter to comment on the statement made by Sheriff Strider in Mississippi regarding a plot by the NAACP in the Till case, Roy Wilkins smiled with confidence and then he replied with quiet force, "Sheriff Strider is a little confused. We do not murder Negroes in order to maintain our point of view. The little Till boy was the second killed in a space of sixteen days and the third since May 7. Strider's ridiculous fantasies about a plot by this organization is a crude cover up too thin to fool any decent human beings."

Later during the night of September third, Mamie arrived again at the church, where the crowd remained, as they continued to file in to view the body of her son inside the church. It was Mamie's plans to have her son buried in Burr Oaks cemetery after the Saturday afternoon funeral service. However, because of the commiseration shown her son, she was so moved by the large outpouring of sympathy from the crowd of people waiting night after night to view her beloved son's corpse that she decided to postpone the burial until Tuesday, September sixth at ten a.m. Earlier that day, Mamie had told a reporter, "They have come here to see my son and they'll see him." Mamie made her way through the crowd thanking as many of them as possible for coming out and showing their concerns. For it became apparent from the tremendous demonstration of commiseration that Emmett Till was not just her child anymore, he had become a universal child to many stirred by his brutal murder in Mississippi. She began to speak to the gathering about mobilizing to fight against inequality in America; "This is not just for Emmett, because my boy can't be helped now, but, to make it safe for other Negro boys. Unless an example is made of the lynchers of Emmett, it won't be safe for a Negro to walk the streets anywhere in America. I intend to fight this case all the way to the Supreme Court, until we get a death verdict for all four lynchers. I am not bitter against all white people. Many good white people will help me, I know, but I do want these lynchers of my boy punished. And it's the federal government's job to punish Mississippi for its refusal to protect colored people. I want to go to the Mississippi trial; I want other people to go with me, to see this thing through. I'm willing to go anywhere, to speak anywhere, to get justice." The people around her applauded her courage and strength, as they informed her that they were behind her fight for justice.

CHAPTER TWENTY-ONE:

NIGHT OF CHAOS

The sun hung hot and bright on the sunny summer afternoon of Sunday, September fourth, where Mamie stood with her cousin, Rayford Mooty on the sidewalk outside the Roberts Temple church watching the stream of mourners entering through the open doors of the church leading to the sanctuary to view her only child lying in state. Rayford Mooty, a handsome, forceful and articulate man in his mid-thirties was President of Local 3911 of the CIO Steelworkers Union in Chicago, and he held employment for many years at Inland Steel where he conducted his union business. A white male reporter, average built and in his thirties stood watching the stream of people of mixed genders and ages entering the church and writing in his notebook the events of the story unfolding before him. Mamie's eyes soon shifted to the reporter from New York as he approached her and introduced himself. Rayford held his grounds at her side and he watched the reporter with an inquisitive stare. During the interview, the reporter made known to Mamie about the charges made by Sheriff Strider in Mississippi, who had stated that he did not believe the body found in the Tallahatchie River, was really that of her son, Emmett Till. Mamie struggled to hide her ire and frustration over the sheriff's erroneous charges and she stated, "I positively say it is my son lying there in the church, if the State of Mississippi says that, he is not my boy, the burden of proof rest upon that State. I will say that as long as there is a shadow of doubt, I will not have the body interred."

The reporter asked suspiciously, "Judging from the condition of the body, are you really sure it's your son?"

She responded indignantly, "The last time I saw him was August twentieth. Certainly, I would remember my son."

Rayford felt he could no longer maintain his silence at the reporter's audacious probes and as he watched the reporter with disgruntlement, and after becoming more irritated at the reporter's line of questioning, he uttered, "Certainly his ludicrous statement does not come as a surprise. As far as the family is concerned, the body is Emmett's."

As Mamie looked on, the reporter responded to his statement and he conveyed, "The sheriff believes that he have proof!"

Rayford replied, "His statement is an attempt to cover up the truth."

Several hours later the same afternoon, the familiar pick-up truck driven by J.B. arrived and parked outside the Leflore

County Jail in Greenwood, Mississippi. The second occupant in the pickup truck with J.B. was his mother, Eula Lee Bryant, a full-bodied, temperamental woman in her mid to late fifties. A steadfast woman deeply rooted in southern traditional etiquette. The two occupants vacated the pickup truck and entered through the door of the two-story structure. Upon their entrance into the building, they stopped at the front desk to converse with Deputy Sheriff Ben Shelby, who was a weighty man in his mid-forties. He was sitting behind the desk preoccupied with a job-related task. J.B. aroused his attention with a friendly greeting, "Afternoon, Ben."

"Afternoon, J. B., Miz Bryant," the deputy replied, as he greeted the familiar occupants.

"Y'all here to see Roy and J.W.," the deputy then asked?

"That's right," Eula replied.

Shelby rose from his chair to retrieve the set of keys, which opened doors to the cellblock area. As they followed behind the deputy, Eula Lee stopped upon observing Sheriff Smith alone in his office filing reports with his back against the door.

Eula Lee remarked to Ben, "I see the sheriff is back?"

"Yes, ma'am…he got back yesterday mawnin'," the deputy replied.

"J. B., go on with yo' visit, I need to talk with the Sheriff," Eula Lee suggested.

J. B. gave her that look of distrust, which she understood to mean, 'don't antagonize the sheriff', Eula told J. B. that she planned to be on her best behavior and she convinced him by saying, "Go on now, and tell the boys I won't be long." He was content with her answer and he exited to the second floor to visit first with his brother, J. W.

Eula Lee knocked on the open door and then uttered, "Sheriff Smith! I wanna talk to you." Sheriff Smith looked up from his occupation and turned his mindfulness toward the direction of the familiar sounding voice and he courteously invited her in as he asked, "What can I do for you, Miz Bryant?" Eula entered the office of Sheriff Smith, and when he turned his attention to her, he extended her the chair in front of his desk and directed her to take a sit, which she refused, and she told him, "I'll stand, mind ya'." He could almost sense the anger in her defiance. The sheriff watched her apprehensively as she remarked, "I'll come rite to the point, how long you gone hold my boys on these false charges?"

"I can assure you ma'am…the charges ain't false," replied the sheriff. Although, Sheriff Smith was sympathetic to her opposition, she became more agitated by his frankness and she replied, "You done gone and took sides with niggers against my boys… red blooded Americans."

"Ma'am, they confess to the kidnappin'," Sheriff Smith interrupted her.

"They ain't killed that niggra' boy," she remarked with emotions.

Sheriff Smith suggested reassuringly, "I'm sorry, ma'am. I got witnesses say otherwise."

Her complexion turned flush and red as she replied, "Theys a damn lie! Just wanna cause trouble down here and you can't see that."

Sheriff Smith made every attempt to alleviate her anger, but her continued accusation caused an argument between them and he asserted, "Don't tell me how to run my affairs. I know the law!" She fired back, "My boys fought in the war for our country and now you takin' sides with outsiders and niggers, hell bent on destroyin' our way of life down here."

"Who put those lies in your head? I don't take sides with nobody. I was elected by the people to uphold the law," the sheriff replied aggressively.

Meanwhile in Chicago, throughout the day and night of Sunday, September fourth until church attendants closed the doors at 2 a.m., there was a consistent procession of mourners filing pass the mutilated corpse of Emmett Till underneath the covered glass of the open casket. As on previous days, the mourners maintained their emotional vigil and the media continued its coverage of the tragic event.

Meanwhile, in the South and particularly in Mississippi authorites had received rumors that "Chicago Negroes with machine guns" were about to invade the State of Mississippi to avenge the brutal murder of Emmett Till. Mississippi authorities were taking the rumors seriously. Mississippi government authorities ordered State Patrol to set up roadblocks and they began stopping cars with Illinois license plates. Highway State Troopers aggressively carried out the ordered stop and search procedures during the next forty-eight hours starting all day and during the night of Sunday, September fourth and ending during the night of Monday, September fifth. During this time, many black motorists traveling south to Mississippi had to undergo being frisked and intimidated for no reason and some were even arrested unlawfully.

Late morning the following day of September fifth, there was a meeting of the Mississippi Council of Negro Leadership in progress in the all black town of Mound Bayou. Attending the meeting were many faces of Southern American blacks from the area whose eyes were concentrated on the articulate speaker. The speaker was an average height, medium built black man in his early fifties whom everyone in Mississippi and the general area knew as Doctor Theodore Roosevelt Mason Howard, known throughout Mississippi as Doctor T. R. M. Howard. Also attending the meeting was Medger Evers, a NAACP field representative. Doctor Howard whom most black leaders referred to as "The Militant Medic", was also a resident of Mound Bayou, Mississippi, and was president and founder of the Mississippi Council of Negro Leadership. He was also a country physician and the most controversial figure on civil rights in Mississippi.

During his speech on "Mississippi's Way of Desegregation", he informed the council that in spite of the murders of Reverend George W. Lee and Lamar Smith whom he called outspoken leaders of injustice; his objective was to, "stay in Mississippi and fight, so long as God gives me strength." He further stated that, "whites in Mississippi are extremely defiant and hostile toward the Supreme Court's decision outlawing segregation in public schools. I believe an example of this might have led to the brutal lynch/murder of that young boy, Emmett Till." There was a silent anger among the assemblage, as they responded to his speech with vigorous applause. Afterwards, the council drafted a plan to protest Emmett Till's lynch/murder publicly.

A short time later in the Leflore County Jail in Greenwood, Sheriff Smith was talking to a reporter about Sheriff Strider's comments regarding the case against Milam and Bryant. During the interview, he quoted Strider as saying that he did not "see how" Bryant and his half-brother, Milam could be indicted for Till's slaying on the slim evidence available. Sheriff Smith informed the reporter that he was confident that they had a strong case against the two men.

In the meantime, District Attorney Gerald W. Chatham, a resident of Hernando, Mississippi was sitting on his porch conversing with a southern reporter about Strider's statement. As the district attorney conversed with the male reporter whom Chatham was acquainted, their conversation was momentarily interrupted by the wife of the district attorney who brought them a pitcher of lemonade and two glasses and then she quietly entered their residence again. As he and the reporter conversed, Chatham declared, "You would certainly have to prove that the body was really the Till boy's body. Strider's statement complicates the issue of whether the two men will face a murder charge as originally planned."

During the night of Monday, September fifth, there were more than three thousand people waiting outside of the Roberts Temple church, as they were waiting their turn to view the body of Emmett Till. Claude Lightfoot, a native American-Indian, was also among the mourners waiting to enter the church that night. Claude Lightfoot was chairperson of the "Communist party" of Illinois with chapters in Indiana as well. He was making his way among the large gathering attempting to pass out inflammatory literature to whoever would take it and only a few in the crowd accepted the literature. The black mourners were apprehensive about any involvement with the communist party, because of their patriotic loyalty, in spite of social oppression, which was a consistent thorn in their daily existence. The communist hand pamphlet that Lightfoot was passing out displayed a nurse holding the body of a child and the captioned read, "Punish the Child Lynchers." The hand leaflet urged the readers to make demands that the federal prosecution punished the "Ku Klux lynchers and their accomplices, the Mississippi officials." More than forty-thousand persons had viewed Emmett's body in the afternoon and night of September fifth. The procession of mourners continued throughout the night until twelve midnight when the doors to the church were closed.

The rumors of a black invasion continued to escalate to such a degree that during the night of September fifth, the National Guardsmen converged on the Leflore County Jail in Greenwood, Mississippi. Governor Hugh White of Mississippi ordered out the military National Guards to preclude any threats of violence to his State or against Roy Bryant and J.W. Milam. Inside the jail, Sheriff Smith and Deputy Sheriff Cothran were arousing Roy and

J. W. from their sleep concurrently. As the men dressed, all the excitement evolving around them confused them and they sought an explanation. Sheriff Smith informed Roy and J. W. that the governor had ordered out the national guards to protect the two men from danger, because of rumors of a black invasion from the north to shoot up the state of Mississippi and Greenwood in particular. The two white defendants were concerned for their safety as well as the safety of their families and were reassured that their families would be protected. Afterwards, the sheriff and deputy drove the two accused men to the Vicksburg County Jail in Vicksburg, Mississippi incognito. They were to remain there until their arraignment in Sumner, Mississippi, the following day.

CHAPTER TWENTY-TWO:

ARRAIGMENT

The following morning, Tuesday, September sixth, at 11 a.m., the funeral cortege of Emmett Till made its way through Burr Oak cemetery in Alsip, Illinois. The long caravan of automobiles followed behind the hearse through the grass covered cemetery to the open crypt where Emmett Till would be laid to rest. Subsequently, the young pallbearers who were friends of Emmett struggled against the weight of the bronze coffin as they gripped their hands around the handles to lift it from the hearse. Patrick Scott a white, slender built man in his early thirties and the assistant pastor of Roberts Temple Church and also a funeral assistant from A.A. Rayner was assisting the young pallbearers who were friends of Emmett Till carry the casket to the open grave. During the emotional service Bishop Ford eulogized Emmett Till, "As we entomb the body of Emmett Louis Till, today. It is my prayer that his mother, family and friends will find comfort and peace knowing that God has brought him unto himself as a sacrificial lamb.

To wake the conscious of America of its racism and from this senseless act, many will be delivered and the move of righteousness will prevail." During the eulogy, the watchful eyes of sorrow ignited into excruciating grief from family, friends and spectators alike. The strain of the service caused the assistant white pastor of Roberts Temple Church to nearly collapse from grief. The heart-rending agony of watching the bronze metal coffin sank into the concrete vault in the six foot deep grave, became too much for Mamie, Alma and her father, John to bear and their emotional grief caused other family members and friends to cry out in lamentation and Mamie collapsed into the arms of Bishop Roberts and sobbed with uncontrollable sorrow and through her tears, she cried, "Oh, God! Why?" At the conclusion of Emmett Till's four-day funeral over one hundred thousand people both blacks and other nationalities had viewed his body, which attracted dignitaries from around the country including white politicians as well as black leaders.

An hour later the same afternoon, Roy Bryant and J. W. Milam arrived by police escort to the small town of Sumner, Mississippi. Inside the courtroom, Roy and J. W. sat facing the Circuit Judge Curtis Swango, Jr., and watching the all-white eighteen-man grand jury with nervous glances as the men on the jury surveyed them with a stern, yet sympathetic foreboding stare. During the hearing, the grand jury, the judge and the two defendants watched attentively, as District Attorney Gerald Chatham questioned Sheriff Smith, Deputy John Cothran and States Attorney, Michael Frasier individually on the witness stand. Each of the men questioned expounded on the evidence against J. W. and Roy. At the conclusion of the district attorney's deposition, the state's evidence was handed over to the grand jury by the judge and afterwards, the foremen stated, "We say, Roy Bryant and John Williams Milam did unlawfully, willfully and feloniously and of their malice aforethought kill and murder Emmett Till, a human being." At the recommendation of the state, the grand jury filed murder charges against the two men, jointly and separately. Later during the afternoon of the same day, Sheriff Smith informed the press that he would be filing a retainer on Roy and J. W. on kidnapping charges in the event the two men were acquitted of murder. In the meantime, the national guardsmen vacated Greenwood, Mississippi.

Sometime later, the same evening of the same day after Roy and J. W. were transferred to the Tallahatchie County Jail in Charleston, Mississippi, as a result of their murder indictment in Sumner, the two men were sitting in the office of Sheriff Strider and they were conversing with him unrestrained. During their relax conversation, the sheriff expressed his indignation as he uttered, "Reckon, I don't know what all the fuss 'bout some dead nigger in the Tallahatchie. Hell, that river's full o' dead niggers!" J. W. and Roy nodded their heads in agreement and Strider continued, "Seem to me the NAACP and outside agitators is tryin' to destroy our Southern way of life, down here. The whole damn State of Mississippi is on trial 'casue of this thing."

Sheriff Strider reassured them that they need not be concerned about a murder conviction, because of the slim evidence against them. J. W. and Roy were pleased about what they were hearing from the sheriff and fearing no threat of reprisal from him, they informed the sheriff about the two field hands who had accompanied them to Preacher Mose tenant shack. Sheriff Strider's concern for Mississippi's reputation let it be known to the two defendants that as soon as the trial date was set that he would make sure the two fields hands weren't around to testify against them.

The following day, Moses arrived at the home of his eldest son, Charles Wright, by his first marriage. They conversed about Moses appearance in local newspapers and the vast publicity concerning the brutal murder of his nephew, Emmett Till. Moses expressed his disappointment that two white men were charged with his nephew's murder in spite of the fact that four white men had arrived at his tenant shack and abducted his nephew at gunpoint. Charles attempted to encourage his father about the arrest telling him that in a state where the arrest of whites who committed crimes against blacks was rare that having the arrest take place was considered important enough. Charles inquired about his stepmother's expected return from Chicago with other family members returning from the funeral the following day, but Moses sadly informed him that his wife was not planning to return and that she decided never to live in Mississippi again. Moses informed his son that once the trial was over that he was planning to leave Mississippi as well. Charles, concerned for his father's safety encouraged him to do so.

Meanwhile the same afternoon on the Clint Sheridan plantation, Willie Reed; his grandfather, Ed Reed, Frank King, Mandy and Alonzo Bradley and Walter Bullup were working the cotton crop in the fields among other sharecroppers on the plantation. During their discussion of the funeral of the little Chicago boy murdered on the plantation where they resided, Mandy conversed with her sharecropper neighbors about contacting Doctor Howard, but the men refused her suggestion because of their fear of white retaliation. Mandy finally convinced them that they needed to take some kind of action to prevent a similar occurrence; they clandestinely engendered a plan to get information to Doctor Howard in nearby Mound Bayou.

Later during the evening of the same day, Velma and her husband, Earl visited her sister Mandy and Alonzo on the Clint Sheridan plantation. Earl and his wife, Velma were residence in the all-black town of Mound Bayou. Mandy had been expecting their visit; therefore, she had prepared a big dinner for them. As the four of them sat at the table consuming the appetizing meal before them, Velma uttered with regret, "Ain't it a shame what them peckerwoods did to the li'l boy from Chicago." Mandy and Alonzo watched each other with uneasy glances of suspicious embarrassment and she was unable to restrain her inner anger, as Mandy replied, "It show ain't right and dey did it right out there in dat shed." Earl and Velma stared at them with shock and concern and then Earl asked, "You sayin' that young boy was killed out yonder?" Alonzo uttered, "That's right…we seen 'em."

Earl offered, "Y'all know Doctor Howard is lookin' for folks who know 'bout that killin'. Y'all gotta tell 'em." Velma's concern for the safety of her sister and brother-in-law caused her to react to her husband's suggestion, since Velma did not think that his suggestion of having them contact Howard was wise. Furthermore, as far as Velma was concerned contacting Doctor Howard would attract too much attention to the plantation and would place her sister in harm's way; therefore, she spoke anxiously, "Now, Earl, you know them crazy peckerwoods. They go talkin'...they'll kill them just like they killed that child."

Mandy reached over to calm the fear in her sister's eyes and then she spoke softly to her, "Velma, he gotta know dis, don't you understand, he's gotta know!" Earl contemplated over the situation and knowing that his wife's concern was not devoid of truth, he decided that it would be easier for him to contact Doctor Howard whom he knew personally, since him and his wife made their home in Mound Bayou. He felt that by doing so, he reasoned that his action would draw attention away from Mandy and Alonzo. Alonzo and Mandy agreed with his proposal and they watched each other with uneasy glances, as Velma watched the three of them with anxiety and concern.

Later during night, Too Tight sat drinking substantially in a bar known around the town of Glendora as King. Too Tight, being a resident of Glendora was a frequent visitor to the bar and tonight he sought to relieve the tormented agony of his mind by drinking repeatedly in the hopes of erasing the brutal images of the child's murder from his memory. Too Tight in his state of intoxication began talking out loud to himself, as others around him were attentive to his rather outlandish digressive utterance. Those present in the tavern with him was his neighbors who also resided in the poor black section of town. They had known Too Tight and Henry Lee for many years and they were befuddled and concern by what Too Tight was saying. Too Tight could neither read nor write and he struggle with his inner state of anxiety over what he and Henry Lee had been through concerning the murder of the young child. The average height bartender and those around him found it difficult to understand his inconsistent muddleheaded conversation at first. Nevertheless, as he continued, they began to piece together a clear picture of what he was agonizing over and slowly they came to understand his involvement in the murder of the little boy found in the river. The bartender asked, "Too Tight, you be there when that li'l boy got kill?" The only thing Too Tight repeated over and over was, "Me and Henry Lee, us seen 'em do it!" The neighbors of Too Tight sat around watching him in dreaded fear as the reality of what Too Tight was revealing through his drunken lips and what the new revelation could mean to their safety if this information got into the wrong hands. Ella Mae, the girlfriend of Too Tight whom he has been living with for over a year, entered the tavern and upon observing his disappointing state of intoxication; she walked over to him and uttered, "C'mon Too Tight, reckon we be git'n' on home." A male friend assisted her as they ushered him out of the King tavern.

CHAPTER TWENTY-THREE:

PROTEST RISING

The following day about late morning, September eighth on Chicago's South Side, Mamie and her father, John was in her second floor apartment watching the late morning news report of the latest information regarding the brutal murder of her son in Mississippi. While searching through the mail, she discovered a letter from District Attorney Gerald Chatham requesting her presence by invitation to be a witness at the upcoming murder trial. They soon diverted their attention to the newscast of a press conference from the courthouse in Sumner, Mississippi, where Circuit Judge Curtis M. Swango, Jr., announced to the press that he had set the murder trial date for September nineteenth. Mamie and her father watched each other with reflective thoughts of anxiety and she uttered, "Lord, give strength to do what needs to be done." John took his daughter into his embrace and he spoke to her in comforting hope, "The Lord will take care of us in this thing, baby."

Mamie called her attorney, William Huff and she informed him about the letter she had received from the district attorney in Mississippi. Attorney Huff disclosed to Mamie that he had some skepticism with regard to her attending the upcoming trial, and he revealed his plan to contact the FBI for protection while she was in Mississippi. Attorney Huff further instructed her that before she made any decision to attend the trial, he would need to contact the district attorney and advise him to issue a subpoena making Mamie a state witness so that she would receive full protection from the State of Mississippi. Mamie agreed with Huff's course of action and she promised to wait until she heard from him, before she decided to accept the district attorney's summons.

Meanwhile, a short time later, the same afternoon of the same day, Mandy Bradley's brother-in-law, Earl who resided in Mound Bayou, arrived at the Friendship Clinic of Doctor T.R.M. Howard. When he entered the clinic, he observed the many dark oppressed weary faces staring back at him and in those eyes revealed years of hard Jim Crow oppression with no compensation or opportunity for social change. Earl walked over to the desk and told Doctor Howard's receptionist that it was urgent that he spoke to Doctor Howard about the ad the doctor had placed seeking witnesses with knowledge about the murder of Emmett Till. The receptionist informed Earl that Doctor Howard was out of town on business, but that upon his return she would see to it that the doctor received his urgent message. The black female receptionist inquired whether she could be of further assistance or if someone else would be able to aid and he enlightened her that it was urgent that he spoke only with Doctor Howard. The receptionist was well aware of the ad placed by her boss as her thoughts were also on the little murdered child. Earl was suspicious and careful not to alert attention and he told her that he would return several days later in an attempt to contact Doctor Howard. The receptionist disclosed to him that she was expecting the doctor's return in a couple of days. Then Earl vacated the office en route to his place of residence.

Meanwhile public pressure continued becoming increasingly insurmountable in the city of Chicago and around the nation, as headlines of Emmett Till's brutal lynch-style murder continued to ignite sorrow and anger. The Chicago press during the week of September eighth headlined the events as the "Mississippi Child Lynching." An editorial in the Chicago Sun-Times read, "A revolting crime against humanity has been committed in Mississippi in the name of white supremacy. The senseless killing of Emmett Till is a shameful blot not only on Mississippi, but also on America. Until punishing his murders to the full extent of the law has done justice, no American with a conscience can have peace of mind. If as is often the case, an all-white jury should be lenient toward the lynchers, decent Americans will demand federal anti-lynching legislation. If the states cannot deal with these criminals, the Federal government must."

Chicago Mayor Richard J. Daley told the press that he had wired President Eisenhower demanding federal action against the lynchers. He also stated to the press, "We join with all decent citizens in urging swift prosecution of those who are guilty of this act." The mayor proposed to the President by wired communications, "I strongly urge that all facilities of the Federal government be immediately utilized so that the ends of justice can be served."

The Governor of Illinois William Stratton had also instructed his Attorney General to urge the Mississippi authorities to make a complete investigation. National organizations with regional offices in Chicago, including various unions and the NAACP had begun to direct the indignation of their members into action. The Chicago district of the CIO United Packing House Workers sent a telegram to Mamie inviting her to speak at a mass meeting at the union center to help launch a plan of action for their membership. Gerald Bullock, regional director of the NAACP, told the Chicago Defender, "The atmosphere in Mississippi reeks of race hatred and defiance of all laws based on democratic principles." He also blamed the lynching of Emmett Till on the "reign of terror" directed against the movement of Americans of African ancestry who were seeking to exercise their democratic rights and he called for federal action.

The Washington Park Forum had also announced to the press of their plans to launch a mass protest rally denouncing the brutal murder of the fourteen-year-old child and a cry for justice. Many black leaders in Chicago and around the country stated that the call for justice was just the beginning of mass rallies in reference to the unspeakable lynching of the Chicago child. The fact that Emmett Till was the son of a World War II veteran killed during the war infuriated their efforts and they promised to touch off the most powerful movement against racism, Jim-Crow and lynch law the city of Chicago or the entire nation had ever seen.

Various Mississippi newspapers had also joined the nation in the rising indignation of the brutal slaying. Most of them united with Mississippi Governor White and local officials in asking for a speedy prosecution of the men accused in the kidnap-murder of young Emmett Till.

The Greenwood Commonwealth reported, "Every decent and respectable citizen of this state will assume responsibility for seeing that justice is administered through the Court of Law and that the guilty parties shall pay for their crime." Another Mississippi Delta paper, the Clarksdale Press Register, wrote, "Unless the guilty parties are prosecuted vigorously, the State of Mississippi and the South may as well burn all of its law books and close its courts." The Vicksburg post also reported, "Only through vigorous prosecution and conviction of the guilty parties, will the death of this teenager be avenged." The Hattiesburg American stated in their commentary, "The whole world is watching the law enforcement authorities of Leflore and Tallahatchie counties to see how they will handle their responsibilities."

It became increasingly clear that while the authorities and newspapers in the South had demanded the punishment of the killers, an increasing amount of their outrage were directed at those who protested against the atrocity of the young child's brutal murder. Mississippi State's Attorney, Michael Frasier, stated to the press, "Outside agitation in the case is not helping the prosecution cause at all." The Jackson Daily News screamed that the NAACP was, "Trying its best to inflame the nation against the South and Mississippi in particular."

The following Friday afternoon, September ninth, one day after the murder trial date was set, two white brothers in their early thirties and members of the White Citizen Council decided to organize a defense fund for the accused murders. During one of the

White Citizen Council's vociferous debates against integration, the two brothers suggested raising money for the two men accused of murdering young Emmett Till. The two men were E. D. Nabus and his brother, J.B. With overwhelming acceptance the Nabus brothers succeed in getting the council to create a Milam-Bryant six thousand-dollar defense fund. After council members travelled from door-to-door throughout the delta region collecting large sums of money from numerous white farmers, several clergymen and neighboring bankers, the generous contributions given by whites in the area amounted to ten thousand-dollars. Members of the White Citizens Council hired five of the best lawyers in Sumner, Mississippi to represent the two defendants from the law office of Breland and Whitten.

Later during the same evening, District Attorney Chatham was on the telephone in his modestly furnish office talking to Attorney General J. P. Coleman, the newly-elected governor of Mississippi about getting someone to assist him in the upcoming murder-trial against the two defendants, whom he heard was being represented by five attorneys. The attorney general realizing that it would be to difficult for the district attorney to prosecute the case against five defense lawyers without the aid of an experience assistant; advised the district attorney that he had appointed a former FBI agent, Robert B. Smith, the third from Ripley, Mississippi to assist him in the upcoming murder-trial in Sumner, Mississippi.

Later during the night in Mamie's second floor apartment, Mamie was conversing with her mother, her father and her Aunt Mama Lizzie. During their conversation, Mamie informed them about the letter she had received from Doctor Howard and the NAACP inviting her to speak publicly around the country in reference to her son's tragic death. Mamie also informed them of her decision to attend the upcoming murder-trial in Mississippi; in spite of the lack of protection, since Attorney Huff had informed her that the FBI notified him by letter that the agency did not provide protection to private citizens. Mamie's announcement caused Alma concern and her concern caused a heated debate between them. Alma distressfully verbalized, "I won't have you going down there, Sister. It's much too dangerous!" Mamie replied, "Mother, I need to be there." "What good would it do if something happen to you down there, "asked Alma? As John and Mama Lizzie looked on with concern, Mamie uttered, "It doesn't matter whether I come back dead or alive I need to see that justice is done, I need to do this for Bo." Alma knew that it was pointless to try and persuade Mamie once she had made up her mind and Alma sat watching her daughter with a troubled look. Mama Lizzie remarked sadly, "She's right, Mamie. I just couldn't take it if something else happen." In spite of their insistence, she was adamant about her decision, which prompted her father to assert, "If that's what you wanna do daughter, I'm goin' with you."

Several days later, mid-afternoon, Monday, September twelfth, in a modestly outfitted newspaper office in New York, James L. Hicks, an average looking man of dignity and pride with a flair for adventure was sitting at his desk typing a report. He was a black reporter for the Baltimore Afro-American Herald and a man in his early forties. While James Hicks was typing, the sound of the telephone ringing on his desk interrupted his thoughts. Hicks' conversation on the phone revealed that he was talking to his managing editor, Arthur (Art) Carter. During their conversation, Art's voice was audible through the phone, "Jimmy, we've got to send a man to Mississippi." James Hicks had been expecting this call for some time, since his return from Memphis the week before, where he was covering the Baptist Convention. With a look of uneasy anticipation, even before Art could finish the question, Hicks interrupted him and ask, "When do you want me to leave?" Art suggest, "We need you in Mississippi by Friday morning to cover the upcoming murder-trial." Hicks replied, "I'll be there." He concluded his conversation with Art and then he pulled out his Rand McNally Atlas from his desk drawer and took a long hard look at the Sovereign State of Mississippi. As James Hicks gazed at the map, his thoughts were on preparing to enter a racially charged combat zone to get a story and he spoke to himself, "How the hell do I prepare for this?"

Later during the night of September twelfth, the night was dark, humid and mysterious around the black section of town in Glendora, Mississippi. The hour was late and the town was quiet as the inhabitants were off the street and in their place of residence. All at once, deputy sheriffs besiege upon the physically undisturbed area with their guns drawn. The deputy sheriffs made their way to and surrounded the tenant shack where Henry Lee and Clara lived as the two were asleep inside. And other deputies surrounded the tenant shack a short distance away, where Too-Tight was sleeping in bed with his girlfriend, Ella Mae. After the deputy sheriffs force their way into the tenant shacks simultaneously, they ordered Henry Lee and Too-Tight to get dress and come with them. Inside Henry Lee's tenant shack, he and Clara were obviously shaken and she anxiously inquired where the law enforcement officers were taking him. One of the deputies attempted to ease her fears by telling Clara that they were transporting Henry Lee and Too-Tight to the county jail in Charleston, Mississippi, because the two men lives were in danger from persons unknown.

CHAPTER TWENTY-FOUR:

PRE-TRIAL BLUES

The following afternoon, Tuesday, September thirtieth, in the Tallahatchie County jail in Charleston, Mississippi, H. C. Strider, the sheriff of the segregated county jail allowed J. W. and Roy to enter the cell to converse with Too-Tight and Henry Lee. In the segregated prison, it was customary in the South to quarantine white and black prisoners from each other. When the two field hands had arrived at the jail the night before, the sheriff reassured them that their incarceration was only for their protection and Strider informed them that he would place no restrictions on their movements throughout the black section of the jail. Sheriff Strider forbidden the two field hands from discussing their incarceration with other inmates, he also registered the two field hands under concealed names during the time that they were held in custody to conceal them from the press. J. W. pulled the unlocked cell gate open and he and Roy came face-to-face with Henry Lee and Too-Tight as the two black men were sitting on the two cots eating their lunch. During the visit between the four jailed men, as usual undemonstrative Roy had little to say and his extroverted half-brother, J. W. did all the talking. J. W. looked sternly into the low self-esteem eyes of the two black field hands and he uttered, "Now you two boys the only one can hurt us in this thing." Too Tight and Henry Lee watched the two white men with uncertain mistrust, as they listened to J. W. converse about he and his half-brother's concerns. J. W. stood over the two black men like a towering threat as he told them that it was imperative that the two field hands keep their promise of silence about their knowledge of the murder of the young child. J. W. reiterated the threat he had made to them prior to his arrest threatening harm to their families as well as themselves. Too Tight spoke to him reassuringly, "Reckon we ain't do y'all no hurt, Mister J. W."

Henry Lee found himself staring at the two white child killers with silent bitter contempt and deep down inside of him; he longed to inflict serious retribution on the men for making him a witness to their depraved immoral appetite. His enmity toward the men did not just derived from the senseless murder of the young child, but also from years even centuries of wretched racist oppression, which had been passed down from generation to generation on Americans of African lineage.Henry Lee's thoughts were on all the unresolved lynchings perpetrated on his race, which he observed staring back at him through the hateful eyes embodied in the two white men standing over him.

J. W. turned his attention to Henry Lee and he asked, "Can we count on you, Henry Lee?" Henry Lee dropped his head as a castrated attack on his manhood and he struggled to answer the question posed to him by the over confident child killer and with silent reluctance he said, "Yessuh!" J. W. boasted with confidence that even the law was on their side. Afterwards, he and Roy abandoned the jail cell of the two field hands unrestrained and as J. W. closed the cell gate behind them, he threw a halfhearted smile and declared, "Reckon, we'll be seeing you boys."

Several days later sometime during the mid-afternoon of Thursday, September fifteenth, the head of the FBI was holding a press conference at the FBI Headquarters in Washington, D. C. Since the brutal murder of young Emmett Till, which had consumed the nation with shock and grief, the Federal Bureau of Investigation and the White House continued in the tenacious bombardment of numerous angry letters from all over the country and parts of the world. The letters urged President Eisenhower, Attorney General Herbert Brownell and FBI Director; John Edgar Hoover to take action under the presupposition that Emmett Till's civil rights had been violated. J. Edgar Hoover, as he was well known was holding the press conference in reference to Emmett's brutal murder in Mississippi. One of the reporters asked during the deliberation why the FBI and other government agencies had refused to enter the murder case, which was obviously a lynch-murder based on the race of the young child. Hoover eyed the reporter with a hostile glance and then he delivered with obvious irritation, "This agency could not act on the kidnapping charges, because no state lines were crossed." The FBI continued to state publicly pertaining to the reason for their lack of inquiries into the brutal murder of Emmett Till. Yet, the FBI under the direction of J. Edgar Hoover maintained a clandestine surveillance over the case, which also included the monitoring activities of national civil rights organizations, national and local unions as well as keeping the Communist Party activities around the country under scrutiny. The Communist Party continued their vociferous public protest regarding the lynch-murder of young Emmett Till in Mississippi to further their communist causes.

Later during the muggy summer night, inside the Tallahatchie county jail in Charleston, a comely looking black woman in her early to mid-thirties and whom everyone in the jail knew as, Sarah was a 'trusty' at the jail and also a cook for the inmates. Sarah was serving a life conviction for killing a rival woman who was dating her husband. Sarah's promiscuous services with Strider and some of his deputies allowed her special privileges around the jail. On this particular night, she pushed a cart with dinner trays on it. As Sarah swaggered along the cellblocks passing out trays to black inmates, she entered the cell of Too-Tight and Henry Lee who watched her with curious intriguing stares. The two field hands unrestricted movements around certain areas of the jail caused curiosity in her and she came looking for answers. Sarah was a woman who made it her business to be in the loop germane to events occurring around the jail. Since the arrival of Too-Tight and Henry Lee, she had been trying cleverly to get information from the sheriff about the reason for their incarceration, but he remained strangely tight-lipped about her concerns. Strider's lack of cooperation in the matter only flamed her inquisitive nature even more. Upon Sarah's entrance into the cell where the two men were housed, she being an outspoken and witty woman began to converse with the men at first with small talk and a little female charm. During their conversation, she soon learned that the two men real names were Leroy (Too-Tight) Collins and Henry Lee

Loggins. Sarah had learned their fictional names from the sheriff during one of her private intimate moments with him. The reasoning behind Sheriff Strider incarcerating Too-Tight and Henry Lee was to prevent their testimony in the upcoming murder-trial.

Sarah's conversation soon focused on the pending trial and she mentioned to them with concern, "hear tell dem white folks gon' git free and clear, cuz ain't got nobody who say dey done it." Henry Lee's silent anger was still seething within him and he did not consider the outcome when he broke his silence and looked sternly at her and replied, "We can say dey done it, cuz we was dar!" Henry Lee's blunt confession alarmed Too Tight and fearing that Henry Lee might reveal more facts related to Emmett Till's brutal murder, Too Tight irritably reprimanded him by saying, "Shut the hell up, Henry Lee! You know we ain't talk on dat!" Sarah was obviously stunned and confused and she asked, "What y'all talkin'?" Henry Lee stared disappointingly at his roommate, as Too Tight had turned his back on them and realizing the danger of his disclosure; Henry Lee refused to comment further on the subject. Sarah vacated the cell concerned about what she had heard.

The following day of Friday, September sixteenth, it was twelve o'clock in the afternoon, when James Hicks arrived in the small town of Sumner and parked his rental 1955 green Mercury in front of the single level building. The inscription across the large front window of the single-level building read 'Sumner Sentinel Newspaper'. James Hicks entered the small somewhat shabby office, where the chief editor, William M. Simpson greeted him. Simpson was a stocky, Southern aristocratic looking man in his mid-fifties. As they conversed with one another, Hicks informed the chief editor that he represented the national newspaper association, which included an Atlanta daily paper. A broad smile thundered across Simpson's face and he indicated, "Good! You are from the South. You can do this county a lot of good by explaining in your article just how things are down here in the South."

Meanwhile, the same Friday afternoon of Sepember sixteenth, Lucy Mae, a full-bodied black woman in her early forties arrived at the Tallahatchie County Jail to visit her sister, Sarah. As she made her way to the visiting area, she passed the open door of the prison laundry room where she observed Too Tight whom she was an acquaintance through her husband, as he was washing prison uniforms. Lucy Mae was surprised to see him there, and she stopped to converse with Too Tight about the reason for his incarceration, and he made up some excuse to ease her curiosity. Satisfied with his answer, Lucy Mae was about to leave when he whispered to her to get in touch with his father. Too Tight told Lucy Mae to let his father know that he was all right and that he was in need of money. A short time later, when Lucy Mae visited with her sister, Sarah, she informed Sarah that Kid Townsler whom they both knew very well had died and that his funeral was scheduled for the following Sunday. Lucy Mae informed Sarah of her and her husband's plan to attend the service. As their chitchat continued, Lucy Mae disclosed to her sister about the encounter she had had with Too Tight and the content of their conversation. Sarah reacted with surprise to learn that her sister knew Too Tight and Henry Lee. Lucy Mae's intense interest in her sister disclosing enlightened revelation regarding Too Tight and Henry Lee's involvement in the much-publicized murder of young Emmett

Till held Lucy Mae hostage with intrigue. Lucy Mae struggled to hide the astonished expression on her face as she indulged the shocking revelation from Sarah.

Sarah spoke to Lucy in whispered clandestine tones as she looked around suspiciously to make sure they had not attracted the attention of other inmates that sat around them in the visiting room with their visiting relatives and families. Sarah also enrich the mind of her sister on how deputies had estranged the two field hands from conversing with other inmates. Lucy Mae divulged to Sarah about her acquaintance with J. W. and his half-brother, Roy and she further shed some light on the subject that the two field hands worked for J. W. This new revelation about the two men working for J. W. explained why Sarah had observed the two white men conversing with them in their cell. Sarah disclosed to her sister that each time she inquired about the two men's incarceration to Sheriff Strider, he was very evasive and he just told her that the men were being held in protective custody. Lucy Mae uttered softly, "That ain't what Too-Tight told me." They stared at each other in quiet concerned fear.

In spite of national and local attention over the terrible crime in his State, Sheriff H. C. Strider was self-assured and unconcerned about rumors spreading with much talk about racial confrontations erupting from tension and uneasiness among the inhabitants of his county. Therefore, he joined several local sheriffs who took off for a trip to Atlanta over the weekend to attend a football game against the State of Mississippi and Georgia. They departed the evening of Friday, September sixteenth.

During the night, Reporter James Hicks arrived at the home

of Doctor Howard in Mound Bayou, for a meeting with the physician. Also attending the meeting was Medger Evers, Ruby Hurley a regional official of the NAACP and Doctor Howard's wife. During the meeting, T. R. M. Howard disclosed about the information he had received from a man, who had identified himself as the brother-in-law of one of five witnesses to the murder of the young child, Emmett Till. As the gathers looked on with excited interest, Doctor Howard imparted to them that according to the witnesses, the murder took place on the Clint Sheridan plantation, which he revealed was near Drew, Mississippi. The disclosure of possible witnesses to the hideous crime caused euphoria among those in attendance. Therefore, they devised a strategic plan to convince the witnesses to testify at the impending trial, and they discussed among themselves about the necessary preparations of safety for the five or more witnesses living on the Clint Sheridan plantation.

Hicks suggested that once they came to know the eyewitnesses on the plantation, in order to secure their safety, he and others could possibly camouflage themselves as sharecroppers and invade the plantation during the late hours of nightfall to lead them to safety. Ruby suggested that they would need to keep the information hidden until the trial. Doctor Howard also told them that the mother of Emmett Till and Congressman Charles Diggs of Michigan made plans to arrive sometime Monday before the trial. As their conversation continued, Howard proposed in a direct manner without hostility, "This trial will demonstrate to the nation just what Mississippi justice means to people of color."

Contrary to what Sheriff Strider had been telling the press

about his self-assurance that there would be no outburst of racial tension anywhere in Mississippi, pertaining to the much-publicized brutal murder of Emmett Till. There were disseminated acts of violence and death threats by white supremacist groups against Americans of African lineage who dared to take a stand for social equality. One particular incident occurred in the town of Greenwood, when four angry white men with guns in their possession confronted a conspicuous looking, middle-aged, black man. The man was Edward Clark and at the time, he was president of the NAACP chapter in the seat of Leflore County. The four angry young white men surrounded him when he was vacating the three-story Greenwood Plaza hotel, which he owned along with several other businesses in town. The incident occurred the Saturday afternoon before the start of the murder trial scheduled to begin the following Monday. During the encounter, one of the men told him, "Boy if you know what's good for you. You better not show up at that trial on Monday." Edward said he knew everyone in town, yet those four white men were men he had never seen before. Fortunate for him his three bodyguards were able to vanquish the attack against him. His three bodyguards often accompanied him when he traveled. The four white men quickly retreated from the possible confrontation and Clark told them, "Before you get me, some of you gonna end up dead. We've had enough tyranny." The white men soon sped away from the area in their vehicles, as the four black men watched after them in anger. It was because of Edward Clark's involvement with the NAACP, that he had received many death threats from racist elements in the surrounding region, which moved him to hire bodyguards to offset for any sudden dangers and bodily harm.

Meanwhile, the same Saturday afternoon in the all black town of Mound Bayou, a station wagon arrived at the resident of Doctor T. R. M Howard. Earl drove the automobile, transporting Mandy, Alonzo, Willie Reed and Willie's grandfather, Ed to converse with Doctor Howard and others invited to Howard's home for the meeting. Inside the single level home, waiting their arrival were Doctor Howard, James Hicks and Ruby Hurley. Earl had to be very careful not to alert attention to his activities on the plantation, as he gathered the four sharecroppers for the planned communed. Upon their entrance into the resident, the five-invited guest stared at the two unfamiliar faces with Howard with anxious glances and Howard being mindful of their uneasiness, soon introduced Hicks, the reporter and Hurley, a representative of the NAACP to them. During the conversation between them, Hicks, Hurley and Howard learned in detail about the beating episode concerning young Emmett Till on the Clint Sheridan plantation.

The four potential witnesses of the plantation conveyed to Howard and his two guests that they heard no gunshot during and after the beating. Reporter Hicks expressed to the four sharecroppers from the Clint Sheridan plantation how important their testimony would be for justice in the impending murder-trial. Mandy, Alonzo, Ed and especially Willie became frighten at the possibility of putting their lives in danger by testifying against white men accused of murdering the young child. Hicks understood their fears and he began to appeal to their sense of compassion and as they looked on, he spoke directly to Willie by saying, "Son, I know how afraid you are. But, I promise you, we won't let anything happen to any of you." Hurley added, "This crime is being watched all over the world. You don't have to worry; the

NAACP can provide protection for all of you." Howard then declared, "Son, you have rights. All of you have rights and you can change things by standing up for what is right." Although, the four sharecroppers had not relinquished their fears, three of them agreed to testify at the astute persuasion of Doctor Howard whose reputation they knew well. Mandy and Willie also informed them of other witnesses.

The following day amid a muggy Sunday afternoon, September eighteenth in the small town of Sumner, there was a mixed race crowd of people consisting of blacks and whites and they were entering the Sumner Baptist church. The church was not far from the courthouse in the Town Square. Blacks and whites of the town had come to attend the funeral of a local black resident by the name of Kid Townsler. Amid the local spectators who had come to attend the service were out of town reporters including James Hicks. The funeral was presided over by a local minister whom everyone in town knew as, Reverend Hill. During the service, Hicks was sitting in the back of the church with fellow reporter, Simeon Booker, a reporter from Ebony publication, who had arrived early Saturday to cover the trial and like Hicks, he had taken up residence at a hotel in Mound Bayou. As they observed the crowd of whites attending the service, Simeon referred to the large presence of whites attending the service and he suggested, "You know their presence here is just a public relations stunt." Hicks did not reply to his statement, but his smile confirmed his agreement.

Outside of the church, an automobile arrived and parked a short distance from the building. In the vehicle, Lucy Mae and her husband, Clay arrived at the church to attend the service of their longtime friend.

Inside the church, Hicks remarked to Simeon, "Man, it's hot in here! I need some air, I'll be back later." He departed the church, walked over to his car, lean against it, and lit a cigarette. As he took puffs from his cigarette, his eyes took in the ambience around the town with veneration and yet disappointment at everything that encompassed the South. He frowned at the separate accommodation signs and then at the local black residents walking abreast and then stepping completely off the sidewalk to let whites pass. Lucy Mae and Clay were sitting in their car and their attention was drawn to his discriminating appearance and Lucy Mae asked her husband, "I ain't ever seen him 'round these parts. You reckon he's one of them news people we been hearin' 'bout?"

Clay replied, "Reckon, it don't hurt to find out."

Clay left the vehicle and walked his medium built frame over to where Hicks was standing and he asked, "Excuse me Mister! Is you a news man." "Yes, I am a reporter. What can I do for you," Hicks asked? Clay told him that his wife sitting in his car would like to speak with him. Hicks followed him to the car and during his conversation with Lucy Mae, Hicks learned about her sister, Sarah and Too-Tight and Henry Lee, their incarceration and the two field hands possible involvement in the publicized murder of the young teen from Chicago. Clay informed him that if he traveled to the Reid's Cafe' in Glendora, someone there could tell him how to get in touch with Henry Lee's common law wife, Clara. At the conclusion of their conversation with Hicks, Lucy Mae and Clay decided not to attend the funeral since they felt they might have drawn suspicion to themselves by talking to the stranger in town. Subsequently, Clay suggested to him, "We best be goin'. If you go to Glendora, good luck! But don't get caught down there after dark." The car pulled away from the curb and Hicks watched after them as the car drove away from the area.

Hicks began the short walk back toward the church as he pondered the important information he had received from the two strangers. When Hick passed by two white men on his way back to the church, he overheard one of them say regarding the funeral, "That boy show picked a convenient time to die." The two white men found the comment humorous.

Meanwhile, many miles away in Money, two black reporters were arriving at the tenant shack of Moses Wright. The two reporters were Cloyte Larsson-Murdock an attractive and outspoken woman who worked for Ebony publication as a reporter and her black male assistant, David Jackson who was a tall, dark and forceful man and a photographer for Jet magazine. They greeted Moses who invited them to sit with him on the screened porch. Maurice, Robert and Simeon were sitting a short distance from the tenant shack and they were keeping a concerned watchful eye on their father. During the interview, Moses told the female reporter how he was looking forward to testifying at the murder-trial when it gets underway the following day in Sumner, Mississippi. Cloyte asked curiously, "You're not afraid of the possible danger of testifying against white men in the South?"

Moses, who was rocking back and forth in his rocking chair, replied with assurance, "Naw ma'am, the Lord is on my side, he'll keep me."

"What about threats, have there been many," she asked?

Moses replied with some concern, "Reckon dare's been some. Ain't lookin' for it to stop me none."

The three youngsters as well as Moses and the two visiting journalist attention was suddenly diverted to the slow moving pickup truck advancing toward them on the gravel road. The three youngsters scurried to the feet quickly and bolted to the porch of the tenant shack. From where Moses and the two journalists were sitting, they could see the shotguns that the six white men were holding in their hands as the gun barrels were gleaming in the hot sunlight. As the truck converged near the tenant shack where they were sitting, the white men on the truck gazed at them with a cold and ageless hostility. The three occupants on the porch stared back at them and the spell was not broken until, suddenly, when the pickup truck picked up speed and raced on down the dusty gravel road leaving a funnel of dust in its trek. As the truck sped down the road in a puff of smoke, David commented to Moses, "Reverend Wright is it hurting season now?"

Moses resumed his rocking and showing no sign of concern and as he continued to watch the fleeting pickup truck, he replied, "Not as I know of, Mister Jackson. Unless it's us dey got in mind!"

Later during the night, Mamie, her father John and her cousin, Rayford Mooty departed a plane at the Memphis Airport. The time was 2:30 a.m., early Monday morning, September nineteenth. When they entered the waiting area, Doctor Howard in the company of two bodyguards greeted them. After Mamie, her father and cousin had arrived in Memphis; they entered the waiting station wagon driven by one of the bodyguards. They departed the airport en route to Doctor Howard's home in Mound Bayou about one-hundred and twenty-five miles away, where they would be his houseguest during their stay in Mississippi. Congressman Diggs would arrive with his party sometime during the afternoon or evening on the same Monday of September nineteenth, the first day of the murder-trial.

CHAPTER TWENTY-FIVE:

MURDER-TRIAL: DAY ONE

The following mid-morning, Monday, September nineteenth, in the town of Mound Bayou, a refurbished two-story structure stood erect with a protruded sign that read: MOUND BAYOU HOTEL. Inside the conference room, a meeting was in progress with numerous black reporters who had come to Mississippi to cover the murder-trial of the two white men accused of murdering young Emmett Till. They were meeting to discuss their strategy in covering the eminent murder-trial getting under way in Sumner, Mississippi, thirty miles away. The black press embodied such reporters as Simeon Booker, James Hicks, Cloyte Murdock, David Jackson and four new arrivals, such as L. Alex Wilson, the editor of the Memphis Tri-Star Defender, which represented Defender publications. Mrs. Nannie Mitchell-Turner the publisher of the Saint Louis Argus and her assistant, Steve Duncan and Abner Berry from a national publication known as the Worker. While they were conversing about the various methods of covering aspects of the murder-trial and the intense charge atmosphere of racial tension and social injustice, which they had anticipated encountering daily; the reporters turned their attention to the white man in his early thirties entering the conference room and sitting among them. Simeon Booker introduced the man as, Michael Shiver, a professional photographer employed by Jet Magazine, an illustrious national black publication out of Chicago, Illinois. During the meeting, the black press decided that it would be wise if they pretended not to know their white companion, because they felt that any interracial encounter would probably arouse suspicion. The white news photographer disclosed how he planned to photograph aspects of the trial and of the countenance of life in Mississippi, which would be impossible for black reporters to cover without intimidation and threats from Southern Whites. Hicks concluded the meeting with the reporters by suggesting possible rendezvous points where they could secretly exchange information with the white photographer. The reporters decided that any exchange of pertinent information should be far away from media cameras and other hostile forces determine to preclude the truth from coming forth in the racially tense and explosive murder trial. Shortly thereafter, they set out in their automobiles for the trial, thirty miles away.

An hour later the same morning, vehicles driven by members of the black press arrived at the two-story courthouse in the town of Sumner, Mississippi. The Black reporters kept a watchful eye on the hostile surroundings as they made their way to the courthouse. All around the town square there was a large media presence as news crews were hastily setting up bulky TV camera equipment on the courthouse lawn. When members of the black press reached the courtroom, they had to present their press passes before white deputies would allow them to enter, although the massive white media that their white companion had joined upon his arrival encountered no opposition from the southern deputies standing guard outside the courtroom. There was a large crowd gathered in the Courthouse Square and they were comprised of white farmers as well as black sharecroppers and members of Emmett Till's family who symbolized courage and tenacity as they waited to enter the courthouse.

Meanwhile inside the courtroom, many white farmers received subpoenas to participate in the jury selection for an all-white, all-male jury as they gathered to wait questioning from the prosecution and defense attorneys. The waiting men were part of a one-hundred and six man jury panel sequestered to form the twelve-member jury for the trial. In Tallahatchie County and throughout the South, the racist separate and unequal system in the South outlawed Americans of African ancestry to serve on any jury anywhere in Mississippi as well as other Southern States. Only qualified voters could serve on the jury and since the segregated system prohibited blacks the right to vote, there were no registered black voters to serve on jury selection.

There were only two-hundred and eighty seats in the courtroom, yet there were more people trying to get into the courtroom than there were seats available. The crowd waiting for the doors to open was so thick in the lobby outside the courtroom that those leaning against a plate glass window caused the window to shatter from the weight. When the two white deputies of Sheriff Strider finally opened the doors, many in the overflow crowd pushed their way into the courtroom and more had to wait outside when the deputies closed the doors. During the time that the courtroom doors were opened, the room quickly filled to four-hundred as the sheriff and his deputies admitted mostly white men and women into the courtroom. Forty-six relatives of Emmett Till's family manage to push their way into the rear rows reserved for blacks, and they sat on the only available wooden benches in the crowded room.

The press arrangement in the courtroom consisted of three press tables with twenty-two seats reserved for white reporters and off in the far rear corner away from court proceedings was a Jim-Crow card table for the eight black reporters. When H. C. Strider came face-to-face with members of the black press, he greeted them with "Mawnin', niggers!" Then after placing his right hand meaningfully on his gun, he directed them to the segregated press table. Sheriff Strider looked around the steamy hot courtroom and observed that the room was completely crammed; he became concerned about the possibility of violence, because of death threats surrounding the case. Before the judge entered the court proceedings, the sheriff announced to news reporters, spectators and witnesses alike in his strong southern voice that thundered over the room that they had to leave the courtroom. He uttered, "I want y'all to get out of here and you can come back one by one after me and my deputies have searched y'all for weapons, ain't nobody in this courtroom gonna have a gun but me and my deputies." Everyone vacated the courtroom and formed a line outside in the lobby as the sheriff and his deputies stood at the door. The big burly deputies and the overweight sheriff searched each person for weapons, as they walked in single file back into the courtroom. Sheriff Strider informed one of the white reporters that he had received more than one-hundred and fifty threatening letters from anonymous individuals from Chicago, New York, Detroit and other cities in the North and he explained assertively, "Tellin' me I wouldn't live through this trial. They ain't scarin' me."

Meanwhile, across the street from the courthouse as court preliminaries were continuing in the packed courtroom. Roy Bryant and J. W. Milam remained in the law office of Breland and Whitten. The entire bar of Sumner surrounded them, which comprised of their five lawyers who were conversing with them. The five attorneys were J. J. Breland, John W. Whitten, Jr., Sidney Carlton, J.J. Kellum and J.H. Caldwell, Jr. The two defendants were sitting in the custody of their attorneys without guard protection. During the conversation between them, Kellum asks Milam; "Did y'all kill that little niggra boy?" Roy and J.W. first glance suspiciously at each other, and then J.W. squirmed somewhat rather awkwardly in his chair and he cleared his throat to speak. However, before he could utter a word, Kellum stopped him and told him that he should not answer and that he and his partners preferred not to know. Shortly thereafter, there was a knock on the door of the law office and the deputy informed the attorneys that jury selection was in the process of getting under way. The attorneys collected their material and departed the law office with the two defendants accompanied by their wives, young children and three of their brothers who escorted them across the street to the courthouse. The three brothers accompanying them were L.C., B.W., and J.B. The other family members including their mother, father and other brothers and sisters were already in the courtroom waiting their arrival.

Meanwhile across the street inside the courtroom, Judge Curtis Swango entered and the Bailiff announced his entrance by saying, "All rise!" As those in attendants took their seats, the judge called the court to order and then he announced during selection of the mostly white cotton farmers who were all attired in shirtsleeves that spectators had permission to remove their jackets and smoke while court was in session. During the court proceedings, Bryant and Milam walked into the courtroom, amid photographer's flashes, each defendant carrying his young son in his arm and each had an older son by the hand. Bryant's older child was three and Milam's was five. In courtrooms all over the State of Mississippi, it was customary for defendants to bring in small children. In many parts of the judicial court system around the country, it was unprecedented. Judge Swango allowed Roy and J.W. to smoke during court proceedings. As the morning court litigation progressed, the two defendants' exhibited no signs of remorse and they appeared calm and relaxed.

Amid the hot steamy day in and out of the courtroom, Sumner residents seemed to resent the national publicity given their small town since they felt the crime began in neighboring Leflore County. The reason for Sumner being the center point of the trial was due to the recovery of the young child's body taken from the Tallahatchie River one-quarter of a mile inside of Tallahatchie County. The news media flocked to Sumner to cover the sensational murder-trial, which brought out the largest collection of newspaper personnel, TV media cameras and national radio columnist to cover a Mississippi story in recent years, as they had converged on the Southern delta town with a population somewhere around five-hundred and fifty or more. They had come from as far away as New York, Chicago, Atlanta and many other cities including coverage by the foreign press. The media came to report how Mississippi dispensed justice when the victim is black and the suspects are white.

Meanwhile in the crowded steamy hot courtroom, Sheriff Strider threw a perfunctory smile and then he directed the eight Black reporters who were the last to reenter the courtroom to the segregated card table. The black reporters coordinated there sitting arrangements so they could view the court proceedings, even from their awkward segregated seating position. The Black reporters watched with interest, as the prosecution and defense attorneys in the tense courtroom questioned prospective jurors. Many of the black reporters said they overheard the sheriff mention, "We ain't mixed so far down here and we don't intend too." During the trial proceedings the Northern reporters, both blacks and whites watched in astonishment while white farmers in attendance munched on sandwiches which they had brought with them and several others were observed with cans of beer, which they opened and drank without rebuke from the bailiffs or the court. The judge himself uncapped a bottle of cola and sipped from it while attorneys fired questions at potential jurors.

Special Prosecutor Robert Smith, a former FBI agent for four years during the 1940's asked each prospective juror during jury selection if any of them had contributed any money to the defense of the two men accused of murder in the case, and when any had answered in the affirmative, he moved to have them excluded from the jury. Prosecutor Smith continued his line of questions of those who had contributed money to the ten thousand dollar defense fund and he asked, "Has any one of you contributed any money to the defense of the men accused of murder in this case?" H. M. Brower, a farmer raised a timid hand to the question and then he replied, "A gentlemen came to my house and said he was collecting money for this trial. I gave a dollar." He was the third among many to get the judicial ax by the prosecutor. The prosecution excused another man because one of the defense attorneys had represented him in a worker's compensation case.

During the jury selection process, District Attorney Chatham emphasized to the court that he was not asking for the death penalty, as he declared, "The State will not ask for the infliction of the death penalty, since a substantial part of the state's evidence is circumstantial." The defense said it would make the State prove that the body pulled from the river was really that of Emmett Till. The district attorney also enlightened the court that there were four possible verdicts in the case, which he outlined by stating, "If the defendants are found guilty as charged it becomes mandatory on the court to send them to the gas chamber. Number two, if the jury finds them guilty, but disagree as to the punishment; life imprisonment is the legal penalty. Three, the jury can find the pair guilty and specify in its verdict that the penalty shall be life. And last, the jury can acquit the men." Throughout the murder-trial, the guns of Sheriff Strider and his deputies including their soiled spittoon and their blackjacks were symbols of tension, fear and crudeness, which were symptomatic of the explosive courtroom drama looming in the murder trial.

During the long jury selection process, Reporter Hicks soon became restless and he told his colleagues that he had to leave to make an afternoon appointment that awaited him. He told them that he would see them later at the hotel in Mound Bayou. Hicks vacated the courtroom and drove away from the one-story shops surrounding the Courthouse Square in Sumner. He headed his rented car south on Highway 49 toward the town of Glendora. During his travel on the back roads leading to the black section of town in Glendora, his observation revealed the dilapidated Delta countryside where he viewed the crumbling tenant shacks scattered throughout the Delta with disappointment, he passed by large black families crammed into small living conditions. Hicks' journey allowed him to perceive ragged poor black children with dreamless faces as they were seen everywhere around the tenant shack in a State where the income of Black families were the lowest in the nation. Hicks soon drove pass Southern mansions and surrounding plantations, which symbolized to his race the horrendous inhumanity of slavery, reconstruction and Jim-Crow, which Southern whites were determined to maintain through an oppressive unjust system that had too some, become passé, in theory at least, but not reality. Because Hicks like many in his race were fully aware that the reconstruction of the Confederate States were alive and flourishing in every area of their lives. Moreover, as a black man and a reporter affected like others of his race by a brutal lawful Jim-Crow system, he pondered about the only escape from such a barbaric and oppressive system that comprised it, was to challenge it and change the system from within to free America from its racism.

When James Hicks arrived in Glendora, he had no difficulty locating the Reid's Café. He parked his car outside the one-story structure and then entered the rather empty diner. Hicks, at first glance, viewed the place and the few strangers with suspicious eyes and they stared back at him likewise. Hicks walked his medium built frame over to the nearest table to sit, unwind and relax from the methodical tension bubbling up inside him and to escape the steaming heat outside the café as well as the racially charged heat he had escaped from in the courtroom. An attractive dark skin female waitress, who had been watching him since his entrance into the café, walked over to him and with a curious stare, she asked, "Can I help you, Mister?" Hicks smiled politely at the woman and replied; "Can I please have a menu?" The expression on her rather blank face seem to question his request, as his voice carried across the inconsequential establishment attracting the attention of the two males and they stared at the polite stranger whom they reason was obviously not from around the area. He perceived from their reaction that the term menu held no familiarity among these slow talking Southern folks and as he adjusted his chair closer to the table, the tall, large frame man behind the counter indicated, "Mister, we don't have no menu, but I can make most anythin' you want." Hicks gestured with his hand that he understood and then he ordered a cheeseburger and a coke. James Hicks reporter impulse soon kicked in and he carefully engaged himself in a conversation with the stranger behind the counter preparing his meal. He rose from his chair, walked over to the counter and sat on the stool and as the waitress and the other man looked on, he asks, "Is it always this quiet around here?" The man behind the counter replied, "Naw sur, just that trial over yonder in Sumner got folks upset is all." Hicks was pleased that the conversation was evolving just the way he planned and he soon came to know the stranger as the owner, Jimmy Lee. Jimmy Lee and the other two occupants in the diner were delighted to learn that he was a reporter after Hicks informed them that he was covering the murder trial in Sumner.

By the time Hicks had finished his lunch at the diner, he had received information on the arrest of Too-Tight and Henry Lee by Sheriff Strider's deputies and they also told him how he could locate Clara who resided a short distance away. The other man in the diner was the same man in the tavern the night Too-Tight was overheard revealing his involvement in the publicized murder and the stranger volunteered to escort Hicks to the resident of Clara. Hicks and the stranger left the diner and they located Clara at her place of residence as she was in the company of her pastor, Reverend Eddie Ware who had been assisting her with food and other necessities during Henry Lee's absence.

During the conversation, Clara was reluctant at first to speak openly about the incarceration of her common-law husband, Henry Lee and his best friend, Leroy (Too-Tight) Collins, but with the persuasion of Hicks and her minister, she told the reporter where the men were jailed and she further stated to him about the sheriff's promise not to harm the two field hands. Pastor Ware also disclosed to Hicks about the confession he had learned from Henry Lee pertaining to Henry Lee and Too-Tight's involvement in the publicized murder case. The minister was disinclined at first to reveal what he knew about the case because of his promise to Henry Lee, but since Hicks knew intimate details about the involvement of the two men; he felt relieved that it was now out in the open and that the truth has exonerated him from a promise that was agonizing and frustrating to keep hidden. Hicks, the reporter was overwhelmed and very pleased about what he had learned about the case and he soon concluded his conversation at the diner and headed back to the hotel in Mound Bayou.

When he arrived at the hotel later in the afternoon, Hicks filed the new information with his Editor in New York first before sharing the shocking revelation with Doctor Howard who was stunned by the illegal incarceration of the two field hands by Sheriff Strider. Reporter Hicks and Doctor Howard knew that the pertinent information regarding Too-Tight and Henry Lee's incarceration and the potential witnesses on the Clint Sheridan was information the district attorney needed to know. Before informing the district attorney about the important information, they decided to disclose the information at the meeting with members of the black press and members of the NAACP when they returned from the first day of the trial proceedings in Sumner, Mississippi.

A short time later in the courtroom in the town of Sumner, court litigation was ending as District Attorney Gerald Chatham addressed ten of the twelve finalists who would officiate over the case and he instructed them on how they should decide the fate of Roy Bryant and John Williams Milam. He told the ten white men sitting in the jury box, "This case is to be tried fairly on the law and evidence and nothing else. The defendants are presumed to be innocent unless proved otherwise and the state will have to prove beyond reasonable doubt that the defendants are guilty." The ten men selected were Gus Ramsay, James Toole, L.L. Price, J.W. Shaw, Jr., Ray Tribble and Ed Devaney who were all sitting in the front row. Sitting in the second row was Travis Thomas, George Holland, Jim Pennington, and Davis Newton. The ten chosen were all farmers from the nearby area. The district attorney also asked the chosen jurors whether race or anything else would influence them and whether they could disregard any 'street talk' or what they had read in newspapers and give the defendants a fair and impartial trial. After the jurors answered in the affirmative, the swearing in of the all-white male jury occurred at 4:30 p.m. and Judge Swango adjourned the court session until the following morning at 9 a.m.

CHAPTER TWENTY-SIX:

STEAL AWAY IN THE NIGHT

Democrat Congressman Charles Diggs from Detroit, Michigan and his two partners, Basil Brown, an attorney and James Del Rio, a businessperson arrived at the Mound Bayou hotel around 3:30 p.m. on Monday, September nineteenth. They arrived one hour before Judge Swango recessed the murder trial in Sumner until the following morning. After Congressman Diggs and his two aids had settled in their rooms, they received an invitation from Doctor Howard asking them to join him and Reporter Jimmy Hicks for a prepared lunch to enlighten them on the latest development in the murder case of Emmett Till. The congressman and his two aids were also invited to sit in on the meeting between Doctor Howard, Reporter Hicks and the returning black reporters and members of the NAACP returning from the trial, later in the afternoon.

In the meantime, in the town of Sumner, Mississippi, Mamie,

her father; John and her cousin; Rayford Mooty was visiting in the home of her Uncle Crosby and other family members including Moses Wright and six of his eight siblings. Moses reiterated known facts about the abduction and the arrival of the four white men and two young black men who had come to his tenant shack on the morning of August twenty-eighth. He told them that he was looking forward to testifying at the murder trial the following day and that in spite of the death threats he had received from whites around the area; he had no intention of placating the facts of what he knew. Moses told his in-laws how he and his three young sons had to live at their tenant shack on a transitory basis by what he called a "here-by-day, gone-by-night- life." Mamie mentioned to them of her plans to attend the trial the following day. She also informed them about the new witnesses found on the Clint Sheridan plantation where witnesses say her only child was murdered.

A short time later the same evening in the town of Mound Bayou, the eight black reporters, Ruby Hurley and Medger Evers representing the NAACP and Congressman Charles Diggs and his two aids were attending a meeting in the Mound Bayou Hotel. The discussion in the meeting entailed the first day of court proceedings regarding day one of the tense murder-trial. The focus of attention from those sitting around the table in the conference room turn their attention to Doctor Howard as he uttered with assurance, "I think the men who will make up the jury basically think the same as the men who committed the crime. I'm willing to bet that no matter what the jury finds neither man will get over ten years if they get that much." Doctor Howard and Ruby Hurley acquainted the gathering about the five or more witnesses on the Clint Sheridan plantation and Hicks told them about the two incarcerated field hands jailed by Sheriff Strider and his meeting in Glendora earlier in the afternoon with more potential witnesses.

Members of the Black press and the NAACP authorities in the meeting agreed among themselves that the information disclosed was too important to suppress and they were also aware of the legal ramifications involved if the new witnesses were not divulged to the prosecution and defense attorneys. The propensity of the conversation necessitated devising strategic plans to relocate the sharecroppers who had overheard the murder, off the plantation to a place of safety without arousing suspicions.

Medger Evers communicated to them that their plan to secure witnesses had to be thought out very carefully, because any mistakes could place their lives as well as those of the witnesses on the plantation in serious jeopardy. Hicks reiterated his plan to those in the meeting and he asked for willing volunteers to accompany him and Ruby to the plantation by clothing themselves as poor black sharecroppers and secretly moving witnesses to a place of safety. Ruby Hurley had gathered all the clothing and make-up needed to camouflage their true identity. Although, those attending the meeting thought Hicks plan to infiltrate the Clint Sheridan plantation dressed as sharecroppers was a workable idea, the thought of infiltrating a racial combat zone in unfamiliar territory did not generate any volunteers. So the enormous tasks rested on the shoulders of Jimmy Hicks and Ruby Hurley to carry out the mission of getting the witnesses safely off the plantation. At the conclusion of the meeting, Hicks and Ruby set out to make preparations for their assignment.

After Hicks and Ruby had arrived secretly on the Clint Sheridan plantation, they were able to locate and meet privately with Mandy and Alonzo at their tenant shack. During the hasty meeting between the four individuals, Ruby and Hicks informed Mandy and Alonzo that they needed to locate as many willing witnesses as they could find. Once they had located them, they were to have them wait at their tenant shack until Hicks and Ruby retuned later in a station wagon to transport them to a place of safety. When Hicks and Ruby had vacated the plantation in his rented sedan, Willie Reed stopped by Mandy's tenant shack and after she informed him about Hicks and Ruby's plan, they set out to locate their neighbors who were also witnesses to the murder of the young child killed on the plantation.

A short time later, the same evening, in the tenant shack of Mandy and Alonzo Bradley, they were conversing with Willie Reed; his grandfather, Ed and Walter Bullup, who had refused to accompany Mandy and the other witnesses to meet with Doctor Howard for the first time at his residence where they had met Hicks and Ruby. Walter was in the barn milking a cow during the morning hours of Emmett Till's savage beating and murder. The conversation between Mandy and Alonzo with five of the possible six or more witnesses to the murder was not an easy conversation among them. Mandy told her reluctant neighbors about James Hicks and Ruby Hurley's visit to she and her husband's tenant shack and about their plans to have them meet there and to use their place as the rendezvous point for the potential witnesses' flight to safety upon Hicks and Ruby's return during the night.

During the meeting, they conversed with concern about the

mysterious disappearance of 47-year-old, Frank King after he attempted to contact Doctor Howard who was unavailable at the time. A white female overseer escorted Frank to the friendship clinic and after he returned to the plantation, he was threaten by white male sharecroppers on the plantation who told him after learning of his intentions that he had better not testify at the trial. After the encounter resulting from Frank's efforts to contact Doctor Howard, Mandy said Frank mysteriously disappeared during the night and his neighbor sharecroppers never heard from him again. Because of Frank's disappearance, the five sharecroppers were even more afraid for their safety if they mustered enough courage to testify at the murder-trial. Walter decided that he did not want to involve himself anymore in the situation, because of fear of white retaliation and after his visit with them, he left Mandy's tenant shack to stay with relatives outside of the State of Mississippi. The other men with the exception of Mandy, the only female began having serious doubts too after listening to Walter's concerns. Mandy pleaded, "We can't turn back now. Doctor Howard says dey keeps us safe." Before Walter vacated Mandy and Alonzo's tenant shack he replied, "Dey ain't keep, Frank safe!" Ed added, "I'm old man now, I done live my life, I just don't won't nuthin' to happen to my grandson." Willie Reed watched his grandfather and the others adults around him with fear and uncertainty as the imminent threat to their lives lingered in the air around them.

Meanwhile, in the all black town of Mound Bayou, Doctor Howard was in his place of business placing a call to the district attorney and informing him about the new witnesses, naming each of them. District Attorney Chatham reacted with indifferent to the information, which Doctor Howard found rather odd. As an officer of the court, Chatham conveyed to Howard that it was his duty as the district attorney to inform the defense attorneys of new witnesses. Chatham indicated that his purpose for disclosing possible witnesses was to allow the prosecution and defense attorney's time to validate the stories of the five witnesses to avoid any preconceived notions about the validity of the information. Doctor Howard suggested to the district attorney that he needed to pressure the court to move the murder-trial from its present location in Sumner to a new location somewhere in Sunflower County since the discovery of witnesses stated that the actual murder occurred on the Clint Sheridan plantation, located in Sunflower County. Howard felt that it would be impossible to continue the trial in Sumner.

Although, District Attorney Chatham agreed with his assessment of the legal dilemma involving the location of the trial, he informed Howard that he felt that the murder trial should remain in Sumner. He also informed Howard of his plans to announce the discovery of possible witnesses in court the following day sometime during trial proceedings. Howard informed him that by then the witnesses should be in a place of safety. The district attorney informed Howard that he would need to question the witnesses as soon as possible and Howard assured him that the necessary arrangements would be made. They then concluded their conversation over the telephone.

A short time later during the night, Sheriff Smith was alone in his office when he received a call from a mysterious caller informing him about the potential witnesses located on the Clint Sheridan plantation 3.5 miles west of Drew, Mississippi. Although, the voice of the mysterious caller over the telephone sounded somewhat familiar to the sheriff, the caller never identified himself. At the conclusion of the conversation, Sheriff Smith sat in his chair troubled yet excited by the mysterious caller informing him about the significant information and the revelation of new witnesses being found, which if proven valid would be momentous to the state's case. After much consideration, the sheriff and his deputies decided to make a trip out to the plantation to investigate and locate the so called new witnesses, because in spite of the circumstantial evidence in the case, it was Sheriff Smith's belief that the two men were guilty of killing young Emmett Till.

Meanwhile in the town of Mound Bayou, two white male reporters arrived at the office of Doctor Howard and he invited them in for an interview. The two white Southern reporters were Clark Porteous of the Memphis Press Scimitar, located in Memphis, Tennessee and James Featherstone of the Jackson Daily News, located in Jackson, Mississippi having arrived in separate cars. During the interview with Doctor Howard, Clark suggested, "I guess it won't be a long trial, considering the State have no clear-cut evidence to convict the men." The physician-social activist listened quietly to the statement in an upbeat manner and then he replied, "Can I speak with you in the strictest of confidence?" They both replied in the affirmative and Howard convinced of their word of secrecy, stated, "I can produce at least five witnesses at the proper time who will testify that young Till was not murdered in Tallahatchie County, but in Sunflower County." On the faces of the two reporters were an expression of surprise and concern at the new revelation. Reporter James asked inquisitively,

"Do you know where?" Doctor Howard replied with confidence, "On the Clint Sheridan plantation in a headquarters shed about three and a half miles west of Drew, Mississippi. I might add that the plantation is managed by L.C. Milam, the brother of J.W. Milam and half-brother of Roy Bryant." He also informed them about the incarceration of the two field hands, Leroy (Too-Tight) Collins and Henry Lee Loggins by Sheriff Strider, the sheriff of Tallahatchie County. Howard revealed to the two reporters that he had facts that the two field hands that worked for J.W. Milam were housed at the Tallahatchie County Jail in Charleston, Mississippi. The two reporters were speechless as they listened to Howard espouse on the damaging evidence.

The two reporters concluded their conversation with Doctor Howard and they vacated his office. As they walked toward their cars parked on the side of the one-story building, Reporter James asked, "Do you know what this could mean to our way of life down here?" His companion Clark replied in his deep southern inflection, "I sure do, we gotta fight this outside invasion." They open the door to their automobiles and before they entered their cars, Clark asks, "How 'bout me and you trek on over to the Charleston jail to visit the sheriff 'bout this thing?" James agreed with his suggestion and they headed their cars east on Highway 32 toward the County Jail in Charleston, many miles away to converse with Sheriff Strider about the new information from Doctor Howard.

A short time later during the night, Sheriff Smith and his deputies converged on the Clint Sheridan plantation to search for any evidence they could uncover. During the investigation procedures, Black sharecroppers who were mingling about in the cotton fields observed the sheriff and his deputies with fear and full-of-mystery. As the law enforcement officers began searching the shed where the murder occurred for evidence of bloodstains on the floor, which had been covered over by cotton seeds, rumors spread swiftly that the men were really FBI agents who had come to interrogate witnesses. Many of the sharecroppers mingling about in the fields were some of the same people who had heard the savage beating in the shed and three of the black men ran into Sheriff Smith and some of his deputies and when the sheriff attempted to question them about what they might have heard on that ill-fated morning, the men said they knew nothing about the incident and scurried off to their place of residence. Sheriff Smith and his officers tried to question other sharecroppers, but many of them fearing that the men were FBI agents, denied any firsthand knowledge of the murder.

L.C. Milam arrived home on the plantation in his pickup truck shortly thereafter, driving one of two vehicles that he owned, he observed the activities of the sheriff and his men mingling about the plantation and their presence caused him a great deal of concern. As he observed their movements on the plantation from the illumination from their flashlights, he became frightened. The movements of the sheriff and his officers around the shed caused L.C. to contemplate in his mind as he watched the men and his thoughts raced inside his brain, "why have they come here? What are they searching for in the shed; do they know that the murder occurred there, do they have knowledge of his involvement in the murder?" He contemplated getting out of his truck to enter his resident, but fear overtook him that the law enforcement officers might question him as a suspect, although, up until that point he had never been questioned. He decided not to stay at his place of residence and he drove his pickup truck in the direction of his relatives, who lived nearby, where he stayed the night.

A short time later after Sheriff Smith and his deputies had vacated the Clint Sheridan plantation, a dark inexplicable enigma overwhelmed the stillness of the night; troubled eyes of black sharecroppers watched from behind closed doors of their tenant shacks. Sheriff Smith's search of the plantation came almost a month after the murder had occurred, which produced no new evidence that would be advantageous to his investigation in the case. They were unable to locate the possible new witnesses and Sheriff Smith never contacted L.C. Milam. They did manage to question some of the white sharecroppers who resided on the plantation and who said they saw and heard nothing.

Shortly thereafter, James Hicks and Ruby Hurley arrived on the plantation in sharecropper clothing of the locality. Hicks parked his loaned 1951 black station wagon in a sequestered wooden section not far from the tenant shack of Mandy and Alonzo. Ruby and Hicks walked very stealthy and carefully through the dark foreboding, gravel patches leading to the resident to which they had become familiar. Hicks pounded on the door of Alonzo and Mandy's tenant shack. When Alonzo opened the door, he, his wife and the others were somewhat startled by Hicks and Ruby's altered appearance. Inside the tenant shack, Ruby and Hicks were surprised to find only three volunteer witnesses rather than the five whom they were expecting. During the discussion between them, Alonzo once again began wrestling with his fears of testifying, but after observing his wife's unwavering tenacious stand to be a witness; he felt a need to summon his own courage. Mandy's bravery caused Alonzo to reveal more of what he knew about the murder. As Mattie, the wife of Ed and the grandmother of Willie Reed looked on, Ed informed Hicks and Ruby who had come to retrieve them about the arrival of the law enforcement officers, whom they perceived to be from the FBI; Hicks and Ruby expressed their concerns about the surprise visitors to the plantation, which could only mean that their secret had now become knowledge to persons of interest. They told the potential witnesses to gather their belongings quickly because it was imperative that the witnesses are moved immediately to a place of safety in Mound Bayou.

As Mandy, Alonzo, Ed and his wife, Mattie and Willie abandoned their homes on the plantation; they pondered whether their lives would ever be the same again. In the meantime, the two white reporters decided that due to the late hour and the distance to the county jail in Charleston, they decided to inform the sheriff by telephone of the incriminating information given to them by Doctor Howard. Sheriff Strider and his deputies moved quickly to hide the evidence of the two field hand's incarceration at the jail and they arranged to hide Too-Tight and Henry Lee as well.

CHAPTER TWENTY-SEVEN:

MURDER-TRIAL: DAY TWO

In the minds of Southern blacks, the recent unsolved murders of Reverend George W. Lee and Lamar Smith in Mississippi as well as the overall dehumanizing barbarity of slavery and Jim Crow, which ensnared indelible imagines derived and etched by decades even centuries of some of the most hideous and inhuman acts of violence against America's native citizens, those citizens being Americans of African ancestry. The brutal murder of fourteen-year-old, Emmett Louis Till just set in motion the whirlwind efforts for social change long overdue for Americans of African ancestry as well as other oppressed non-whites living in America during the 1950's. The persistence for social oppression was tantamount to the tenacious drive for social equality. One case in point began the following day after the start of the explosive murder-trial in Sumner, Mississippi. On plantations managed by white ultra-conservative overseers, black male and female sharecroppers perpetrated the unthinkable. As the trial proceedings were about to get underway in nearby Sumner, black sharecroppers in large numbers walked off plantations around the site of the trial, leaving their chores undone. In spite of opposing strategic barriers along the route even at the point of violence, sharecroppers forged ahead without fear. The decision of the black sharecroppers to boycott their chores on the plantations throughout the area stemmed from a unanimous feeling of anger and frustration over the brutal murder of young Emmett Till, which had become a highly publicized case. In many instances the white overseers stood with their shotguns drawn on the courageous sharecropper, yet, their threats did not avert the sharecropper's tenacity to vacate the plantations. The open defiance and insubordination of the black field hands caught their white overseers by surprise and they watched stunned as they walked down the dusty gravel road in large numbers heading for the murder trial. As the white managers watched their recalcitrance sharecroppers, they began to realize the emergence of their greatest fears of the darker race coming together to challenge centuries of inhumane racial oppression. Moreover, for the first time they feared that their control of political and social domination was on the verge of collapse.

Meanwhile in the town of Sumner, court proceedings were already underway with the continuation of jury selection. With the selection of ten white male jurors chosen on the previous court session and two more with one alternate scheduled at today's session. Again, a throng of white cotton farmers and sharecroppers were pushing their way into the second floor courtroom, not built to accommodate the crowd pressing their way into it. Outside the courthouse in the Town Square, there were more people in the town of Sumner than its entire population. Throughout the town, black sharecroppers who had earlier walked off plantations were now arriving among the crowd of country white folks convening in the town of Sumner as the black sharecroppers began approaching the hot Southern town from all directions. Many whites observed the unexpected invasion with fear and suspicion.

Members of the black press arrived with Congressman Charles Diggs and his party of two and authorities from the NAACP. Ruby chose not to attend the trial and she stayed behind in Mound Bayou to coach the witnesses before their scheduled meeting with prosecution and defense attorneys later in the afternoon. Congressman Diggs and the NAACP's decision and purpose were to attend the murder-trial as observers. Amid the crowd the congressman, his aids and members of the NAACP waited their turn to enter the two-story courthouse building.

Shortly thereafter, Mamie arrived at the courthouse accompanied by her father; John, her uncle; Crosby and her cousin; Rayford and they viewed the large black crowd gathered around the courthouse with a profound and curious observation. Because of the large crowd, both blacks and whites, they were unable to get near the courthouse, therefore, they had to park a block away and walk to the building and the potential walk caused Mamie some concern. When the black sharecroppers recognized that Mamie was the mother of the little boy brutally murdered, they formed a human shield on either side of the street all the way to the courthouse entrance to protect Mamie and her family from any possible harm. Resentful Southern whites and the press watched with interest, as Mamie and her family walked through the middle of the crowd to the courthouse. When Mamie and her family approached the courthouse, a white reporter asks Mamie, "Are you willing to identify the picture of a body taken from the Tallahatchie River as that of your son?" Mamie replied to his question with quiet dignity, "I will tell the truth. It was Emmett's body."

Meanwhile outside the double doors of the courtroom on the second floor, the crowd of people was forming two lines, as Sheriff Strider and his deputies allowed white reporters, white farmers and white sharecroppers to enter first. When the sheriff came face to face with the black press, he greeted them with the same embittered smile and said, "Mawnin' Niggers!" After members of the black press filed passed the sheriff, he personally escorted them to the segregated press table after instructing his deputies at the door not to allow any other blacks to enter, except for the mother of Emmett Till whom they were expecting. When Congressman Diggs and his two aids attempted to enter the crowded courtroom, two burly deputies guarding the door impeded their futile attempt. One of the white deputies addressed the congressional representative in a voice charged with hostility and the deputy intoned, "You just hold on their, boy, ain't no more room!" Congressman Diggs was deeply mortified and shocked by the treatment on a United States Congressman by the southern deputy. Congressman Diggs would later tell the press that being a northerner; he had never been exposed to such raw open racism, which confronted him with such brutal reality in the South, he went on to say that he was more familiar with racism of a more subtle temperament, which people of color often encountered in most northern states. Reporter Hicks observed the confrontation and attempted to intervene on the congressman's behave and he explained to the deputy that he was addressing a United States Congressman from Michigan and the two deputies at the door found the statement hilarious.

The two stocky built deputies began to converse about the predicament with each other and ignored Hicks and the Congressman as if the two black men were invisible to them. The deputy informed his partner and other deputies standing nearby and he explained, "This nigger here (pointing to Hicks) says that this nigger (pointing to Congressman Diggs) is a United States Congressman." The other deputies who were observing the encounter gasp in unbelief at the statement and they made racial sarcastic comments among themselves. The deputy's partner stared with an expression of astonishment on his face and he asked, "A nigger congressman?" The deputy who had received the sheriff's instructions replied, "That's what this here nigger, say!"

Reporter Hicks knew painfully well that to try reasoning with the deputy at that point was useless, therefore, he retrieved Congressman Diggs card and entered the courtroom to converse with the judge about the dilemma. While the congressional representative and his aids waited outside the courtroom, their attention were temporally diverted to the activities of reporters surrounding Mamie and her three family member's arrival on the second floor outside of the courtroom chamber as reporters clamored to get interviews by shoving microphones in her face.

Meanwhile, Hicks informed Judge Swango whom many considered as being an impartial judge, about the dilemma preventing Congressman Diggs entrance into the courtroom by the deputies guarding the double doors. The judge carefully looked over Diggs credentials and content with the information on the congressional representatives' identification card, the judge asked, "Sheriff Strider, I hear you got a niggra congressman out there? Have that boy come in and sit over there with those niggra reporters." The sheriff's disrespect and embittered mannerism was evident as he escorted Congressman Diggs and Hicks to the segregated black press table. The two aids of Congressman Diggs and authorities of the NAACP received permission to sit in the sequestered back rows reserved for Americans of African ancestry.

Shortly thereafter amid rapid flashes from photographer's hand held cameras, Mamie pushed her way through the crowded courtroom, accompanied by her father, uncle and cousin. One of the deputies pointed her in the direction of the black press table and she sat among the press and the congressional representative. Mamie was wearing a dark gray suit with a white collar and a black bow and in her hand; she was carrying a black silk fan to diminish the impulsive heat. Upon her entrance into the courtroom, the attention of the white spectators watched her every movement with silent blank faces void of remorse. Sheriff Strider then pushed his way through the crowd, walked over to Mamie sitting at the table and represented her with a subpoena and he uttered, "You are now in the State of Mississippi...you will come under all laws governing this State." Mamie graciously accepted the legal document and Strider demonstrated no commiseration or concern toward her and as quickly as he appeared, he soon disappeared through the crowd again.

Congressman Diggs whispered to Mamie, "He's quite a

character, isn't he?" Mamie's smile as well as the other reporters' sitting around the table confirmed their agreement with his comment as well. The congressional representative and the reporters offered their condolences to Mamie regarding the death of her only child. Mamie thanked them for their continued news coverage and she personally thanked the Congressman for coming from the State of Michigan to join her in what she called her darkest hour.

Black sharecroppers sitting on the rear-segregated benches who were friends of Crosby relinquished their seats to him and his visiting in-laws who had accompanied his niece from Chicago. John and Rayford kept a watchful eye on Mamie from their observation as they sat in the isolated rear seats. Amid the crowded court proceedings, Mamie informed the reporters that of the two-thousand letters she had received concerning the murder of her son in Mississippi only a few were nasty and threatening.

During the morning court session, the prosecutors and defense attorneys began their questioning of the remaining prospective jurors. Their line of questioning was the same as on the prior court proceedings. The hostile white potential jurors responded when asked, if any had contributed to the defendant's defense fund and if race would have an influence on and prevent them from judging the case fairly. The judge immediately excused those who answered in the affirmative to the questions. Inside the packed courtroom, the two defendants, Roy Bryant and J.W. Milam were sitting with their wives and holding their children in their laps as they watched the court proceedings with unconcerned interest. The children became restless during the hot crowded court session and they began to wander about in the courtroom, climbing on and off chairs. The little boys frolic playful activities occasionally drowned out the words of the lawyers during the questioning of white jurors. Many times their parents had to leave their seats to retrieve one or two of the young lads.

During the questioning of the prospective jurors, the behavior of District Attorney Chatham and Special Prosecutor Smith was more elated than on the previous day, because of their anticipated meeting with the new witnesses, which they had not disclosed to the court or defense attorneys during the morning court session. At the conclusion of the jury interrogation, both the prosecution and defense attorneys agreed on Howard Armstrong, an insurance man Bishop Matthews, a carpenter and the selection of one alternate juror. The jury consisted of one bachelor and the rest were married and fathers. The crowd of people was so thick in the courtroom that they were cutting off air from around the windows, as they prevented any breeze from being forced in by the morning air.

Meanwhile, in the witness chamber, Moses waited to testify with his youngest son, Simeon along with Sheriff Smith and Deputy Cothran. They were waiting to testify for the prosecution. Simeon was neatly dressed and he leaned to his father for comfort against the unfamiliar surroundings, which in his eyes seem charged with uncertainty. They were four of thirteen witnesses scheduled to testify in the racially charged murder trial for the State. Sheriff Smith and Deputy Cothran sat across from each other and conversed among themselves.

The defense listed nine possible witnesses with Carolyn

Bryant as the main witness for the defense. Circuit Court Judge, Curtis M. Swango, Jr., adjourned the morning session after the completion of jury selection and after all available witnesses had been sworn in for the prosecution and defense, the judge called for a one-hour recess before the start of the afternoon session.

As the crowd of people vacated the courtroom, the twelve selective jurors strolled back to the Delta Inn, their temporary home during the trial. The Delta Inn was a short distance from the courthouse within the Town Square. Upon the juror's arrival at the Delta Inn, they settled down in the lobby to watch a television set borrowed for them by Sheriff H.C. Strider. Several white men serving on the jury who resided on back wood farms and who never had access to a television set watched the moving visual images on the screen with fascination.

CHAPTER TWENTY-EIGHT:

THE MEETING PLACE

Meanwhile several miles away from the site of the murder trial, Ruby Hurley was gathering the four witnesses together for their journey to the delta town of Sumner to meet first with the prosecuting attorneys and then with the defense attorneys. They vacated the safety of the Mound Bayou Hotel and entered the rented black station wagon, the same station wagon which had transported them away clandestinely from the Clint Sheridan plantation on the previous night. Mandy positioned herself on the front seat next to Ruby and Alonzo, Willie and Ed sat on the back seat. Willie Reed and his grandfather, Ed smiled uneasily at each other as they attempted to hide their fears. Alonzo focused his attention on his wife sitting on the front seat of the vehicle as he struggled with his own fears and uncertainty regarding the ordeal of testifying against white men charged with killing a black youth. Ruby drove the vehicle away from the hotel and headed east then northeast toward the town of Sumner, which was thirty miles away.

An hour later, the same afternoon in the courthouse Town-Square in Sumner, the crowded courtroom proceedings were just getting under way. Again, the courtroom was packed as people were standing and sitting. Young white peddlers were walking the length of the courtroom selling cold beverages including cans of beer to thirsty white spectators and they flatly refused to sell to those sitting at the black press table. Members of the black press elected a pool reporter to retrieve cold drinks from the general store blocks away from the courthouse. The judge even allowed the two defendants to use the restroom in his chambers, yet he would not allow blacks the same privilege no matter what position they held, they had to use a lavatory, which was also a block away from the courthouse, clearly identified by the colored only signs.

Judge Swango observing the overcrowded condition in his courtroom caused him much concerned as he called the afternoon session to order. The white spectators turned their attention to the two defendants, J.W. Milam and his half-brother, Roy Bryant and their wife's and children with feelings of remorse, as they waited in quiet anticipation at the opening of state evidence against the two defendants. In spite of the sympathy shown toward the two men on trial, J.W. and Roy sat erect in stern assurance that every Angle-Saxon person in the courtroom viewed them as proud defenders of Southern white womanhood. After the judge banged the gavel for order a wave of quiet mutter fell over the room, then he asked, "Is the state ready to present its case?"

District Attorney Chatham rose from his relaxed posture, he

threw a confident smile toward the two defendants and their five attorneys, and then he replied, "We are your honor, but may I address the court?" Judge Swango replied, "You may!"

Attorney Chatham uttered eagerly, "Your honor, the state has uncovered five new witnesses to the murder of Emmett Till." The announcement caused an excited eruption of murmurs among the white spectators. The confident demeanors of the two defendants dissipated into a mounting agony of fear and anxiety. Concerned misgivings fulminated across the facial expression of the attorneys and their reactions, which was conducive to their anxiety regarding the direction of the case. Amid the euphonious whispers, the wife's of the two defendants and their families watched the adversity unfold in dreaded anguish. The district attorney tried to continue his address, but the mumbling noise prevented his articulation. The judge briskly banged his gavel several times and called for order before the excitement in the courtroom seethed into a state of quiescence. As the murmurs quieted down around him, the district attorney continued his utterance by stating, "Your honor, the prosecution is requesting a recess to allow more time for us to question the new witnesses."

Distressed by the request of the state's recess, the defense attorneys voiced their objection. Attorney Breland was the first to voice his opposition and he accused the prosecution of not disclosing knowledge concerning the discovery of new witnesses. Assistant Special Prosecutor, Robert Smith challenge his opposition by stating that the prosecution had only found out about the witnesses on the previous night and that they had every intention of sharing the information with the defense. Attorney John

Whitten complained, "Your honor, we object to this recess. The prosecution is using this recess to prolong the trial longer than necessary."

Judge Swango moved to relinquish the debate before the situation spiraled out of control. Because of the disclosure of new witnesses, both the defense and the prosecution passed up their opening statements. The judge informed the defense attorneys that he felt that the request for a recess by the prosecution was reasonable. However, Judge Swango admitted that his main concern was over crowded conditions in the courtroom as the real reason for granting the recess. He asserted emphatically, "There are too many people gathered in here. If a fire develops any place in this courtroom, great tragedy will take place." The judge also ordered the court officials to limit Wednesday's spectators to only those who were able to find seats. The judge further stated to photographers that he would not allow them to take anymore pictures during trial proceedings and he warned that he would reprimand violators openly.

District Attorney Chatham informed the judge that he was asking him to issue five subpoenas for the five prospective witnesses that he and his assistant was scheduled to meet during the afternoon. After the district attorney presented the names to the defense, he made known to the court the names of the individuals scheduled to testify in the murder trial. At the conclusion of the prosecution's request, the judge adjourned the court until the following day at 10 A.M. Shortly after the judge had ordered the courtroom cleared, Ruby Hurley, members of the NAACP and James Hicks escorted the four potential witnesses into the empty courtroom to converse with District Attorney Chatham and Special Assistant Prosecutor, Robert Smith. District Attorney Chatham inquired about the whereabouts of the fifth witness and Ruby briefed him that Walter Bullup refused to testify and vacated the plantation because of fear of white retaliation.

Meanwhile across the street in the law office of Breland and Whitten, the five attorneys were conversing with the two defendants, their wife's and other defense witnesses about the development. Carolyn was the star witness for the defense and she was told that if the defense strategy fell apart by the testimony of the new witnesses to the murder; she must be prepared to testify that the youth attempted to assault her while she was alone with him in the store. Attorney Carlton explained to Carolyn that he was using "assault" in the legal sense, which implied any untoward incident such as indecent advances, but that it did not imply actual physical attack or rape. Carolyn informed the attorneys that she was willing to say or do whatever was necessary to exonerate her husband and brother-in-law. The attorneys began to rehearse her with the details of her story in an attempt to counterattack the prosecution case. In spite of the defense concerns about the testimonies of the potential new witnesses, they continued to express doubt that the prosecution would be able to prove a murder case against the two defendants.

Meanwhile in the courtroom across the street from the law office, the four witnesses were each giving their statement of events to the prosecuting attorneys. Each of the prospective witnesses communicated to the two attorneys about what they observed and heard during the early morning brutal murder of young Emmett Till on the Clint Sheridan plantation. Each of the witnesses also enlightened the two prosecuting attorneys that they heard no gunshot. Willie Reed also told Chatham and Smith that he was able to identify the two missing field hands that many of the witnesses knew, as the two who had accompanied the victim into the ill-fated shed. However, both attorneys were pleased with how the witnesses conducted themselves during their intense questioning; they warned them that the tactics from the defense would not be as easy. The two attorneys conversed with Ruby and Hicks about the incarceration of the two field hands by Sheriff Strider. The states' attorneys informed Ruby and Hicks about their plans to issue a search warrant requesting Sheriff Strider of the county jail to allow authorities to search the premises, where they believed the sheriff held Too-Tight and Henry Lee against their will.

A short time later, the same afternoon in the Delta Inn Hotel, Sheriff Strider and a few of his deputies, three Southern white reporters and the twelve jurors were playing cards and watching television. The conversations evolved around the interest of their anticipation of watching the outcome of the Marciano-Moore fight scheduled for the following night. The three reporters were Clark Porteous, James Featherstone and Arthur Everett, all representing Southern newspapers.

During the conversation between the sheriff and the three reporters, Clark asked, "Sheriff Strider, you take care of that problem we told you about last night?" Strider looked up at him with a confident smile and he assured him that the dilemma ceased to be a problem anymore, because he and his deputies did what was necessary. Clark placed an assured slight squeeze to Strider's shoulder, "we wanna see you come through this thing, ya' hear!"

Sheriff Strider understood the full meaning of the reporter's statement and he took full advantage of the opportunity, which had presented itself and Strider, a true ultra-conservative southerner at heart, used the media to further his defense of the State of Mississippi, which prompted his decision to make a statement to the press. While he continued his aggressive card playing, Strider stated to the white press, "I want you reporters to take this down. I like for the NAACP or any colored organization, anywhere, to know that we are here giving all parties a free trial. And intend to give a fair and impartial trial. And we don't need the help of the NAACP and we don't intend for them to help us. We never seem to have any trouble until some of our Southern niggers go up North and the NAACP talks to them and they come back home." The twelve jurors who were listening to the exchange between the sheriff and the reporters found the sheriff's statement meaningful and embolden in southern pride.

Meanwhile in the law offices of Breland and Whitten, the five attorneys were waiting the arrival of the four witnesses. The defense attorney's allowed J.W. and two of his brothers to sit in on the meeting. Outside the office of Breland and Whitten, Ruby, Hicks and two members of the NAACP were encouraging the four witnesses who were about to meet with the defense attorneys, not to be intimated by any questions asked by the attorneys. The lawyers from the defense team were aware of the new witnesses and members of the NAACP's arrival outside their legal establishment, as Ruby and Hicks had spoken with John Whitten upon their arrival. Whitten had also informed Ruby that she, the NAACP or the black press would not be allowed to sit in on the interview while they were questioning the new witnesses. Neither Ruby nor Hicks were comfortable with the decision made by the defendant's attorneys, but they knew they could do little to overturn their predetermination.

C. Sidney Carlton entered the small outer office area and he inquired if the witnesses were ready to meet with them. Mandy, Alonzo, Ed and Willie turned their attention to Ruby for her acknowledgement and she gave her consent. First Mandy and Alonzo followed Attorney Carlton into the law office and then Ed and Willie followed behind them. Inside the office, J.W. had his legs propped on one of the lawyer's desk and smoking a big cigar. He watched and recognized the witnesses who were surprised by his presence as they entered the office.

When J.W. came face to face with Willie Reed, the encounter caused his facial expression to contort with surprise and concern. His thoughts reflected back to the morning of the murder when he confronted Willie after leaving the shed where the brutal beating occurred. His two brothers, J.B. and B.W. also stared at the familiar faces with threatening glances.

The interrogation process from the defense attorneys first began with Mandy, as they surrounded her sitting in a chair near J.W. Mandy watched the unfamiliar faces of the five attorneys and J.W. staring at her with apprehension and mean-spirited perception. She was first overtaken with fear, but the thought of the young child's brutal murder ignited courage to face the task at hand. When asked by Attorney Kellum, she again reiterated what she saw and heard during the morning of the beating and murder. Attorney Whitten asked her about the pickup truck and she mention to him that she had seen the truck many times before on the plantation before that fateful morning. She also asserted that she knew the truck belonged to J.W., the brother of L.C. Attorney Breland asked her if she ever came face to face with either J.W. or Roy on the morning in question and she replied that she had not. Mandy was asked by Attorney Carlton if she ever saw them carry the little Niggra boy into the shed and again her answer was no.

Alonzo was next to sit in the interrogation seat, as the attorney's questioned him with the same line of questions that they had presented to his wife, Mandy. During the questions from each of the five lawyers, his eyes moved from J.W. throwing threatening glances at him, to the two brothers of J.W. who were watching him with hate filled eyes. He then searched the room and found his wife and he looked to her for support, as he struggled within himself to relate what he saw and heard. Attorney Caldwell and Attorney Carlton questioned him and they attempted to trap him, as he elucidated to inform each of the attorney's that he saw the pickup truck, which he knew belonged to J.W. leave the shed where he had heard a savage beating-taking place on the morning of the murder.

When the attorneys questioned Ed, they found that his answers were like those which they had heard from Mandy and Alonzo. Ed informed each of the five lawyers that he had heard the savage beating in the shed and then he later saw the pickup truck leaving the plantation with three men in the truck and that the rear cargo area of the pickup truck was covered. The defense lawyers concluded their inquisitive probe of the three potential witnesses. Content with the accounts of the three individuals, they asked them to leave the inner office. When the four started to leave, Whitten asked Willie Reed to remain. Ed inquired about his grandson and he was told that they wanted to question him privately. As Mandy, Alonzo and Ed vacated the office, Attorney Carlton closed the door behind them.

Ruby and Hicks queried them about why Willie had to remain behind with the attorneys. Ed filled with anxiety told them that he was told that his grandson had to be questioned privately. They all pondered what the defense lawyer's true intentions were and many felt their intentions were esoteric and not advantageous to the state's case.

Meanwhile, Willie Reed watched the rigorous faces around him and fear at times became insurmountable like a lightning charge filling him with consternation and a bundle of nerves. Attorney C. Sidney Carlton walked over to the door leading to an external office and opened the door. A white man with a receding hairline and the same built as J.W. entered the room and sat in the chair next to J.W. Willie observed the situation with curious suspicion as each of the five lawyers began to question him. First Attorney John Whitten asked, "Now, boy! Tell me exactly what you saw that morning?"

Willie began to squirm nervously in the wooden uncomfortable chair to relieve the tension he felt and he replied, "I saw Mister Milam truck comes toward me on the road. I stopped to let it pass and it went straight into the shed." Attorney Breland asked again, whom he had saw on the truck and Willie replied, "I saw Mister Milam and his brother, Roy in the truck with another man. Then I saw Too-Tight and Henry Lee and that boy, Emmett Till." Attorney J.J. Breland walked behind the unidentified man sitting next to J.W. and he asked, "is this the man, J.W. who you saw that mawnin'?" Willie stared nervously at J.W. who was sitting in the second chair and he replied, "That's Mister Milam, right there!"

J.W., his brothers and the unidentified man watched with humorous intrigue as each of the five lawyers used every possible modus operandi to manipulate Willie's testimony, but Willie remained adamant about his knowledge of the events surrounding the murder and his identification of J.W. Milam. Shortly after the concluding interrogation of Willie Reed, he left the law office and joined the others waiting for him in the small lobby, shortly thereafter; Ruby drove them back to the hotel in Mound Bayou, Mississippi.

Later during the night, for the first time in the history of Mississippi, Sheriff Smith, and his two deputies teamed up with the two states attorney's, NAACP officials and the entire black press in a move to locate the two missing field hands. After searching several plantations with ties to the two missing field hands, on the second day of the murder trial, they made a surprise visit to the county jail in Charleston, Mississippi. The bad blood between Sheriff Smith and Sheriff Strider was no secret since the publicized brutal murder of young Emmett Louis Till from Chicago. Neither of them was pleased with the way the other had handled the case thus far. Sheriff Smith presented the sheriff of the county jail with a search warrant, but Strider informed him that the search warrant would not be necessary, as he invited them in to search the premises without interference from him or his deputy staff.

Sheriff Strider's willingness to allow the search convinced District Attorney Chatham that the search for the two missing field hands would prove nothing; therefore, he decided that perhaps the sheriff was innocent of the charges stated against him of possibly preventing the testimony of the two important witnesses. Sheriff Smith asked to see a register of names of prisoners listed at the jail and upon close examination, he was unable to locate the names of Leroy (Too-Tight) Collins or Henry Lee Loggins. Due to the late hour of the night, the two prosecuting attorneys agreed that it would be useless to search the entire jail for the two missing men as members of the black press and officials of the NAACP looked on disappointingly at the exchange between the sheriff and the states' attorneys. It was clear the search of the jail would not continue based on the word of Sheriff Strider. Suggestions made by the black reporters that other plantations and jails around the general area needed to be search during the remainder of the night, and the black reporters knew that it would be impossible to accomplish and much too dangerous without the aid of the sheriff and his deputies. Sheriff Smith was unhappy and frustrated with the decisions made by the prosecuting attorneys not to search the county jail and he soon felt that the region was much too large to cover with the limited man power available to him; therefore, he called off the search about midnight after leaving the Tallahatchie county jail in Charleston, Mississippi.

Sheriff Strider had been expecting a visit from Sheriff Smith and his party; therefore, he had made provisions to hide the two missing field hands away from the search party. In addition, he covered any traces of evidence that would conceivably incriminate his deputies and or himself.

CHAPTER TWENTY-NINE:

MURDER-TRIAL: DAY THREE

The following morning, Wednesday, September twenty-first in the steaming hot Mississippi delta town of Sumner, Mississippi, the third day of the captivatingly publicized murder trial was already in progress. Inside the second floor courtroom, the twelve jurors all in shirtsleeves and smoking occasional cigarettes and cigars, listened attentively to the state's opening testimony in the crowded courtroom session. The packed courtroom continued as on the two previous days, but Wednesday's session had fewer people standing in the aisles, because of the judge's order. In spite of efforts on the previous night to locate the two missing field hands by members of the black press, the state's attorney and law enforcement officers, the morning court session continued as scheduled. Sheriff H.C. Strider and his deputies were again in court and he was elated after succeeding in keeping Too-Tight and Henry Lee hidden from the search party.

Amid the large assembly of white spectators, the white news media and the black press sat eagerly awaiting the testimony of scheduled quarantined witnesses in another room. The judge banged his gavel for order and then he asked, "Is the state ready to call your first witness?" District Attorney Gerald Chatham rose from his seat and replied; "We are your honor. The state call, Mose Wright."

As the courtroom ignited into serious whispers from interested and concerned spectators, Moses walked into the courtroom from the rear entrance and he pushed his way firmly through the crowded courtroom and sat down in the witness chair. Moses was attired in black dress denims, white shirtsleeve with black tie and yellow suspenders, and he watched from the witness chair at the hate-filled stares directed at him from the white spectators in the courtroom. After informing the burnished dressed sharecropper that he was still under oath, the district attorney asked Moses to describe the events of August twenty-eighth. Moses positioned himself comfortably in the chair and then he explained, "Early Sunday, 'bout 2 o'clock in the mawnin'…somebody was at the door. He say, "Preacher, Preacher, this is Mister Bryant. I wanna talk to that boy who done the talkin' at Money." His eyes shifted away from the district attorney who was asking the questions and for the first time he came face to face with the two defendants, Roy Bryant and J.W. Milam in court together. Moses eyes were transfixed on them, as he stared with confidence at the two men without dropping his eyes. Roy, J.W. and the white spectators watched him aggressively with eyes of hatred and he continued his stare at them without intimidation.

District Attorney Chatham directed his attention to the questions again and Moses continued, "I got up and opened the door." The district attorney asked him to explicate what he saw when he had opened the door to his resident. Moses replied, "Mister Milam was standin' at the door with a pistol in his right hand and a flashlight in the other." The district attorney interrupted him, "Uncle Mose, do you see Mister Milam here in the courtroom?" Moses then rose from the witness chair to his medium built frame of five feet, six inches and pointed his long gnarled finger and replied, "Dar he!" Attorney Chatham walked over to the two defendants sitting with the five attorneys, and he pointed directly at J.W. and he asked, "Are you referring to this man as Mister Milam?" Moses who was still standing answered in the affirmative.

During Moses testimony and identification of the two defendants, Roy an ex-paratrooper during the Korean War sat quietly and showed no visible signs of emotion. However, J.W. sucked on his cigar and shifted nervously in his seat. Moses identification of the two men caused awestricked silence in the courtroom, except for the gyrating fans held by many of the white female spectators and several black female sharecroppers sitting in the rear of the courtroom as they watched Moses on the witness stand.

Attorney Chatham continued, "Uncle Mose, did Mister Milam say anything to you that morning? Moses replied, "He ask, if I had three boys out of Chicago, here? And I told him I had."

District Attorney Chatham asked, "What did he say?" Moses replied with assurance, "He say, "We wanna talk to that boy who done the talkin'." Moses then reiterated how when the three men had stalked uninvited through his house that Milam told him upon seizing Emmett from his bed that, "If he ain't the right boy, we'll bring him back in put him in bed again." The district attorney then asked, "How did you know which boy they wanted?" Moses reply was, "A neighbor told me Emmett had done some talkin' at the store in Money." The district attorney continued, "Was anything else said?" Moses paused a moment to the question and then he replied, "Mister Milam axed me how old I be and I say sixty-four. Then he say, "If you give anybody our names, you won't live to be sixty-five."

Attorney Chatham continued his line of questions and he asked if Moses wife, Elizabeth said anything during the commotion? Moses reply to his question was, "She offered 'em money. She said, "We'll pay you whatever you want to charge if you just release him." Chatham asked Moses what the two men responses were and he replied, "Dey ain't say nuthin', dey just left with Emmett." Moses then testified how he and his wife watched as the men took Emmett to the car parked on the gravel road about fifty feet from the screened porch. He said he heard one of the men ask, apparently to someone in the car, "Is this the boy?" Then Moses said he heard a lighter voice from the car reply, "Yes, he's the one!"

District Attorney Chatham asked, "Was that a man's voice or a woman's?" Moses replied with certainty, "It seemed a little lighter than a man's voice." He continued by telling the district attorney that he and his wife stood watching the pickup truck with his nephew in the back with two unidentified young black men and the car drive away toward Money with no headlights from the two vehicles. Grief filled Moses voice as he sadly replied, "I never saw Emmett alive again. An unconventional quietness filled the courtroom, as Mamie, Congressman Diggs and the black reporters observed the proceedings from their segregated location in the courtroom.

Bryant and Milam continued to watch Moses intently as they listened to his testimony. For the first time the two defendants were without their wives and children in court. The two small sons of each of the men were absent from court during the third day of trial proceedings. The wives of J.W. and Roy was in another room quarantined, as were all scheduled witnesses, as each waited their call to the stand.

The district attorney then suggested, "Uncle Mose, I want you to tell us about that afternoon when you saw the body removed from the river." Moses struggled to control his inner torment as he reminiscence on the attorneys' question. Moses reacted to the terrible images in his mind of that afternoon as if he was reliving it all over again; he saw the bludgeoned body of his nephew as anglers removed it from the muddy waters of the Tallahatchie River. As he wrestled to fight back tears, he told of how he and his brother-in-law, Crosby Smith were watching when the boat arrived on shore with the body, which was badly beaten. Chatham then asked him, "Whose body was it?" Moses replied firmly, "It was Emmett Louis Till." He continued to speak with assurance, as he informed the attorney of how they had watched authorities remove from the body a ring like the one Emmett wore-an initialed signet ring originally worn by Emmett's father who died in World War II. The district attorney then concluded his questions by stating, "I have no further questions for the witness at this time."

Judge Swango then turned his attention to the defense and he asked, "Does the defense have any questions for this witness?" One of the defense attorneys, C. Sidney Carlton stared at Moses sitting on the witness stand; he leaned back in his chair with a confident smile, and replied, "We do your honor." Attorney Carlton rose from his chair, walked in front of the defense table, and asked, "Now, Mose. You claim you can positively identify these two men as the ones who came to your place that mawnin?" Moses sat contemplating the meaning of his question, finally he answered, "Yessuh!" Attorney Carlton, who was determined to cut down Moses' identification of Milam and Bryant in his cross-examination, asked, "Was there ever any lights turned on in that house?"

Moses watched the movement of the Attorney carefully with concern, as Attorney Carlton watched him with a sarcastic smile as he waited for Moses to answer his question, with hesitancy Moses cleared his throat and then he replied, "No, suh."

Attorney Carlton fired with another question, "Didn't you tell me and the other attorneys last week that the only reason you thought it was Mister Milam was because the man at the door was big and baldheaded?" Moses sat quietly, as he attempted to remember the conversation to the question. The attorney asked again, "All you saw was a baldheaded man?" Some of Moses answer in response to the defense lawyer's rapid-fire questions seemed to be more confused rather than evasive or contradictory.

Nevertheless, in his state of obvious confusion he paused then answered, "That's right." During the cross-examination by the defense, Moses admitted that he did not know Roy Bryant very well and that he had never met J.W. Milam before until that morning of his nephew's abduction.

At one point during the intense cross-examination of Moses, the district attorney who objected to the line of questions by the defense voiced his opposition and demanded, "Why don't you quite badgering the old man, can't you see he is trying to do his best to answer the questions?" Judge Swango saw nothing wrong with the defense line of questions and he allowed him to continue.

Defense Attorney Carlton continued with his aggressive interrogation and he turned to the jury and uttered, "Now Mose, you want this court and this jury to believe that you could identify two men in the dark whom you did not know, is that right?" Moses sat in silence pondering his question and reflecting back on Milam holding the flashlight and observing the illumination from the flashlight filling areas of the room. When the attorney turned to face him again, he replied, "Yessuh!" Attorney Carlton asked, "The first time you ever saw Mister Milam was here in court wasn't it?" Moses replied with assurance to his question, "No suree, I saw him that night."

"Didn't you tell us there was a third man, a Negro, at your place," ask defense attorney, J.J. Breland?

Moses replied, "Yessuh, 'cause he was tryin' to hide his face. He acted like a colored man."

Defense Attorney J.J. Breland attempted to exploit the fact that the aging sharecropper, Moses' identification of Roy Bryant was less positive than that of Milam. Nevertheless, Moses stood firm, and he insisted that the second man was Bryant and although he did not get a good look at his features in the dark, he felt that he saw enough to convince him that it was Roy Bryant. One interesting thing the prosecuting attorneys failed to emphasis was the fact that Roy Bryant had identified himself when he arrived at Moses tenant shack the night Emmett Till was abducted.

The defense then raised the question of Emmett's signet ring, which Moses had testified that he saw authorities remove from his nephew's finger. Defense attorney, John Whitten decided to cross-examine Moses while sitting at the defense table and he asked, "You never saw that ring before you saw it on the body that afternoon, did you?"

Moses replied out of his frustration of attempting to respond to every question from the various defense lawyers using clever psychology to confuse him and he finally replied, "That's right!" Moses tried to explain to the defense attorney that his knowledge of the ring came from his brother-in-law and his children who were able to identify the ring wore by his nephew, but the defense lawyer interrupted him and prevented his explanation.

"Somebody told you that was his ring, isn't that right," asked defense attorney, J.J. Kellum?

Moses was unable to control his anxiety and frustration by what he felt was a distortion of the facts by the defense and he replied with an aggressive outburst, "I know it was Emmett's ring."

Judge Swango instructed the jury to disregard his affirmative outburst. The defense attorneys felt confident that they had succeeded in creating doubt of Moses identification of the two defendants, therefore, Attorney Kellum concluded by saying, "We have no further questions for this witness, your honor."

Circuit Judge Curtis Swango turned to Moses on the witness stand and he uttered, "The witness is excused." He watched as Moses vacated the witness stand and then exited the courtroom through the rear door. As Moses passed by the black press table amid hostile stares from white spectators, he glanced at Mamie and dropped his eyes in disappointment, and then he departed through the door he had entered. The judge then asked, "Is the state ready to call your next witness?"

Special Prosecutor Robert Smith rose from his sitting position and he addressed the court, "We are your honor. The state calls, Chester A. Miller." Chester Miller, the black undertaker from Greenwood entered the courtroom from the rear entrance, made his way uncomfortably to the witness stand and sat somewhat nervously on the chair. During the questions by the special prosecuting attorney, the undertaker informed the court that when he removed the ring from the finger of the corpse he gave it to Moses Wright one of the relatives.

"When you arrived at the river that afternoon, whose body was you told to pick up," Prosecutor Smith asked.

"I was told to pick up the body of Emmett Till," Chester replied.

"Chester, describe the condition of the body upon your examination," Smith asked?

"There was barbed wire around the head and neck and it was attached to that gin fan machinery," Chester replied.

"Let the record show that the witness has identified this machinery here in court, exhibit number one, whom he identified as being attached to the victim's body," Prosecutor Smith enunciated.

Special Prosecutor Smith allowed the undertaker to continue with his testimony, and the undertaker told of how he had observed the head of the victim, and the top part had been crushed in. Miller further explained how he also saw a hole in Emmett's skull about one inch above the right ear. When asks if he thought the hole above the right ear might have been caused by a bullet, the black undertaker stated that he could not say for sure what caused the hole or other wounds. Sheriff Strider had said a bullet caused the hole above Emmett's right ear. At the objection and request of the defense, the undertaker was required to limit himself to saying that there was a round hole at this place and that the wounds were sufficient to cause death.

The next two state witnesses for the prosecution during the morning session were Sheriff Smith and his deputy, John Cothran. Sheriff Smith was first to take the witness stand and the prosecution attorneys guided him through a line of questions concerning the case. County Sheriff Smith testifying before the court said Roy Bryant, a back road grocer admitted kidnapping the little fourteen-year-old black boy on August 28, but denied killing him. At this point, the defense objected vigorously to any admission of any putative confession. The defense argued that because the evidence in the case was mainly circumstantial, the prosecution had yet to prove the two defendants were guilty of a crime. They moved to have the jury dismissed during the sheriff and deputy's testimony. In spite of the objection by the prosecution, the judge agreed that the state had to prove a crime was committed before it could ask to introduce any such statements before the jury.

In spite of the testimonies of Moses Wright, undertaker, Chester Miller, and Sheriff Smith and Deputy Sheriff Cothran, Judge Swango added that all the state had done thus far in the trial was to show that Emmett Till was dead. He also advised the prosecution that pending the testimony of new witnesses; he would permit both men to testify before the jury regarding the confessions of the two defendants. He then dismissed the jury from the courtroom and had them sequestered in the judge's chambers.

During the absence of the jury, the prosecution and the defense continued asking questionings of Sheriff Smith on the stand.

The sheriff replied to the district attorney's question and he responded, "Roy told me he went and got the boy and brought him to the store."

Chatham then asked, "Who did he say went down to Mose house with him?"

Sheriff Smith replied, "He didn't say."

"What did Roy tell you after he took the boy to the store," the district attorney asked?

"He said his wife looked at the boy and said he wasn't the right boy," the sheriff replied.

"How far is the store from old Mose Wright's place," Chatham asked?

"I judge 'bout three miles," he replied.

"Did you ask him why he didn't carry the boy back to Mose place," asked the district attorney? The sheriff replied, "I did. He said he reckoned the boy knew the way."

During the testimony of Deputy Sheriff Cothran, he stated that Milam had told him exactly the same story. Cothran replied to a question by the prosecution, "I asked J.W. if they went out to get the boy? He said, "Yes, but they put him out at the store."

Defense Attorney Sidney Carlton disclosed during cross-examination of the sheriff that the two defendants supported both the sheriff and the deputy the year before when the sheriff had run for the legislature and the deputy when he was a candidate for sheriff, although both lost their bid for election. The defense attorney tried to make the half-brothers admission seem like a cozy, private confidential chat among friends, not to officers of the law. Both Sheriff Smith and Deputy Cothran during their cross-examination by the defense uttered that they were just during their duty as officers of the law. However, the sheriff and deputy conceded that they did not warn the two defendants regarding the use of their words that might be used against them in court.

Later during the afternoon of the murder trial, Floyd Hodges, the seventeen-year-old angler and B.L. Mims testified to finding the body of Emmett Till in the Tallahatchie River on August thirty-first. Both testified that they lived in the area where the body was uncovered and B.L. stated that he operated an outboard motorboat in the area. The two witnesses both said the boy's legs and feet were visible from the water, but the heavy cotton gin exhaust fan held down the rest of the body. After their testimony, the judge called for an adjournment until the following morning at 9 A.M.

CHAPTER THIRTY:

MURDER-TRIAL: DAY FOUR

The following morning, Thursday, September twenty-second as a streaming rain drummed hard against the outside of the Sumner courtroom, inside the packed courtroom, the sensational murder trial had endured another tough day of court proceedings. The driving rain outside provided little relief from the steam bath temperature and buzzing flies in the courtroom. The curious spectators jammed into the courtroom had turned their focus of attention to District Attorney Gerald Chatham as he announced, "Your Honor! The state call, Mamie Bradley to the stand." Amid fiery energetic whispers and hard stares from white spectators, Mamie vacated her seat from the segregated press table where she had been sitting among the twelve black reporters and Congressman Diggs from Michigan. She walked toward the witness chair attired in a black hat, a dress with black and white prints on it, black bolero jacket, and she was wearing green earrings and two rings on her fingers. She was also carrying a black silk fan with her, as she made her way to the witness stand with quiet dignity, she could feel the stares of the white spectators eyes hanging tightly around her neck as she passed each row of the white cotton farmers in the courtroom.

During her testimony on the witness stand, both prosecution and defense lawyers addressed her as 'Mamie' and never as Mrs. Bradley as was customary in speaking to an American woman of African ancestry in the Deep South. Once she placed her somewhat corpulent built frame on the witness chair, the district attorney approached Mamie and he informed her that she was still under oath. Mamie nodded her head acknowledging her confirmation of his statement. She stared rather circumspectly at the sea of hostile white spectators who appeared to watch her every move. Her eyes came face to face with the two defendants who had brutally murdered her only child, Emmett Till and her gaze was at first fixated on them. Roy, J.W., and their wives stared back at her without any show of remorse.

During Mamie's testimony in court, she testified with calm, even-tempered demeanor and quiet proper etiquette. Mamie's firm clear voice carried conviction as she answered the lawyer's questions. She related how she had talked with her son many times before she allowed him to travel to the Delta of Mississippi on a summer vacation to visit his great-uncle, Moses Wright and other family members.

"I told him that he had to adapt himself to a new way of life in Mississippi," she said.

"I warned him to say 'Yes, Sir' and 'Yes, Ma'am' at all times. I told him to be very careful of how he spoke and when he spoke. I also told him that if an incident came up, he should apologize and if necessary he should humble himself and go on his knees," she continued.

District Attorney Chatham then asked, "Did you direct his attention to his conduct toward white men?" Mamie replied, "I impressed it on him carefully, Sir." "Did you caution him not to insult a white woman," he asked? "I believe I just said white people," she replied.

At the conclusion of the district attorney's questions regarding admonition of her son prior to his visit to Mississippi; Special Prosecutor Robert Smith began to take her through the identification process of her son's body in Chicago. Mamie's testimony was highly valuable to establish the identity of the body fished from the muddy waters of the Tallahatchie River on August thirty-first of the previous month.

"Did you see the body of your son in Chicago?" Smith asked.

"Yes Sir, I saw it first on a slab and then in a casket at the funeral home," she said.

"Could you identify it?" Smith asked.

"I positively identified it. It definitely was my boy beyond a shadow of a doubt," Mamie replied.

Special Prosecutor Smith presented the photograph to her that he was holding in his hand and he asked, "I have a police photograph, can you tell me if this was your son?"

Mamie sat motionless for a long duration obviously in shock; as she stared at the police photograph of her son's body on the day that it was first removed from the river. In a voice drained of expression, she finally replied, "That was my son, Emmett Louis Till." Her facial expression collapsed into wrinkled grief as her anguish mushroomed inside of her; she bit her top lip, took off her glasses, dabbed at her eyes trying to stop the tears flowing down her cheeks and wept with emotional sorrow on the witness stand. Some of the spectators watched her with heartfelt pity and others observed her with faces void of sympathy. Throughout her testimony on the stand, she was a portrait of misery after seeing the picture of her son's body, made by a Greenwood police photographer. It was the first time Mamie had seen the picture before the body was prepared for burial in Chicago. Mamie managed to compose her grief as best she could under the adverse circumstances and she then moved forward in answering the lawyer's questions. Special Prosecutor Smith asked Mamie in a tone filled with sympathy, "Mamie… you able to go on?" Mamie answered with more control in her voice, "Yes, I can go on."

Special Prosecutor Smith continued with his line of questions and he asked, "How were you so certain in identifying the body of your son?" "I was able to identify him by his nose, his lips, the chin, the hairline and his ears. I know it was him," Mamie replied. He then inquired of her about the ring found with the body and she said the ring belonged to her late husband, Louis Till who had died in military service overseas on July 2, 1945. "The ring bore his initials, "L. T." and the date of May twenty-fifth, 1943," she replied with assurance.

"How did you get the ring?" he asked. "The Army sent it to me with my husband's other things, Sir," she answered.

"What did you do with it?" Smith queried. "I kept it in my jewelry box for Emmett. It was too large for him to wear at first. Since he was twelve he wore it, occasionally with either Scotch tape or string to make it fit," Mamie continued.

"When did you last see it before now," Smith asked? "It was in Emmett's personal jewelry box. I was getting cuff links for him the day he went away, August 20th, and he tried on the ring and said, "Look, ma' it fits." "I said he was getting to be a big boy and…" Mamie continued. "Did he wear the ring," Smith inquired interrupting her? Mamie replied, "Yes, Sir!"

The two defendants were sitting in court with their children as the fourth day of the murder-trial continued. As the special prosecuting attorney questioned Mamie, the older children's activities in the aisles and playing with toy guns at times disrupted court proceedings occasionally. During Mamie's testimony on the stand, Milam's older child walked over to her and pointed his little cap pistol at her and he shouted, "Bang, bang, you're dead!" The children's parents and many of the spectators found the child's antics hilarious. Special Prosecutor Robert Smith concluded his questions of Mamie as she continued to watch the hate filled eyes of the white spectators staring at her.

Judge Swango than asked the defense attorneys, "Are you ready to question this witness? Attorney J. J. Breland replied, "Defense is ready, your honor!"

On cross-examination defense attorney, J.J. Breland remained seated while questioning Mamie, which many reporters considered an unusual tactic. During the defense attorney's questions, he brought out the fact that she was born in Webb, Mississippi only a couple of miles down the road from Sumner and he also stated that she left her native birth place at the age of two and moved to Chicago. Breland also repeated her statement of talking to her son several times before his trip to Mississippi from Chicago. Attorney Breland then hammered at Mamie from various angles.

"Was that kid in any trouble up there in Chicago when he left?" Breland asked.

"No Sir, Emmett was never in trouble in his life," Mamie replied.

"How much insurance did you have on that kid's life?" he hammered.

"Two polices that equaled about four hundred dollars," she replied.

"Have you collected from those companies, yet?" Breland asked.

"No, I have been waiting to receive a death certificate," Mamie responded.

Attorney Breland and the four other defense attorneys challenged the prosecution by stating that the body found in the river was not that of Emmett Till. Moreover, since they felt that they could prove it, they informed the jury that they must acquit Milam and Bryant of murder. In spite of the defense tenacious arguments of acquittal, the state continued their charges that the two defendants beat, shot and threw the body of fourteen-year-old, Emmett Till in the Tallahatchie River with a weight attached to his ankles and neck with barbed wire. Breland mentioned in court concerning charges based largely on the accusations made by Carolyn Bryant that the teenage youth, Emmett Till insulted her.

Judge Swango dismissed the jury before he allowed the defense to continue with their cross-examination of Mamie on the witness stand. He based his reasoning on the defense argument and strategy that the state had not connected the victim to the defendants. Once again, the judge said he would allow Mamie's testimony in court records if the evidence warranted it. After the all-white male jury had vacated the courtroom, Breland continued his line of questions to Mamie sitting on the witness stand.

"Had Emmett done anything in Chicago to cause you to caution him?" he asked.

"No sir, never," Mamie replied.

"Do you read the Chicago Defender?" asked Attorney Breland.

"I don't subscribe to the Defender, but I do buy it and read it," she replied.

He then asked her whether she had read the September 17 edition and she replied, "I might have seen the city edition, but

I don't think I have seen the national edition." Attorney Breland continued to ask whether 'colored people' edited the newspaper and she replied, "I would assume they did." He then inquired whether she had observed the picture, which showed the body of her son in the paper.

"No! I saw it in another publication," she replied. The publication Mamie was referring to was the pictures of her son's brutally beaten body which appeared in Jet magazine.

The defense attorney asked her if she had furnished pictures to the press. She informed the attorney that she knew of three copies reporters had released on her son to the press. During Mamie's cross-examination by the defense, the judge permitted the defense to offer in evidence a picture of young Emmett Till taken with his mother during the Christmas season of the previous year of 1954. The judge also allowed a newspaper picture of Emmett's body as it was prepared for his funeral in Chicago. Both the prosecution and defense attorneys concluded the examination of Mamie's testimony on the witness stand and she returned to the black press table to watch the continued progress of the trial. After Mamie vacated the witness stand, Judge Swango allowed the jury to reenter the courtroom.

Defense lawyer, C. Sidney Carlton in the presence of the jury attempted to demonstrate that the state failed to establish that Roy Bryant or J.W. Milam had murdered the victim in the case. He then called John Cothran, the deputy sheriff back to the witness stand again. During his questioning of the deputy sheriff, Carlton talked of auto accidents and the 80-pound cotton gin fan which the corpse was weighted.

"Isn't it true those injuries to the head could have been inflicted in an auto accident?" Carlton asked.

"I suppose they could," Cothran replied.

"Or on the other hand, by the blades of that there machine fan that was found with the body, right?" Defense Attorney C. Sidney Carlton asked

"They could have been, I reckon," the deputy sheriff replied.

"Now the small wound in the head, which the state contends was a bullet entry could have been made by a snag in the river," the defense attorney asked?

"Could be," Cothran answered.

"You have no way of knowing it was really Emmett Till's body, do you?" the attorney asked.

"I sure don't," Cothran replied. Carlton then smiled with emboldens reassurance at the twelve white men on the jury as they were allowed back into the courtroom to hear the testimony by the deputy sheriff.

While on the stand the deputy sheriff used the vernacular of the Delta cotton country in telling of the chat he had with Milam in the white prisoner's jail in Greenwood. The deputy sheriff cogitated for a moment then he uttered, "I recall it was a lazy hot afternoon with the summer breeze whistling through the cotton fields when I asked Milam did they carry that boy off? He said they carried him up to Roy Bryant's store in the village of Money and turned him loose out in front." During Sheriff Smith's testimony on the stand again before the jury, he reiterated that Roy Bryant told him much the same thing while he was in jail.

The prosecution called its next witness, Willie Reed to the stand. As Willie, one of the anticipated surprise witnesses for the state entered the courtroom; an old ageless hostile stare followed him as he walked with apprehensive strides to the witness stand. Willie's cautious fear was evident, when he sat on the chair his face revealed a look of uneasy nervous tension. He slowly raised his head and panic overwhelmed him, as he perceived the sea of hostile white spectators staring at him on the witness stand, as well as the two defendants. The fearful glint in Willie's eyes moved toward the five lawyers who also stared at him with hate-filled eyes.

Special Prosecutor Smith attempted to ease his fear by saying, "Now, Willie Reed. I don't want you to be afraid. Just tell the truth of what you saw and heard that mawnin. Can you do that for me?" Willie sitting on the witness stand focused his attention on the attorney asking him the questions and made every effort not to look at the white spectators in the courtroom staring at him and he finally replied quietly, "Yessuh!" Willie began his testimony by saying that he resided on the Clint Sheridan plantation not too far from Drew, Mississippi in Sunflower County. He revealed that he was also a neighbor of L.C. Milam and that he knew J.W. Milam. During his testimony, he testified so softly that the judge repeatedly urged him to speak louder.

Willie complied with the request of Judge Swango and he continued to place J.W. Milam and three others together with

Emmett Till in a shed on L.C. Milam's place from which he said he heard sounds as if someone was being beaten and crying in pain. His testimony was explosive and damaging as the courtroom exploded into agitated whispers from spectators and shock stares from the two defendants and their five attorneys. Although several defense attorneys had protested vigorously to have Willie's testimony excluded, Judge Swango overruled their motions. The previous self –assurance posture of the two defendants soon turned to an expression of anxiety and concerns etched on their faces as well as on the faces of their wives and families, which caused reporters on both sides to conclude that during this court session that the web of evidence against Milam and Bryant was growing with insurmountable validity.

After Judge Swango banged his gavel for order, the special prosecutor commented to Willie on the stand, "Willie, I want you to point to J.W. in this courtroom." Willie Reed rose from the chair and pointed his finger at the heavy-set balding defendant, J.W. Milam sitting with his lawyers, who stared back at him with threatening glances. Disclosing the most damaging testimony thus far, Willie continued his testimony against J.W. from the witness stand. During Willie's deposition, he explained that on the fourth Sunday of August about 6 o'clock in the morning, he was on his way to the store, when he saw a green Chevrolet pickup truck with a white top approach L.C. Milam's place. He said he saw three white men in the cab and two black men and a young black boy in the rear of the cab. He informed the court that two of the black men were sitting on the sides and the third person was sitting on the floor facing him with his back against the cab. At this point in the trial, the special prosecutor gave

Willie a photograph of Emmett prior to his death and he asked him if the person in the photograph was the same person, he saw on the pickup truck driven by J.W. Willie took a hard look at the photograph of Emmett Till and his mother and he identified him as the person he saw that morning.

Willie's identification of Emmett from the news photograph, which the defense permitted as evidence backfired on their strategy when the state used the picture to secure the identification of Emmett whom he placed with J.W. Milam near a back wood shed outside of Drew, Mississippi. Willie said after he had returned from the store, he saw J.W. come out of the shed with a pistol strapped to his side, get a drink of water at the well near the road and return to the shed again where the beating was continuing.

"Willie, what did you hear?" Smith asked. "I heard somebody hollerin'," he replied.

"And what else did you hear?" the special prosecutor asked. "I heard some licks, like somebody git'n' a whippin'," Willie replied.

The defense objected to his use of the word whipping and the judge had it stricken from the record.

"Can you tell the court in your own words, what the hollering sounded liked?" asked Smith.

"He was hollan' …oh, oh, oh!" Willie answered.

"And was it one holler or more than one holler?" Smith asked.

"It was more than once, it was a whole lot o' licks," he replied.

Willie continued by saying that he then went on to Mandy Bradley's resident, then he returned to the well to get a drink of water, and he uttered, "I could still hear somebody hollerin' in the shed." He informed the prosecuting attorney that after he had returned to his residence, he and his grandparents watched as the pickup truck left the area with a cover over the cargo area.

Defense attorney John Whitten attempted to have Willie Reed's deposition excluded on various grounds. One of the grounds concerned his evasiveness of Willie's identification of Roy as one of the men he saw in the pickup truck. Whitten suggested that since the witness testimony mainly involved J.W. and not Roy Bryant; he made a motion to have Bryant exonerated since he felt the affidavit did not relate Roy with the crime.

Special Prosecutor Smith argued that the defense had chosen not to separate the case of the two half-brothers, a right they could have exercised and that not every piece of evidence need apply directly to both. Judge Swango sustained the state's position and he moved to silence the debate between the two opposing attorneys. Defense Attorney, J.J. Kellum sought to bring out contradictions between what Willie was testifying in court and what he had told defense lawyers in a conference with them the day before. By an exasperating idiosyncrasy of Mississippi law, the defense had the right to subpoena all state witnesses and to consult with them in advance of their formal testimony before the court, outside the presence of prosecution attorneys. Although, the defense tried to repudiate Willie Reed's testimony, the young field hand stuck firm by his story, in spite of the harsh cross-examination by the five-defense attorneys of Sumner, Mississippi.

The prosecution called their last witnesses and they were Mandy and Alonzo Bradley and Ed Reed to the stand. During each of the witness's deposition, they helped substantiate the affidavit of Willie's account of the events surrounding the morning of the brutal murder on the Clint Sheridan plantation. At the conclusion of their testimony on the stand, the judge terminated the morning session by calling for a two-hour recess.

CHAPTER THIRTY-ONE:

MURDER-TRIAL: AFTERNOON SESSION

The afternoon court session began in an atmosphere of strain racial tension set ablaze by the damaging and explosive testimonies given by Willie Reed and Mamie Bradley during the morning court proceedings. Particularly with Mamie's positive identification of her son's brutally beaten and waterlogged body, which she had outlined very carefully in court and Willie Reed placing J.W. and Roy with Emmett Till four hours after the young teen was abducted from his Uncle Moses Wright tenant shack in Money, Mississippi. The afternoon court session began shortly after 2 p.m. Inside the packed courtroom, the concerned uneasy expression on the faces of Roy, J.W. and their five attorneys revealed how detrimental the morning court proceedings were to the case of the two defendants. Carolyn and Juanita whose faces were flushed and upset sat tight lipped and clutching their husband's arms with tears in their eyes fearing the possibility that if their husbands were found guilty of murder, they could be put to death. Adding to their agony was listening to the district prosecuting attorney suggest to the all-white male jury that one of their options available to them was to send Roy Bryant and J.W. Milam to the gas chamber for the brutal murder of fourteen-year-old, Emmett Louis Till from Chicago.

The voice of the district attorney vituperated through the antiquated courtroom, as he urged the twelve male jurors to find the two defendants guilty of nothing less than first degree murder. Chatham opened with two hours and twenty minutes of flaming oratory over the lives and freedoms of twenty-four-year-old, Roy Bryant and thirty-six-year-old, John Williams Milam as white men living in Mississippi. White men like other whites throughout Mississippi, the South and the country, relishing in freedom and privileges denied the Negroes living in the South under harsh Jim Crow laws. As District Attorney Chatham articulated his closing arguments, the only noise in the packed courtroom was the continued rat-tat-tat noise of the hard rain hitting the outside of the two-story courthouse, as spectators sat spellbound listening to Chatham's recapitulation of the facts in the case.

Roy nervously puffed on a cigar while his half-brother; J.W. looked mostly at the scarred, littered floor. Chatham paced back and forth in front of the jury and declared, "I say to you that the killing of Emmett Till, a little fourteen-year-old Negro boy from Chicago; was a cowardly act. It was a brutal and unnecessary killing. If the two half-brothers believed young Till had insulted Mrs.

Bryant, they should have taken a razor strap, turned him over a barrel and given him a beating." Chatham pounded his fist as he elucidated the evidence of the kidnapping and he informed the jury that the facts in the case were without contradictions. He also told the jury that the two defendants confessed to the sheriff and his deputy that they had indeed taken the child. Chatham reiterated to the jury that the two defendants claimed that they had turned the little boy loose, three miles from the tenant shack of Moses Wright at 3 a.m., after being convinced that he was not the boy who had made remarks to Bryant's wife. He even expounded that a witness saw the child with the men on the Clint Sheridan plantation four hours after the young teen's abduction from his uncle's tenant shack.

The district attorney admonished scornfully the defense contention that a body taken from the Tallahatchie River had never been proven to be that of Emmett Till's. Chatham further enlightened the jury that even the little boy's mother, Mrs. Mamie Bradley had made a positive identification. "So did young Till's uncle, Moses Wright," Chatham replied. In demanding the guilty verdict, the district attorney stated his case to the twelve-member jury. He said, "I was born and bred in the South. I live in the South and I will die in the South. I'm not paying any attention to any outside organizations set on destroying our Southern way of life, when I ask you for this verdict." At the conclusion of his oratory at 1:56 p.m., he concluded by saying, "The State rest, your honor." The district prosecuting attorney in his closing statement regarding outside organizations was obviously in reference to the National Association for the Advancement of Colored People, this also included other black organizations and the American

Jewish Congress, which had joined with others in the continued efforts in demanding swift justice in the highly publicized lynch/murder of young Emmett Till. District Attorney Chatham's closing statements thereby rested the state's case against Roy Bryant and his half-brother, J.W. Milam.

With such damaging testimony by witnesses and flaming oratory by the district attorney, it was now up to the defense to prove their client's innocence. During the excitement in the courtroom, Judge Swango banged his gavel for order and then asked the defense to call their witnesses. Before the defense had called any witnesses, J.J. Breland of the defense made a motion for a direct verdict of acquittal of Roy Bryant in the case, but the judge denied his request. Judge Swango then commented to the defense attorneys, "The motion is overruled because the court is of the opinion that the evidence presented by the State of Mississippi presents issues for the determination of the jury."

Defense Attorney, C. Sidney Carlton announced, "The defense call, Mrs. Carolyn Bryant to the stand."

Carolyn walked the short distance from where she was sitting with her husband and placed her small built frame on the witness chair. She was still slightly emotional, as she gazed out at the packed courtroom and the white spectators in attendance watched her with heartfelt pity. Judge Swango ruled that Carolyn Bryant's testimony before the jury was inadmissible for consideration by the jury, because previous testimony about events at the general store referred only to the "boy that done the talking." In spite of objections by the defense, the judge excused the twelve white male jurors. The judge ruling blocked plans by the defense to establish that the young unidentified assailant had made a physical assault on the wife of Roy Bryant.

Attorney Carlton walked over to Carolyn on the stand and he asked very politely, "Are you comfortable Mrs. Bryant? Do you need any water or anything?" Carolyn addressed the attorney as she wiped the tear stains from her eyes; "No thank you…I'm fine!"

"Now Mrs. Bryant can you tell us what happened that evening when that niggra boy came in your store?" he asked.

"I sure can…he came in and asked for some candy and soda pops. And when I gave it to him, he grabbed my arm and used ugly words and said 'how about a date, baby?' And then be bragged of having gone out with other white women," she responded.

The white spectators especially white females stared aghast, as they sat listening to her testimony on the stand. Carolyn was very careful not to mention the name of Emmett Till as the one whom she was accusing as the person who had attacked her in the store. Carolyn continued to explain that the assault got so bad, "that another niggra boy had to come in and get him" and pull him off her. She continued, "And he did not go peacefully."

"When the niggra boy was finally pulled outside of the store, he made a noise that sounded like a whistle," she continued.

Attorney Carlton gave his version of a wolf-whistle and she replied, "Yes, it sounded like that."

Mamie, Congressman Diggs, members of the NAACP and the twelve black reporters listened to her testimony in quiet astonishment by what was obvious to them was her mendacious statements regarding the actual events.

Carolyn persevered in her testimony, as she explained how the male Negro, whom she assumed was from the North, since she had never seen him before, had entered the store while she was alone and purchased the items, he had requested. Carolyn said when she held her hand out for the money; she said he grabbed her hand "with full force."

"What did you do at that point?" the attorney asked.

"I pulled away from him and started to the back of the store, but the niggra caught me at the cash register around the waist," she replied.

"Did he say anything?" asked Attorney Carlton.

"Yes! He said, "What's the matter baby, can't you take it?" she responded.

Again, the courtroom exploded in vociferous whispers from white spectators and especially those sitting near the black reporters as they turned their attention of animosity toward those sitting at the black press table. Judge Swango permitted her story into court records at the request of the defense. At the conclusion of her testimony, the attorney excused Carolyn from the witness stand. Carolyn Bryant's testimony was very convincing to the white spectators in the courtroom, but to the many black observers, they were far too familiar with stories like that which lead to many race riots, lynchings and blacks being burned at the stake or hanged throughout the South and parts of the North.

The defense called its next witness, "Mrs. J.W. Milam to the stand." Unlike her sister-in-law, her testimony disclosed that she was in the rear of the store at the time and that she could not recall much about the incident between the young intruder and her sister-in-law in the store. Juanita said she could not recall the incident, but did recall how upset Carolyn was when she told her about it.

Attorney Carlton only asked her questions about her family and her husband's war record. The defense attorney disclosed regarding her husband's war record that he was a soldier in the Platoon manner. Carlton also informed the jury and the court that although, J.W. only had a ninth-grade education, it did not prevent him from enlisting in the Army and the 75th Division commissioned him in battle. Attorney Carlton characterized him as being an expert platoon leader, an expert fighter, expert in night patrol and a specialist with the "grease gun" which he had mastered for close-range killing. Carlton further explained that during World War Two, a German bullet had torn through her husband's chest, which his body now bears multiple shrapnel wounds, the jury and many of the white spectators were moved with patriotic pride; as they listened to the attorney explain the many medals which J.W. had received during his year of war service. He said J.W. only cherished one medal, the combat infantry badge.

During the testimony of both women, the prosecution did

not cross-examine either Carolyn or her sister-in-law, Juanita. In spite of damaging testimony that the murder actually occurred on the Clint Sheridan plantation in Sunflower County, the prosecution was content with Sumner as being the appropriate location for the murder-trial. District Prosecutor Gerald Chatham said no attempt was necessary to change the location of the murder trial, since it was not determined in which county the young child was actually murdered. After the jury had reentered the court proceedings again after Carolyn's testimony, the defense presented other evidence in an attempt to discredit Mamie's identification of her son's body.

The defense called Sheriff H.C. Strider as their next witness. All eyes in the courtroom followed the heavy built sheriff as he walked with confidence to the stand and placed his 290-pound frame in the chair. In an unusual move, the sheriff of Tallahatchie County testified for the defense and not for the prosecution, which was usually the case. During his deposition on the stand, he informed the defense attorney that the body he saw taken from the Tallahatchie River appeared to have been in the water at least ten to fifteen days.

John Whitten, the defense attorney who was questioning the sheriff turned and smiled sardonically at the twelve white male jurors and he responded, "This body was ten to fifteen days in the water and not three days as the prosecution would like you to believe." Whitten the defense attorney then commented, "Tell me Sheriff Strider, when you saw that body removed from the river, were you able to tell if it was a Negro's body?"

"Naw, sir, I couldn't tell for sure whether the body was that of a Negro…all that I could tell was that it was a human being," the sheriff said.

At the black press table, one of the female reporters, Cloyte Murdock, quietly spoke to her colleagues, "If he wasn't sure whether the body was a Negro, why did he get a Negro undertaker to examine it?"

It was the opinion of all sitting at the black press table that the sheriff was obviously not telling the truth. Sheriff Strider was considered by many of the opposition including the black reporters and the NAACP, as being the originator of the wrong body argument theory. Strider was a well-to-do cotton planter who employed thirty black sharecroppers' families on his plantation of 1,500 acres. At the conclusion of Strider's testimony for the defense, he vacated the witness stand at the request of the judge.

The next witness called to the stand by the defense was a white country undertaker, H.D. Malone, who also told the defense that he had estimated that the body had been in the water from 10 to 25 days. Malone, a resident of Cleveland, Mississippi who had embalmed Emmett's body, said that according to scientific methods he had learned at embalming school, "the body had been dead for a minimum of ten days."

Attorney C. Sidney Carlton then informed the jury of his theory that troublemakers had learned of the incident at the store and determined to make an outrage of it, decided to hide Emmett Till up North in some city away from his relatives. Then he continued his theory by stating that he believed that some outside agitators found a dead body somewhere, weighted it and threw it in the Tallahatchie River after bashing the facial features beyond recognition. He went on to say that Emmett Till's ring was taken from him and placed on the dead body found in the river, because just like Sheriff Strider, he too believe that Emmett was alive and living in the north somewhere. The black spectators and the prosecuting attorneys sat flabbergasted by the defense attorney's theory, which was based on a lack of evidence. As the defense continued to attack the prosecution's identification of the body found in the river as that of Emmett Till's, they called their next witness to the stand, a Doctor L.B. Otken, a physician from nearby Greenwood, Mississippi.

Defense Attorney, John Whitten questioned Doctor Otken sitting on the witness stand and asked how long he thought the body was in the river, as he was the one who had made the medical examination of the decomposed body. Doctor Otken stared at the attorney with a frown expression, in retrospect to the image of the body in his head and he replied, "I would say the body was in the water about eight days to two weeks." Defense Attorney J.J. Breland then asked, "In your opinion, could anyone have been able to identify that body, as you heard the mother say this morning?" Doctor Otken replied, "I don't think so, because the body was in an advanced state of decomposition and I don't think anybody could possibly identify it. You couldn't tell whether it was colored or white." The defense considered the three points made during the depositions to be very important, as all three witnesses said that the body was bloated and badly decomposed. This was a critical point because only three days had elapsed from the time of Emmett Till's abduction from his uncle's tenant shack until Floyd Hodges; the teen-aged angler had found the body three days later.

On cross-examination, Special Prosecutor Robert Smith drew agreement from Doctor Otken, Sheriff H.C. Strider and undertaker Malone when he asserted that a decomposed body, badly injured would decompose more rapidly than a normal body submerged in water. The strategy of the defense continued to concentrate its questioning on identification, which they felt, was the heart of the State's case. If the State failed to prove in jurors' eyes that young, Emmett Till had been murdered, it would be impossible to get a murder conviction on Bryant and Milam for killing him. At the conclusion of the defense witnesses, the judge recessed the court at 5 p.m., until the following morning.

CHAPTER THIRTY-TWO:

MOUND BAYOU HOTEL

Members of the NAACP, the black press and Congressman Diggs and his two aids met in the conference room of the Mound Bayou Hotel during the night of September twenty-second with Doctor Howard also in attendance. The topic of conversation during the meeting involved the current events in the murder trial thus far and about the escape plan to get the black witnesses out of Mississippi and to a place of safety before the trial ended in Sumner, Mississippi, the following day. As the meeting progressed, Ruby Hurley entered the conference room a short time later and joined the conversation of her associates sitting around the table.

Ruby returned to the meeting with her colleagues after conversing with Willie Reed and his grandparents in their hotel room and then with Mandy and Alonzo in a separate room on the same floor. Her conversation with them was to convince them of the importance of leaving Mississippi permanently. Ruby's conversation with her compatriots in the NAACP and with members of the black press outlined recommendations regarding the proposed escape plan to get the sharecroppers from the Clint Sheridan plantation safely out of Mississippi with all hasten urgency. Ruby's conversation she had had with the sharecroppers from the Clint Sheridan plantation was not well received at first as she suggested that they had to relocate to unfamiliar locations away from their homes in Mississippi. She told them that she understood their reluctance to leave a home they had known all their lives, yet she sought to encourage them as she reassured the sharecroppers that the NAACP would do everything in its power to assist in their relocation to a place of safekeeping.

Meanwhile, while Ruby Hurley conversed with her colleagues in the conference room down the hall, Willie Reed conversed with his grandparents in their hotel room about his concerns and fears about leaving his grandparents in Mississippi. Their anxiety was a constant battle within them as they moved about in the simple quarters of the room. Mattie viewed her grandson and husband with her own inner battle over the repugnant situation, which had brought this dilemma into their humble lives and she voiced her concerns with Ed and Willie about her fears for their safety, after their testimony in the racially charged southern murder-trial in Sumner. Mattie and Ed's devotion was to their grandson whom they had raised from a very young child and they put Willie's safety before their own well-being. In view of their fears, Ed and Mattie decided that it would be wise and benefical if their grandson left Mississippi and moved North to live with his mother in Chicago. The decision made by his grandparents displeased Willie and he found their suggestion difficult to endure and he opposed the thought of leaving the grandparents who had raised him and the only parents he had ever known. Willie looked into the faces of his grandparents filled with uneasiness and remarked, "Mama, Poppa…I ain't wanna leave y'all. I don't wanna go!" Mattie insisted that Ed also leave Mississippi, but Ed refused her proposition. He took both her hands and placed them in his hands and replied, "Ain't nobody gonna separate me from you but God." Ed went on to tell his wife, Mattie that he was not concerned for his safety nor would the threat of any white retaliation force him from the home they shared together.

Willie came to the realization that if they convinced him to leave Mississippi and move to Chicago to live with a mother he hardly knew, the thought consumed him with fear that he would never see his grandparents again. Willie's apprehension and torment was deep within him as he struggled to accept what he was hearing from them. Mattie and Ed embraced their grandson in their arms and as Willie fought hard to prevent the tears swelling up in his eyes from falling, his grandfather said with sadden encouragement, "Go on up norf and make somethin' outta yo' life, son."

Meanwhile in the next room where Mandy and Alonzo were staying, they were conversing about the possibility that they might have to leave the home they had come to know in spite of the harsh reality of segregation in their daily environment and migrate to the North with the aid of the NAACP. They were poor sharecroppers with no money and trying to come to terms with the sudden changes, which were about to occur in their simple lives. Changes brought about since they had courageously testified for the first time in their lives against white men in an arresting, publicized murder trial, which held the nation and parts of the world spellbound. Mandy was painfully aware that she could never return to the plantation again, because she was cognizant of the fact that some whites on the plantation would surely attempt to kill her. Alonzo was of the opinion that since he did not finger any of the accused men directly, to him, his participation in the murder trial was of little significance. Therefore, he felt that his concerns about white retaliation against him were not as big a threat as it was against his wife, Mandy. Alonzo in his reasoning believed that since he knew his white neighbors and they was well aware that he knew his place that he could possibly continue to reside on the Clint Sheridan plantation until he could raise enough money to relocate to a new location with his wife up North.

In the meantime, in the conference room where the meeting continued, those in attendance listened as Doctor Howard voiced his disappointment at the prosecution attorneys whom he felt was not prepared to present the State's case in the murder trial. He stated with confidence that had it not been for the black press, the NAACP and his participation in their efforts in securing important witnesses who had presented vital evidence to the case, the prosecution would have moved forward with circumstantial evidence. Because of Doctor Howard's busy schedule, which prevented him from attending the trial, he relied on his colleagues to keep him informed about events in the trial. The militant medic expressed his concerns, as Hicks informed him that the defense lawyers had obviously built a strong case on the wrong body theory, and Doctor Howard told him as the others looked on that any experience physician could have easily refuted the defense theory. Doctor Howard's suggestion revealed that the prosecution could have established the age of young Emmett Till's body by an examination of his bone structure, which would have invalidated the fantastic contentions of the defense that the body taken from the Tallahatchie River was that of an older person.

"During the past 35 years, white men have had to pay greater penalties for killing deer out of season than for killing Negroes," Howard uttered.

He further stated, "It is impossible for a Negro to get justice where the races are involved."

At the conclusion of his statement, Doctor Howard declared that, "If the Federal government does not realize how extremely serious this situation is in Mississippi…there is going to be an outbreak of violence…that's going to shock the very imagination of the American people and the world."

Ruby Hurley told the gathering that she had discussed some of the escape plans which they had decided on in the meeting with Mandy and her husband, Alonzo and Willie Reed and his grandparents and they were tentatively leaning toward Willie and Mandy leaving Mississippi. Ruby said that after the meeting she was planning to meet with them again to get their final decision on the matter. Ruby and her partners devised various rendezvous points of interest near the plantation where they could secretly pick up the sharecroppers and get them out of Mississippi and away to Memphis, Tennessee where they were to meet Mamie and her family at the conclusion of the trial. Ruby told them that she would convey any new escape plans to the sharecroppers for their consideration. It was Mattie's insistence that she and her husband and grandson return to the Clint Sheridan plantation for their last night on the plantation as a family before her grandson departed Mississippi permanently. Mandy and Alonzo wanted to return so that Mandy could retrieve clothing and items important to her.

Later during the same night in the Tallahatchie County Jail in Charleston, Mississippi, Sheriff Strider was conversing with his deputies about his plans for Leroy (Too-Tight) Collins and Henry Lee Loggins at the conclusion of the murder trial in Sumner. In spite of concerns from his deputies about the possible outcome of the trial, the sheriff boasted that he was confident that the verdict would not be any different from those in the past. During his discussion, one of his deputies suggested that perhaps it would be to their best interest to release the two field hands during the night instead of waiting for the verdict scheduled for the following day. Sheriff Strider considered and decided that his deputy was right in recommending the release of the two field hands and he determined that now would be the ideal time to carry out his plan. Strider vacated his office and headed for the cell occupied with Too-Tight and Henry Lee sleeping on separate colts to inform them of his plans to release them.

Shortly thereafter, Henry Lee awoke to the sound of dangling keys as the sheriff unlocked the cell door. At first sudden terror struck Henry Lee as he observed the dark silhouette figure entering the cell, yet Too Tight continued to sleep untroubled by the intrusion. Since the unexpected visit by Mississippi authorities and members of the black press to the county jail in search of the two missing field hands, Strider decided to limit their free movement around the jail, even though Too Tight and Henry Lee were not legally under arrest. He even ordered the cell locked during the night for security purposes. The sheriff did not want to run the risk of having his scheme exposed to the public, especially with the murder trial ending. Henry Lee watched Sheriff Strider with restless glances, as he aroused Leroy Collins from sleep. The two field hands watched the sheriff with an inquisitive stare curious of his visit, as Strider stood over them with a superlative posture.

Sheriff Strider scrutinized their insignificant status like an authoritative overseer and he explained to them, "I come to let you boys know my deputies will be in shortly to take you boys back to y'all places." The idea of finally going home after over two weeks in the county jail caused the two field hands much elation. The sheriff suggested further, "Let me give you niggers a word of advice. When y'all git home don't go talkin' to that niggra press and if I was y'all, I'll be high tailin' it outta Mississippi as fast as a bolt of lightnin' hittin' a tree." The two incarcerated men realized deep down inside of them that their promise to the sheriff was a promise they knew they had to keep or else risk the danger of death.

It had been over an hour and a half since Sheriff Strider's conversation with Henry Lee and Too Tight informing them of their pending release. Miles away in the black section of town in Glendora, Mississippi, the quiet mysterious darkness masked the Jim Crow surrounding area as the residence slept in their tenant shacks around the impoverished town. Inside the two-room tenant shack, Clare and the three small children were also asleep. Clare was soon aroused from sleep by the continued sound of a fist pounding on the door of her residence. In her state of somnolent, she made her way to the door and she cautiously asked, "Who there?" An anxious and whispered voice came through the door, "It's me Clare, let me in!" Clare hastily opened the door and she could hardly believe what her eyes was seeing as Henry Lee entered the tenant shack and embraced her, as she threw herself into his arms. The same excited encounter was taking place between Leroy (Too Tight) Collin and his girlfriend, Ella Mae, who resided a short distance away from where Henry Lee and Clare lived.

CHAPTER THIRTY-THREE:

THE VERDICT

    The following morning, Friday, September twenty-third, inside the tenant shack of Henry Lee and Clare, they were discussing his concerns about staying in Mississippi especially with so many people having knowledge about Too-Tight and his involvement in the publicized murder case of Emmett Till. With the threat of death made by the two defendants and others entrenched forever in his mind, Henry Lee was painfully aware that it would not take long before word of his release from jail hit the streets. Information he knew would send members of the press, both black and white and members of the NAACP to his door. Henry Lee knew that any affiliation with the NAACP would cause eminent danger to his family and Clare was painfully aware of the danger as well. In Henry Lee's state of anger and frustration over events, which he felt he had no control over, he informed his common-law wife of his decision to leave Mississippi for a while and make arrangements to stay with relatives in Saint

Louis, Missouri. He had gotten word to his father from a relative that lived nearby and they made arrangement to drive him to a relative home in Saint Louis shortly after his visit with Clare. He told her of his plans to return once he felt that the danger had subsided and their humble lives could return to some sense of stability in spite of the segregated oppressed environment, which they and other blacks in the South knew so well.

In the meantime, on the Clint Sheridan plantation, Willie sadly watched his grandparents as they gathered his belonging for his impending departure to Chicago. Reporter Jimmy Hicks and Ruby Hurley had returned Willie Reed and his grandparents to their place of residence on the previous night to spend their last night together there in the tenant shack that they had come to cherish over the years. Mattie was content that her persuasive efforts to return to their tenant shack on the plantation was worthwhile even though it was a bitter sweet moment because of the fact that the grandson she loved so much was leaving her. She carefully placed his clothes in a sack and then tied knots around a stick so that he could carry the sack with ease. Willie and his grandparents embraced each other tightly and as tears crawled down their weary beaten faces, his grandfather uttered with sorrow, "You better go on son…dey be waitin' for ya."

As his grandparents watched after him, Willie departed the tenant shack with tears in his eyes and the sack of clothes on his back and he walked toward the cotton fields, as if he was going to perform his duties, which he had performed since he was a small child. There was very little activity around the plantation as many of the white inhabitants were en route to the murder trial in Sumner. Active in the cotton fields was some of his black sharecropper neighbor's busy picking cotton. Amid the cool early morning breeze quietly capering its way through the vast countryside, and with the cotton plants fluctuating effortlessly from the breeze whistling through the fields; Willie engaged the plantation around him with cautious glances and then he took off running across the field to the planned rendezvous point where he and Mandy were scheduled to meet members of the NAACP.

Meanwhile, in the tenant shack of Mandy and Alonzo, he too watched his wife as she struggled because of the inflammation in her right hip and leg due to arthritis, as she fought her way across the field to the waiting car, waiting to transport them to Memphis, for their departure North. Upon their arrival in Memphis, they were to wait for Mamie and Congressman Diggs as well as those who had escorted them to Mississippi. The NAACP plans were to have Willie Reed and Mandy Bradley in Memphis before the conclusion of the murder trial in Sumner.

Several hours later the same morning, the murder trial was just getting underway. As on previous days inside the crowded courtroom, Judge Swango banged his gavel for order. As the quiet whispers collapsed throughout the dilapidated room, white spectators as well as blacks continued to watch every detail of the proceedings with inquisitiveness. It was common knowledge with everyone in the courtroom that the litigation would probably conclude with the testimony of six character witnesses called by the defense. The two defendants, their wives and families observed the trial with guarded optimism, as they awaited a possible verdict sometime later during the afternoon.

During the court proceedings, the defense attorneys appeared confident that the all-male, all-white jury would free Roy and J.W. Primarily, the defense based its self-assurance entirely on the testimony of the three medical witnesses. The three whom they had called the day before, to attack the identification of the battered body of the fourteen-year-old teenage, pulled from the river thereby creating doubt of the body really being that of Emmett Louis Till. The defense lawyers were so secure by what they felt were damaging testimony by the three defense witnesses that they felt no need to call Roy and or J.W. to testify. The defense called six individual character witnesses who were mainly friends and relatives of the two defendants. The mother of the two defendants, Eula Lee testified that her sons were never into any meanness in their lives. She expounded on how they were red-blooded Americans who had courageously fought in World War II for the freedom of their country. Other character witnesses talked about how they were good old boys who worked hard and who would safeguard their families with their lives. At the conclusion of the testimonies of the six-character witnesses, the defense rested its case at 10:22 a.m., during the final day of the sensational murder trial in Sumner, Mississippi.

Circuit Judge Curtis Swango again overruled defense motions for a direct verdict of acquittal for Roy and J.W., and then he ordered a brief recess before State prosecutors began their final summation to the jury. In Mississippi in 1955, the State opened and closed the final arguments. The defense arguments were sandwiched between the State's arguments. Judge Swango called the crowded courtroom to order after the one-hour recess. He then instructed the prosecution attorneys and the defense attorneys that he was allowing them one-hour each to submit their final summations before the jury.

District Attorney Chatham rose to his feet from his reclined posture and he walked over to the twelve white men sitting in the jury box. He attempted to hide his uneasiness as he stared at the twelve white jurors with confidence. He knew that his argument to the jury had to overshadow the defense that concentrated their questioning on the identification of the body, which was the heart of the State's case. The district attorney and the special prosecutor for the State were arduously aware that if the State failed in the eyes of the jurors to prove that Emmett Till was murdered, the two defendants could not be convicted of killing him. Earlier during the start of the murder trial, the district attorney had informed the press that the State would not seek the death penalty, since a substantial part of its evidence they felt were circumstantial. During the district attorney's closing address to the jury, he reiterated on some of the evidence by the surprise witnesses, the uncle and mother of Emmett Till; points which he had made earlier when the State had rested its case on the previous afternoon. Chatham summed up the State's case by stating, "If you found a child's unidentified body, you wouldn't go to an undertaker who didn't know the child, you'd go to his mother. Here in this courtroom she told a forthright story of how she was able to identify the body of her only child. What mother wouldn't know her on child after carrying him for nine months and nurturing that child as a babe on her breast? If there was one ear or hairline or mouth, she would have known it."

In presenting the final summary for the defense, John Whitten told the jury, "I am confident that every last Anglo-Saxon one of you has the courage to perform his duty." Mamie, Congressman Diggs and the black press pondered with a sense of meaning about Whitten's term "perform his duty." As those at the black press table continued to observe and listen with interest to the closing arguments by the defense and prosecution attorneys to the jury, they eyed each other with doubt that a conviction was possible. In the strained atmosphere in the courtroom, Attorney Whitten uttered with confidence, "Now I admit for the sake of argument that Milam and Bryant had abducted Emmett Till on the night of August 28. But they said they had turned him loose and ordered him to walk back to Uncle Mose Wright's cabin. Now it's not a far-fetch idea to know what happen next. Mose Wright took that boy to meet a friend- unidentified and unnamed- from the National Association for the Advancement of Colored People. This here friend persuaded Mose Wright to put his nephew's ring on a rotten stinking corpse, which when taken out of the river, would be identified by simple people as that of Emmett Till. There are people in the United States, who want to defy the customs of the South and would commit perhaps any crime known to man in order to widen the gap. These people are not all in Gary and Chicago; they are in Jackson and Vicksburg and if Mose Wright knows one he didn't have to go far to find him. And they include some of the most astute students of psychology and they have ready access to a corpse which could meet the purpose." During his summation, the white spectators listened to his speech with pride and confident glee and the black spectators observed the ordeal with a stunned expression of uneasiness and disbelief at what they were hearing.

The next defense lawyer to speak was J.W. Kellum and he assured the jury by making them keenly-aware that they form, "a peerage of democracy and that they were 'absolutely the custodians of American civilization." He continued to say, "I want you to tell me where under God's shinning sun is "the land of the free and the home of the brave if you don't turn these boys loose; your forefathers will absolutely turn over in their graves."

The remaining defense lawyers made much of police and medical testimony by the three medical witnesses who had stated that the body appeared to have been dead at least ten days whereas the young child, Emmett Till was missing only three days. Both sides bitterly denigrated outside interest for raising a furor over the case and trying to destroy "the Southern way of life."

Special Prosecutor Robert Smith in his closing arguments to the jury called the theory suggested by the defense as nothing less than ludicrous and asinine. In reference to the defense suggesting that Emmett Till and his uncle Moses Wright, whom young Till was visiting, might have acquired some assistance from outsiders namely the NAACP and then suggesting that, "these same people who were trying to create ill will among the whites and blacks by conspiring to carry out a plot to stage the young child's death." Then as the defense suggested arranging to put "some deceased person" in the river wearing Emmett's ring, as the most ludicrous and far-fetched argument he had ever heard in a courtroom.

He then suggested, "But so long as any citizen of this Nation, whether black or white, is denied his constitutional rights of life, liberty and the pursuit of happiness, then we can't complain about what happens to us. Emmett Till, down here in Mississippi, was a citizen of the United States; he was entitled to his life and his liberty. Their claim that the body had to have been in the water at least ten days due to decomposition is not factual. What is factual is that a badly wounded body will decompose faster than a normal body not wounded. That child's body was badly wounded. His mother identified the body as her only child; Willie Reed placed the defendants with the child four hours after he was taken from the home of his uncle. I say to you men of this jury with such evidence, how can you not convict."

At the conclusion of Attorney Smith's address to the jury, the judge dismissed the jury to deliberate the verdict. Judge Swango did not make a formal charge to the jury. He explained that the jury's possible findings were outlined by the state early in the case. The jury then vacated the courtroom.

Mamie, her father, her cousin and Congressman Diggs and his two aids departed just as the jury vacated the courtroom and they first drove to Mound Bayou where they decided to wait for the verdict there, instead of in Sumner, where the black press remained behind to hear the outcome before they joined Mamie and the remaining party in Mound Bayou. After the verdict, their plans were to travel immediately to Memphis where Mandy, Willie Reed and members of the NAACP were anxiously waiting their arrival for the departure to Chicago.

Meanwhile during the short recess by the judge, the two defendants with their lawyers and families along with many spectators remained inside the courtroom, as they waited on edge for the verdict. The jury was assigned the case at 2:35 p.m. Inside the enclosed jury room across the street from the courthouse, the twelve white jurors debated over the evidence. They frowned as they examined the police photograph of the decomposed corpse of Emmett Till. The deliberation process over the evidence was not a lengthy one, as the twelve men began to take a vote on the verdict. The first vote was nine for acquittal and three not voting on the first ballot, ten for acquittal and two not voting on the second ballot. The third ballot was unanimous. At the conclusion of their unanimous decision, they withdraw to purchase soda pops at the nearby one story shop before returning to the jury room and then notifying a bailiff after their arrival that they had decided on a verdict. Meanwhile within the Courthouse Square, hundreds of persons were mingling about or standing under the massive oak trees around the shabby yellow courthouse building in the Village Square.

At 3:42 p.m., Judge Curtis Swango called court to order and the male jurors filed back to their seats. Judge Swango then addressed the jury by asking, "Have the jury reached a verdict." The foreman of the jury, J. A. Shaw, Jr. rose from his seat and handed a slip of paper to the bailiff, who read the verdict. "Not guilty," he said loudly. White spectators from the rear of the courtroom leaped from their seats and vacated the courtroom, down a short stairway and the refrain, "not guilty" carried in shouts from person to person through the corridor and into the courtyard, and many southern whites cheered excitedly at the verdict. There was a slight mishap, however, when Judge Swango reported that the verdict had not been given in the proper form and the jury had to go back and rewrite it, but it was only a technicality.

In the meantime, Roy and J.W. kissed their pretty wives for

the news cameras after the verdict was read until lipstick smeared their faces from their chins to their eyebrows. For the benefit of the TV cameras, the two defendants smiled and smoked big black cigars and they told the press they were, "glad to be turned loose." Carolyn Bryant told the press, "I'm very happy. I feel a lot better than I did yesterday on the witness stand." It only took five minutes for the proper verdict to be presented and this time the bailiff read it, "We the jury fines the defendants, Roy Bryant and J. W. Milam, not guilty." Many people in the crowd had already left the area. And as white spectators leaving the courtroom had filed pass the black press table. They stopped to stare at them and in that moment of southern hostility, that hate filled stare, which seemed to suggest that in the South at least, no white man would ever be convicted of killing a nigger; they exited the courtroom in celebration. The celebration was shot lived, as the two defendants were turned over to Sheriff Smith of Leflore County under kidnapping charges for abducting Emmett Till. They were taken to the Leflore County Jail in Greenwood after the verdict. A grand jury was expected to hear the case against them in Greenwood for kidnapping sometime in the month of November of the same year of 1955. After consulting with attorneys, Judge Swango announced kidnapping charges against the two defendants were being dismissed in Sumner, thereby placing the prisoners in the jurisdiction of Sheriff Smith in adjoining Leflore County. They were charged with, but not indicted for kidnapping in Leflore, where young Emmett Till was actually abducted.

After the verdict, the jury foreman told the press that the jurors, after looking at a photo of a battered body fished from the Tallahatchie River, did not think it could be identified by anyone, "that was the biggest point with us," he told the press. He also told the press that the jury which took one hour and seven minutes to reach a verdict, had ignored the testimonies of Moses Wright and Willie Reed and was unimpressed with the appearance of Mamie Bradley, the widowed mother of the young child victim.

The State had built its case around eyewitnesses such as, sixty-four-year-old, Moses Wright and eighteen-year-old, Willie Reed and Mamie's identification of her only child's battered waterlogged body. District Attorney Gerald Chatham had no quarrel with the verdict as he told the press, "The right of trial by jury is a sacred guarantee of the United States Constitution. I accept the verdict and abide by it." He felt no need to elaborate further. Special Prosecutor Robert Smith said that, "outside influences wanted Bryant and Milam freed. If they are turned loose, those people will have a fund-raising campaign for fifteen years."

Shortly after the press announced the verdict nationally, a statement from the New York headquarters of the National Association for the Advancement of Colored People stated, "The verdict is as shameful as it is shocking. The jurors who returned it deserve a medal from the Kremlin for meritorious service in communism's war against democracy."

The Federal Bureau of Investigation (FBI) reported that in Moscow, the Kremlin was watching and continued monitoring the Mississippi murder-trial of Emmett Till more closely than almost anything else happening in the United States during that time.

Short time later reporters converged on the all-black town

of Mound Bayou to interview Mamie and Congressman Diggs about their reaction regarding the acquittal of the two defendants in Sumner. Mamie informed the press, "The trial was just a farce, so I was expecting an acquittal and I didn't want to be there when it happened. I was a little amazed by the brevity of the jury session." Congressman Diggs and a member of the NAACP told the press that they were pleased with the way Judge Swango handled the case and they were moderately warm with the prosecution. After the interview with the press, Mamie; her father, cousin, and Congressman Diggs in his aids departed en route to Memphis.

Two hours later, the same evening inside the Memphis airport, Mamie and her family and Congressman Diggs and his two aids were conversing with Ruby Hurley, James Hicks and Willie Reed and Mandy Bradley. As they waited to board their planes, which would transport them home to their destinations, Mandy announced that she was afraid to fly by plane and that she would prefer to travel by bus or train. Rudy understood her dilemma and they left the airport en route to the train station a short distance away from the airport.

Upon their arrival in Chicago the following day, Mandy stayed with Mamie for a brief time, like several months until she was forced to settle in Detroit with relatives. Willie Reed who had never been on a plane before was also afraid, but he reluctantly accepted the challenge. During the following day in Chicago Willie Reed settled in with his mother, Wilma. Mamie; her father and cousin were excited about being home in Chicago and Congressman Diggs and his aids held a press conference in Detroit about the verdict.

Meanwhile, during the night of September twenty-third, after the conclusion of the murder-trial in Sumner, Moses arrived at his tenant shack alone and mentally exhausted because of the acquittal verdict of the two men whom he strongly believed had brutally murdered his young nephew. He entered his resident unconcerned about the dangers around him and decided to bed down for the night. Moses was so distraught over the verdict that his fatigue caused him to fall asleep. Suddenly, he was awakened by a voice calling out to him and saying, "Moses, Moses, get up! It is not safe here." He sat up in bed and looked around the room, but the room was empty. Thinking that he was having a bad dream, he reclined on the bed to sleep, when he heard the voice again, "Moses, get up! It is not safe here." Moses later told the press that he was not afraid of what he was hearing because he believed that it was the Spirit of the Lord warning him. He soon obeyed the voice and he got dress and drove to his church in East Money. Shortly after Moses departed, two truckloads full of white men arrived at his tenant shack. They were carrying shotguns and baseball bats. Several of them began to shout toward the tenant shack, "Uncle Mose, come on out here. We just wanna talk to you, nigger! You better come on out o' there boy or we coming in." The white mob soon entered the tenant shack and as Moses neighbors watched nearby, they ransacked his resident. After the near death experience, Moses and his three younger sons (who were staying with relatives during the night) boarded a train, the following day bound for Chicago to join his wife who had taken up residence with relatives living in the Northern city.

CHAPTER THIRTY-FOUR:

STEPS TOWARD SOCIAL CHANGE

Reaction to the acquittal of the two white men accused of brutally murdering young Emmett Till came swiftly around the country. On Sunday, September twenty-fifth, two days after the murder trial ended in Sumner, Mississippi, the NAACP held a rally in Detroit, Michigan with six thousand persons in attendance. Congressman Charles C. Diggs was the main speaker and he was speaking to an enthusiastic crowd determined to fight against racial oppression in the South and other parts of the country. Congressman Diggs attacked the acquittal of Milam and Bryant who were charged with the brutal murder of the 14-year-old teenager from Chicago. He told the crowd that he had "never witnessed such sheer perjury and fantastic twisting of facts." Diggs also told the gathering that he was delighted to breathe, "The clean, fresh air of Michigan after returning from the jungles of

Mississippi." As the crowd cheered him on he charged Mississippi as a State which "represented a shameful and primitive symbol of disregard for the essential dignity of all persons which must be destroyed before it destroys all that democracy is to represent." He further stated that "until every Negro is allowed to vote, we intend to challenge the sitting of every Mississippi congressman." The congressman told the press that he would seek a conference with the White House "to get support on the question of needed Civil Right laws from the Eisenhower Administration " when he returned to Washington D.C. Medger Evers, who also attended the Detroit rally and a Mississippi NAACP field secretary, said the NAACP would appeal to the Justice Department to intervene in Mississippi civil rights cases.

Three days after the murder-trial had concluded in Sumner, Mamie travelled with her father to Harlem, New York, to join Ruby Hurley and other NAACP officials attending a huge rally held to honor her son outside and inside the Metropolitan Community Church. Inside the church, Mamie spoke to the congregation about her life with her child and the dreams and aspirations she had planned for his life and his own dreams of one day becoming a professional baseball player or maybe a TV newsman when he grew up. With grief swelling in her throat, she asked the captive audience, "Have you ever sent a loved son on a vacation and had him returned to you in a pine wood box, so horribly battered and waterlogged that someone had to tell you that this sickening sight is your only child, lynched?" During her heartfelt speech, many in the congregation wept openly as well as many in the large crowd gathered outside the church numbering in the thousands and stretching three city blocks.

Meanwhile in Baltimore, Maryland, Dr. T.R.M. Howard told an audience of two-thousand-five hundred people attending the membership meeting of the National Association for the Advancement of Colored People (NAACP) at the Sharp Street Methodist Church that he was calling for an investigation into the conduct of Southern agents of the Federal Bureau of Investigation. He said addressing the members, "It's getting to be a strange thing that the FBI can never seem to work out who is responsible for killings of Negroes in the South." Dr. Howard referenced the two unsolved murders of Reverend George W. Lee and Lamar Smith who were both apparently active in the movement to get more Mississippi Negroes to vote. He strongly suggested that the President, the Attorney General and J. Edger Hoover are called into a conference by national Negro leaders in solving the dehumanizing conditions of Negroes in Mississippi as well as in the South as a whole. He reiterated, "We must find out why Southern investigators of the FBI can't seem to solve a crime where a Negro is involved." Dr. Howard as you recalled acted as a liaison between the prosecution and the attorney general of Sunflower County in Mississippi and he told the gathering, "The wave of terror has hit the South; it is in Mississippi." He continued to cite several examples of race difficulties which involved daily violent confrontations in Mississippi against blacks living there. He told the enthusiastic crowd, "I'm a mark man. I keep two body guards on duty at my home twenty-four hours a day," there were times during his speech that he became agitated when he outlined the hideous living conditions in the South as he spoke from the alter. Dr. Howard delivered his speech to the member flock for almost two hours. He informed his listeners, "Just getting simple justice from state officials in Mississippi is difficult for

Negroes on every level." He went on to characterize the charge that fourteen-year-old, Emmett Till insulted the wife of the white store owner in Money, Mississippi, as, "a lie…that stinks. Every time they get ready to lynch a Negro in the South, it's got to be about a white woman." Howard further indicated that he felt the Till trial, in which the two white defendants were acquitted was like a "Roman holiday." The congregation broke out into thunderous applauds as he continued about the racist terror in the South and the newly formed Mississippi White Citizen's Council, which he called, "the start of an organized campaign of violence against Negroes who dared to take a stand for their God given rights." In closing, he recommended four points necessary for a successful integration and desegregation plan in Mississippi and the South. They were: Equality in education; unrestricted balloting; maintenance of racial identity; and religion.

Roy Bryant and his half-brother, J. W. Milam was incarcerated in the Leflore County jail immediately after their acquittal in the five day murder-trial until they were freed on ten-thousand dollars bond each, posted by Leflore plantation owners, B. C. Walker and F. B. Steinback on September thirtieth, seven days after the murder-trial ended. After the two men were released from jail, J. W. returned to his overseer duties on one of the Glendora plantations and Roy returned to operate his general store with his family in Money, Mississippi. They performed their daily tasks with their families as they waited for a grand jury to convene in early November of the same year to hear kidnapping charges against them. It is interesting to note that when Roy Bryant returned to his store in Money to do business as usual. The black sharecroppers in the area took it upon themselves to boycott his business and he eventually had to close the store because of the loss of his biggest customers.

During the second week in October, 1955, an article entitled, "THE TILL CASE MAY MAKE MORE PROPAGANDA FOR REDS" written by Mrs. Eleanor Roosevelt, wife of former President Franklin Delano Roosevelt appeared in the Washington News. In her own words this is what she wrote, "In the current issue of Life Magazine there is an editorial on the Till case which is an appeal to the conscience of all our people.

The editorial says quite rightly, that human justice often falls far short of being justice, but that divine justice sooner or later is meted out to all of us according to our just dues. After reading this editorial, I think the jury that allowed itself to be persuaded that no one had really found and identified the body-tho it was granted that a boy had disappeared, but the body found might not be his- and, therefore, the accused men could not be convicted or punished in any way, will find their consciences troubled.

It is true that there can still be a trial for kidnapping, and I hope there will be. I hope the effort will be made to get at the truth.

I remember a train trip I made many years ago between Atlanta and Warm Springs, Georgia. I was with my husband. At one point we were delayed for a long time, and later we heard that a white man had shot a colored man on the train. Both of us were upset, and we asked if the white man had been arrested. "Oh, no" we were told, "but he might later come up for trial."

Months later I was driving my husband thru the county seat near Warm Springs when he pointed out to me a white man standing on the corner near the courthouse and said with a wry smile, "There is the man who delayed us so long that day on the train. He is as free as he ever was; tho the colored man is dead."

I never forgot this incident, but now it has taken on added meaning. I know everywhere in this country we must prove that what we say about equality before the law for every American citizen is a reality and not a myth.

The colored peoples of the world, who outnumber us, will watch the Till case with interest, and if justice in the United States is only for the white man and not for the colored man, we will have again played into the hands of the communist and strengthened their propaganda in Africa and Asia."

Rallies protesting the acquittal verdict continued to intensify around the country as decent white, Jewish and black Americans responded to the exoneration of the two white men with shock and anger. Southern race haters applauded the verdict. Shad Poltier, chairman of the National Executive Committee of the American Jewish Congress and the main speaker said, "The death of that young child, Emmett Till shows that the forces of blind hate and unbounded prejudice still dominate Mississippi. The failure to convict shows it is impossible to obtain justice for Negroes who live in that State."

Three thousand persons filled an Auditorium in Philadelphia days after the acquittal was announced for a rally to protest the exoneration of the two white men and to hear many leaders like

William Edward Burghardt Du Bois (W. E. B. Du Bois) age 87 who was very outspoken about the mere facts that a child could be the object of such race hatred and brutality in the South and as an historical figure in his own right continued his historical writings on the ills of racism in America and abroad, as he and others at the rally urged the crowd to write their protest and strong opposition to their Congressmen. In 1905, it was Du Bois who had launched the Niagara Movement advocating the immediate ending of racial discrimination and segregation and in 1909 was one of the founders of the NAACP, which grew out of the Niagara Movement. Roy Wilkins, executive secretary of the National Association for the Advancement of Colored People (NAACP) in New York told the press, "There are nineteen thousand Negroes in Tallahatchie County, Mississippi, where the trial was held, and none of them was allowed to register to vote in last month's primary election."

During the month of October in 1955, as rallies organized by the NAACP continued to explode across the nation over the brutal murder of young Emmett Till in Mississippi, James O. Eastland, an ultra-conservative senator from the State of Mississippi and a Southern Democrat had directed the United States Army to make public the reason for the misconduct charges placed against Louis Till, the father of Emmett Till who was hanged in Italy over alleged murder charges and rape of two white woman in Italy. While in Washington D.C. at one of the rallies, Mamie and her family learned publicly about the misconduct charges placed against her late husband by the Army. Senator Eastland highly agitated by the bad reputation his State had received around the naiton and parts of the world had the information released ten years later in the aftermath of Emmett Till's brutal murder in the hopes of revealing a pattern of 'like father like son' to diminish charges of racial brutality against black people living in the State of Mississippi. The rape and murder charges were strongly repudiated by friends of Louis Till who had served with him in the Army at the time. Racial segregation was a way of life in the military and it was also a well-known fact that Southern white soldiers refused to tolerate black soldiers and especially those who were confident, self-assured and proud. And particularly black soldiers who were in relationships with white women even in other parts of the world. Racism in the military was the same as it was in the states and when racial Jim Crow laws were violated, the punishment was met with violence or even death. On many occasions, black soldiers in the military during the war in the early nineteen-forties said that white military officers and white soldiers deeply rooted in southern racist traditional values who had knowledge of black soldiers involved with white women would allegedly commit rape and sometimes murder of local white women and then would go so far as blaming outspoken black soldiers of the crime by convincing their white superior officers with alleged evidence and often the black soldiers were the ones arrested late during the night and then were for the most part accused, judged and hanged for the crime.

The brutal murder of young Emmett Louis Till, a mere black child of fourteen years aroused black America in 1955 like it had never been in decades. Mass meeting continued to ignite in every section of the country. Mamie Bradley, Ruby Hurley, Medger Evers and Doctor T. R. M. Howard, militant medic from Mississippi and advocate of "equal rights," were the principal speakers. Crowds overflowed a New York church with ten-thousand in attendance, big auditoriums in Baltimore, Philadelphia, Cleveland, Pittsburgh, Detroit and other places were jammed to capacity. The NAACP sponsored a Mamie Bradley speaking tour during the month of September and October along with Ruby Hurley, but after speaking to massive crowds on the East Coast and the Mid-West, and after being well received and especially observing the large amounts of money being raised at those rallies, Mamie began demanding a five thousand dollar guaranty per speaking engagement per city tour. The organization felt that her demands were unreasonable as it became marred in financial difficulties and the NAACP declined her demands and demised her as part of the tour and continued their protest rallies around the country with Ruby Hurley and others including Moses Wright on occasion. Mamie attempted to resolve the dilemma between her and the NAACP by writing a letter to Roy Wilkins. She wrote, "Dear Mr. Wilkins, The objective of the NAACP is of much greater concern to me than my pocketbook. I set out to trade the blood of my child for the betterment of my race; and I do not wish to deviate from that course. Please let me go forward for the NAACP. It is a duty; I would not want it said that I did anything to shirk it." Mamie was scheduled to speak in eleven West Coast cities sponsored by the NAACP during several weeks in the month of October.

Henry Moon, director of NAACP public relations said that for the last three weeks Mamie Bradley had been speaking in Eastern and Mid-West cities under the NAACP sponsorship at an agreed rate of one-hundred dollars for each appearance, plus expenses. He said the same arrangement was to have applied for the West Coast tour, scheduled to begin in Seattle. Roy Wilkins, executive secretary of the NAACP told the press, "The NAACP does not handle such matters on a commercial basis." Mr. Moon said that Mrs. Bradley had asked the NAACP to sponsor her tour and had told the association that she was not trying to exploit her son's death, though she asked for a fee for each appearance and expenses. Mrs. Bradley had taken a leave from her job as a clerk for the Air Force and it was understood she needed funds, he said. With the Air Force in Chicago, she earned about four-thousand dollars a year. Mr. Moon went on to say, "We are not raising money for the Till case. Collections taken at Mrs. Bradley's appearance are to fight the situation and the conditions out of which the Till case developed." The sudden demand of Mrs. Bradley for a five-thousand dollar guarantee, or a small guarantee plus one-third of the proceeds, plus all expenses led the organization officials to believe that "advisors got to her," Mr. Moon added. Therefore, the movement continued to emerge without Mamie Bradley as an important figure in the fight by the NAACP for freedom and justice for Americans of African ancestry and other oppressed people in America.

CHAPTER THRITY-FIVE:

MURDER CONFESSION

Strong labor unions rallied there members into actions in various parts of the country to rigorously protest injustice in the South and in Mississippi in particular, since the brutal murder of young, Emmett Till and the exoneration of the two adult white men who committed the crime. Decent white Americans galvanized their outraged against the barbarous act inflicted on the young black child and they bombarded the White House, the State Department and the FBI with letters demanding justice for Emmett Till.

In mid-October a large anti-lynch rally occurred in New York's garment district sponsored by District 65 of the CIO-Retail, Wholesale, and Department Store Union (RWDSU) in cooperation with the NAACP which attracted almost twenty-five thousand people of mixed races that included, blacks, Jews and whites who had come to protest the acquittal verdict in Mississippi and to hear speakers such as, Representative Adam Clayton Powell (D-NY), Rabbi Israel Goldstein, president of the American Jewish Congress, Roy Wilkins, executive secretary of the NAACP, Max Greenburg, president of the RWDSU-CIO, Mrs. Ruby Hurley, Southern Director of the NAACP and Cleveland Robinson, Vice President, Secretary and Treasurer for District 65. Also attending the rally was Thurgood Marshall, future first black Supreme Court Justice and at the time in 1955, an NAACP general council who helped in the full mobilization of the 65 shops to map out the giant rally. The many unions participation in the District 65 rally was the first large scale action of its kind protesting the murder of Emmett Till and the acquittal verdict to take place in a predominantly white community. Previous mass rallies up to that point had occurred in Harlem and other black communities around the country. Since the District 65-NAACP rally was held in the heart of New York's heavily unionized garment market, the rally attractive many other trade unions such as, the twenty-five thousand members Local-22 of the AFL-International Ladies Garment Workers Union (ILGWU) and Macy Local-IS in the big department store with some eight-thousand active members. Also participating was the Jewish Labor Committee composed of AFL and CIO unions in the garment area, which denounced openly the acquittal verdict and called for federal action.

The Retail, Wholesale and Department Store Union (RWDSU) placed an editorial in their current issue of the RWDSU records titled the "unmistakable connection between the moves to end school segregation and the recent wave of lynching's and murders by die-hard racist." Cleveland Robinson told the crowd at the rally, "Americans who love democracy have a responsibility as long as Negroes continue to be lynched and denied basic rights as human beings in a free society. We must make our protest heard so that our Federal government will take steps to protect the life and liberty of every human being. Federal civil rights legislation cannot be used as a political football."

It was the International Ladies Garment Workers Union (ILGWU) Local-22 in their recently held membership meeting called on Congress, "to make the first order of business the passage of a federal anti-lynching bill." The Emmett Till case had such a powerful impact on public officials in the government that to illustrate the point there was a report regarding an incident, during a meeting in the House Banking subcommittee hearing on fair housing on Capitol Hill. Representative Ralph Gamble (R-NY) was overheard grumbling to a fellow member, "They're going to have a meeting of twenty-five thousand people at that rally I hear. A lady got hold of me and wanted to know what I was doing about the Till case. I told her it was a problem for the State of Mississippi. She said nothing was being done by the state and that the federal government would have to do something."

With the kidnapping trial of J.W. Milam and his half-brother, Roy Bryant scheduled to convene on November seventh in Greenwood, Mississippi. Willie Reed (18) after arriving from the terror of Mississippi and the overwhelming anxiety of adjusting to a new environment in Chicago soon became ill after suffering from extreme despair after learning that in less than a month he would have to return to Mississippi again to testify in the upcoming kidnapping trial. The ordeal and the weight of it was so heavy on his mind that he had a slight nervous breakdown and had to be hospitalized for almost a week. While Willie Reed was in Michael Reese hospital under a doctor's care recuperating from his condition, two white supremacist agents, William Spell and W. J. Crisler arrived at the hospital to threaten and intimidate him about testifying in the upcoming kidnapping trial. The two white agents had arrived in Chicago from Mississippi in a Mississippi State National Guard plane.

Upon their arrival, they immediately contacted the Chicago police department and received clearance from Police Commissioner, Timothy O'Conner. The two agents were directed to the Prairie Avenue police station where they secured further help from Police Captain Thomas Kelly in locating not only Willie Reed, but Mandy Bradley as well. During their private meeting with Willie Reed in his hospital room, they intimidated him so severely that doctors said he had suffered a relapse and had to be fed intravenously. When the two Mississippi agents had located Mandy Bradley at a relative's home, they began terrorizing her but she stood her ground and contacted an attorney from the NAACP and told of their intrusion and the two agents immediately vacated her location. The two white agents also attempted to locate Moses Wright, but he had left earlier to visit relatives in Detroit, Michigan. When contacted in Detroit and told about the incident by reporters, he told them that he was ready to stand against any terrorism in Mississippi and he divulged that he would return to be a trial witness, if necessary. He continued, "Dey can't do nuthin' more than kill me."

During the height of the continued rallies erupting around the country demanding justice for Emmett Till, Moses Wright and Willie Reed returned to Greenwood, Mississippi in early November to testify at the grand jury trial of J.W. Milam and his half-brother, Roy Bryant on kidnaping charges. A twenty man all-white grand jury was formed to hear the evidence regarding Milam and Bryant's confession of admitting that the two men had abducted the young fourteen year old from his uncle's tenant shack in Money, Mississippi. Moses Wright and Willie Reed travelling under NAACP protection were called to testify before the twenty member grand jury, which also included testimonies from Sheriff George Smith and his deputy John Ed Cothran. Moses testified for twenty-four minutes telling the grand jury how the two white men had come to his tenant shack on early Sunday morning of August 28 and forced his young nephew out of bed at gunpoint and how after someone in the car identified his nephew as the one, they drove away and he never saw his nephew alive again. Willie Reed testified a little less than twenty minutes and he told of seeing young Emmett Till on J.W. Milam's pickup truck and watched it as it drove into the shed on the Clint Sheridan plantation where he later heard a brutal beating and cries coming from the dilapidated structure. Willie Reed told the grand jury that he had saw J.W. vacate the shed where the savage beating was occurring, get some water and return to the shed again. Sheriff Smith and Deputy Cothran both told of the two men confession of taking the young teen from Moses Wright's tenant shack, but said that the two defendants told them that they had released him after they found that he was not the right one. Milam and Bryant did not attend the grand jury trial, but awaited the outcome at their place of residence. Mamie was not called to testify. The grand jury pondered all the evidence for several days and declined to indict J.W. Milam and

Roy Bryant on kidnapping charges freeing the men of all state charges.

After hearing about the verdict in Chicago, Mamie told the press, "Just about everything has run out of me now. I don't know what to say. I don't see how they could fail to indict those men." She further told the press that she was thinking about filing a civil suit, but she had no money and any further action would have to come from the NAACP. The verdict in the grand jury trial brought to an official close one of the most notorious race base cases in modern history, which led to a turning point in the fight for justice and human rights in America.

The State of Mississippi officially closed the Emmett Till case on November eleventh, 1955 and twenty-one days later on December first, 1955, a forty-two year old black woman angered by the injustice done to fourteen-year-old, Emmett Till and as an active member of the NAACP refused to give up her seat to a white man on a Montgomery, Alabama, city bus. That woman was Rosa Louise Parks, a black seamstress in Alabama and according to Emmett Till's mother and grandmother was a distant cousin of the family. Rosa Parks' courageous act of standing against racial injustice set in motion the modern day civil rights movement, which emerged a year later with the success of the Montgomery bus boycott.

In late January, 1956, five months after the brutal murder of Emmett Till in Mississippi and in the mist of the growing Civil Rights movement slowly emerging with the spotlight being on a young, articulate, and educated twenty-six year old black minister new to Montgomery- Dr. Martin Luther King, Jr. J. W.

Milam and his half-brother, Roy Bryant after being exonerated for both murder and kidnapping charges and after being paid four-thousand dollars allegedly told William Bradford Huie, an independent writer for Look Magazine that they had indeed murdered young Emmett Till. According to William Bradford Huie in the article he wrote, he said that J. W. Milam told him that it was Emmett Till's bravado in the face of a pistol-whipping by his confessed kidnappers and his boasting of being better than the two white men were and also saying repeatedly that he had relations with white women to which Milam said sealed his doom.

Milam also stated in the article that the beating episode took place in a tool shed behind his home in Glendora. Milam even told Huie that during the brutal beating that Emmett Till never hollered and kept articulating the perfect speech to insure martyrdom. J.W. allegedly quoted Emmett as saying while he and Roy had him on the river bank of the Tallahatchie River alive, "You bastards, I'm not afraid of you. I'm just as good as you are. I've been with white women before. My grandmother was white."

Milam apparently summed up his true feelings during the interview with Huie, "As long as I live and can do anything about it, niggers are gonna stay in their place. Niggers ain't gonna vote where I live. If they did, they'd control the government. They ain't gonna go to school with my kids. And when a nigger gets even close to mentioning sex with a white woman...he's tired of living. I'm likely to kill him."

J. W. Milam wanted decent human beings to believe that this fourteen year old child in the face of such dehumanizing brutal conditions, enduring such a savage beating stood with tremendous fortitude and tenacity taunting his attackers who was pistol-whipping him. Milam's revelation of events had been the same systematic mendacious justification by white racist to inflict heinous violence on Americans of African ancestry, which resonated throughout American History. When the Look Magazine article entitled, "Approved Killing in Mississippi," hit the newsstands in late January, 1956, it caused a fire storm of protest and Southern criticism against the article and of course it continued to outrage and anger the nation and parts of the world. After the enormous outcry for justice and the immense backlash against the two exonerated men confessing publicly that they had murdered fourteen-year-old, Emmett Till; Milam and Bryant moved expeditiously to recant their story by saying they planned to sue Look Magazine for libel and said they never talked to William Bradford Huie about the case. Look Magazine and William Bradford Huie stood by their story as being the truth and they were never sued by Mlilam and Bryant.

The hideous murder of young Emmett Louis (Bobo) Till set off a series of events electrifying decent white Americans into action joining in the fight for freedom and justice which galvanized Americans of African ancestry who stood unified, determined and entranced in the fight against injustice, oppression and Jim Crow laws. From rallies occurring in Birmingham to Tallahassee to the Montgomery bus boycott, from the West Coast to the East Coast and the Mid-West in between. The atrocity of this young child's death became a symbol that ignited a flame for justice and freedom for all oppressed non-whites living in America during the 1950's and 60's. Twenty-two million and politically strong Americans of African ancestry who stood unified, determined and fighting for rights that were rightfully theirs as American citizens. Demanding equality and freedom which the United States government had promised them since President Abraham Lincoln had signed the Emancipation Proclamation during the Civil War on January 1, 1863. In spite of Emmett Louis Till's tragic death, he did not die in vain, his life was sacrifice as a ranson freeing an oppressed people from physical and moral servitude.

Emmett Till was murdered on Sunday, August 28, 1955 and eight years later on Sunday, August 28, 1963, Dr. Martin Luther King, Jr., gave his famous "I Have A Dream" speech where he spoke of the atrocities that Emmett Till had to face.

And the struggle for civil rights continues.....

www.ingramcontent.com/pod-product-compliance
Lightning Source LLC
Chambersburg PA
CBHW022101150426
43195CB00008B/226